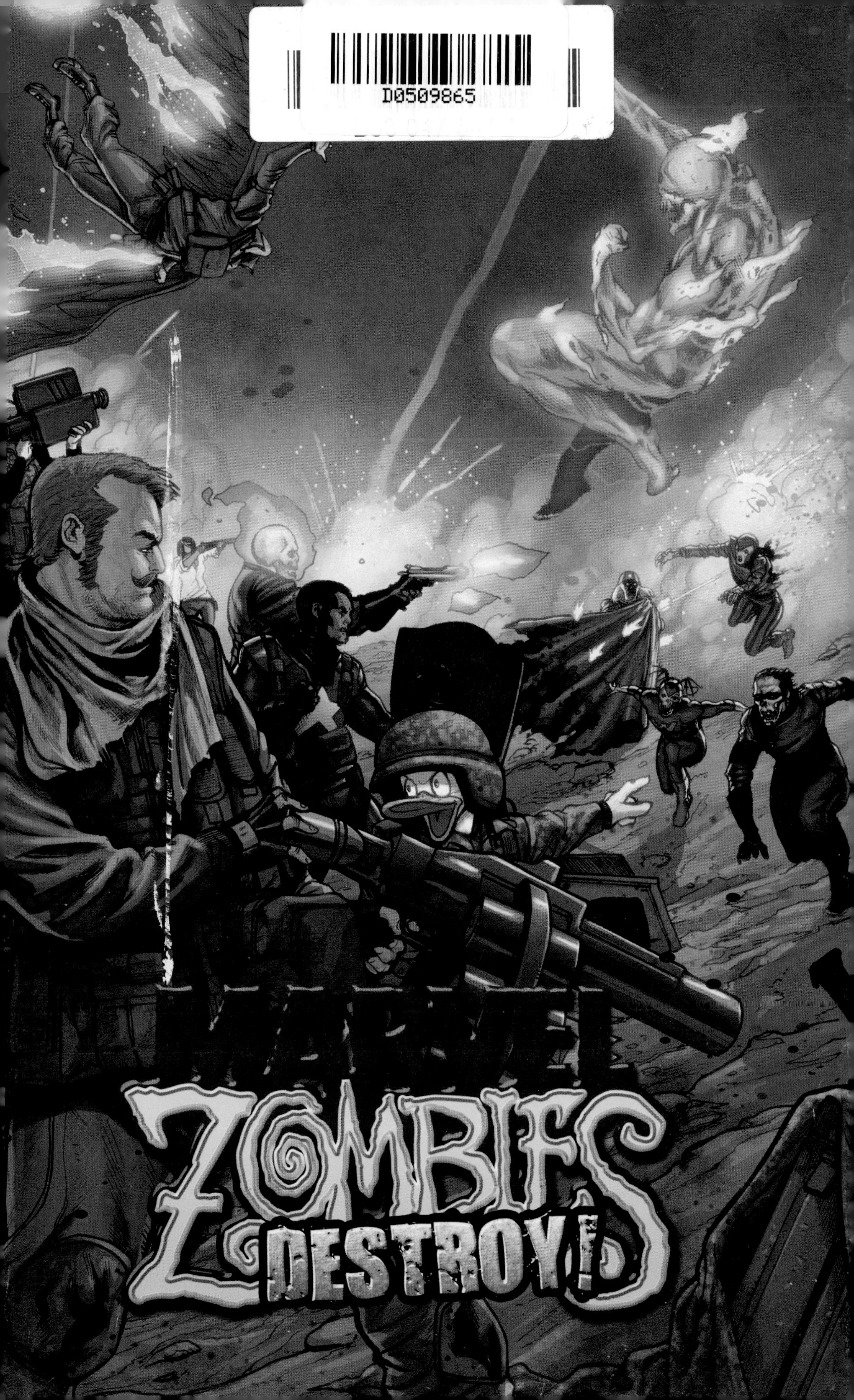
ZOMBIES
DESTROY!

ZOMBIES DESTROY!

WRITERS
FRANK MARRAFFINO (ISSUES #1-2)
& PETER DAVID (ISSUES #3-5)

ARTIST (ISSUES #1-2 & #4-5)
MIRCO PIERFEDERICI

PENCILER (ISSUE #3)
AL BARRIONUEVO

INKER (ISSUE #3)
RICK MAGYAR

COLOR ARTIST
GARRY HENDERSON

LETTERER
VC'S CLAYTON COWLES WITH JOE SABINO (ISSUE #2)

COVER ARTIST
MICHAEL DEL MUNDO

EDITOR
JAKE THOMAS

SENIOR EDITOR
MARK PANICCIA

MARVEL ZOMBIES DESTROY! Contains material originally published in magazine form as MARVEL ZOMBIES DESTROY! #1-5. First printing 2013. ISBN# 978-0-7851-6385-5. Published by MARVEL WORLDWIDE, INC., a subsidiary of MARVEL ENTERTAINMENT, LLC. OFFICE OF PUBLICATION: 135 West 50th Street, New York, NY 10020. Copyright © 2012 and 2013 Marvel Characters, Inc. All rights reserved. All characters featured in this issue and the distinctive names and likenesses thereof, and all related indicia are trademarks of Marvel Characters, Inc. No similarity between any of the names, characters, persons, and/or institutions in this magazine with those of any living or dead person or institution is intended, and any such similarity which may exist is purely coincidental. **Printed in the U.S.A.** ALAN FINE, EVP - Office of the President, Marvel Worldwide, Inc. and EVP & CMO Marvel Characters B.V.; DAN BUCKLEY, Publisher & President - Print, Animation & Digital Divisions; JOE QUESADA, Chief Creative Officer; TOM BREVOORT, SVP of Publishing; DAVID BOGART, SVP of Operations & Procurement, Publishing; RUWAN JAYATILLEKE, SVP & Associate Publisher, Publishing; C.B. CEBULSKI, SVP of Creator & Content Development; DAVID GABRIEL, SVP of Print & Digital Publishing Sales; JIM O'KEEFE, VP of Operations & Logistics; DAN CARR, Executive Director of Publishing Technology; SUSAN CHESPI, Editorial Operations Manager; ALEX MORALES, Publishing Operations Manager; STAN LEE, Chairman Emeritus. For information regarding advertising in Marvel Comics or on Marvel.com, please contact Niza Disla, Director of Marvel Partnerships, at ndisla@marvel.com. For Marvel subscription inquiries, please call 800-217-9158. **Manufactured between 1/16/2013 and 2/18/2013 by R.R. DONNELLEY, INC., SALEM, VA, USA.**

10 9 8 7 6 5 4 3 2 1

ASSISTANT EDITORS: ALEX STARBUCK & NELSON RIBEIRO
EDITORS, SPECIAL PROJECTS: JENNIFER GRÜNWALD & MARK D. BEAZLEY
SENIOR EDITOR, SPECIAL PROJECTS: JEFF YOUNGQUIST
SVP OF PRINT & DIGITAL PUBLISHING SALES: DAVID GABRIEL

EDITOR IN CHIEF: AXEL ALONSO
CHIEF CREATIVE OFFICER: JOE QUESADA
PUBLISHER: DAN BUCKLEY
EXECUTIVE PRODUCER: ALAN FINE

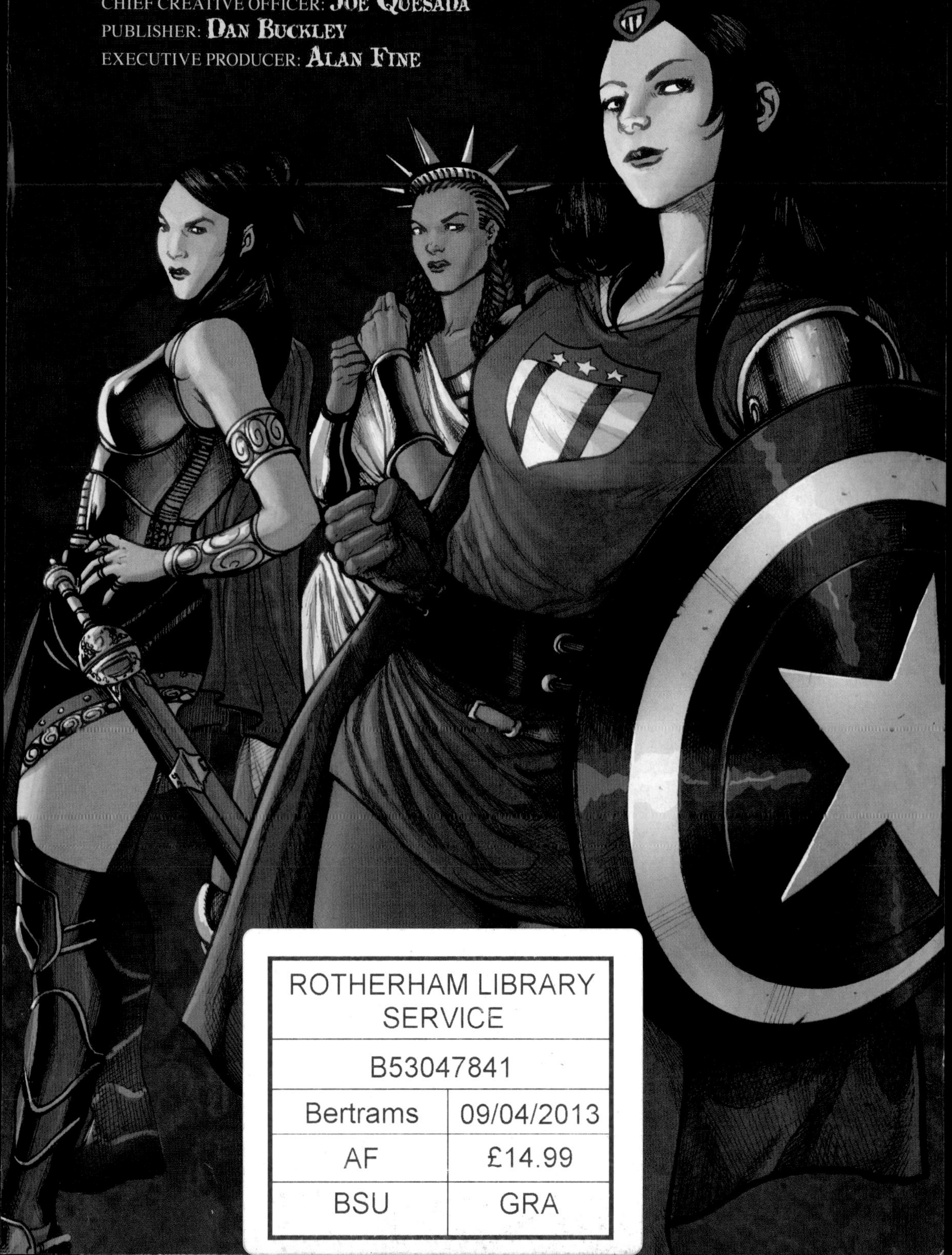

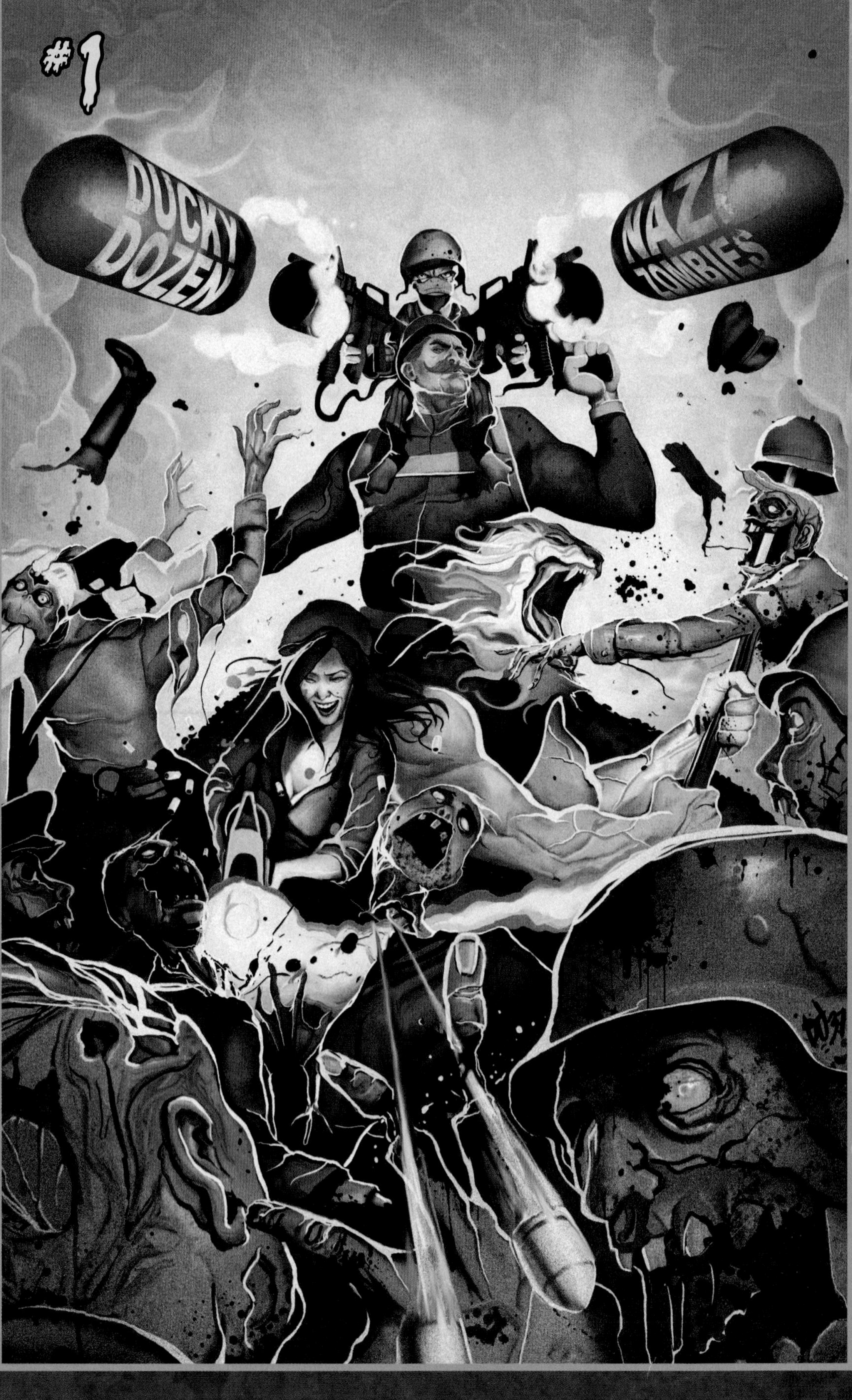
#1
DUCKY DOZEN
NAZI ZOMBIES

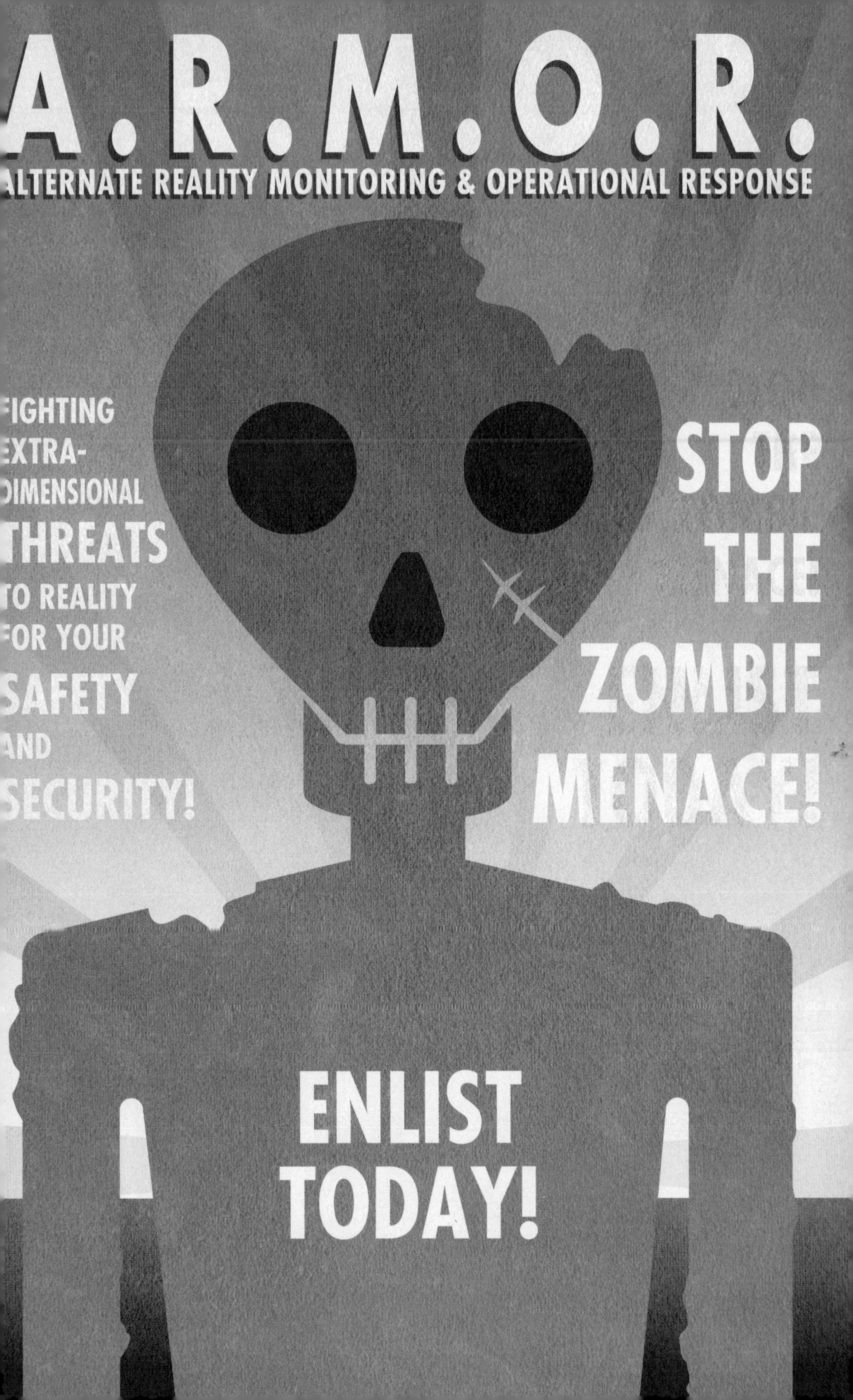
A.R.M.O.R.
ALTERNATE REALITY MONITORING & OPERATIONAL RESPONSE
FIGHTING EXTRA-DIMENSIONAL THREATS TO REALITY FOR YOUR SAFETY AND SECURITY!
STOP THE ZOMBIE MENACE!
ENLIST TODAY!

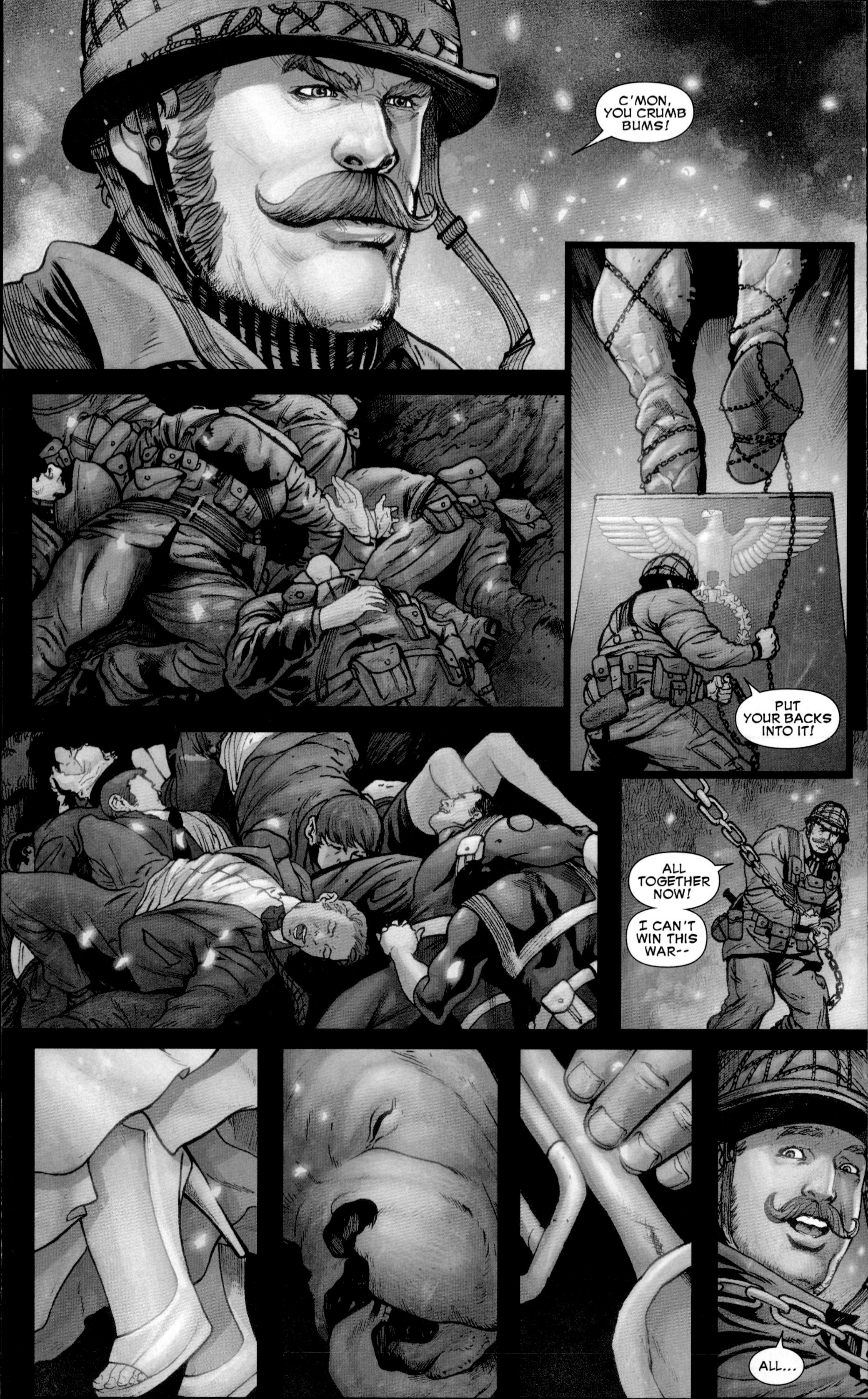
C'MON, YOU CRUMB BUMS!
PUT YOUR BACKS INTO IT!
ALL TOGETHER NOW!
I CAN'T WIN THIS WAR--
ALL...

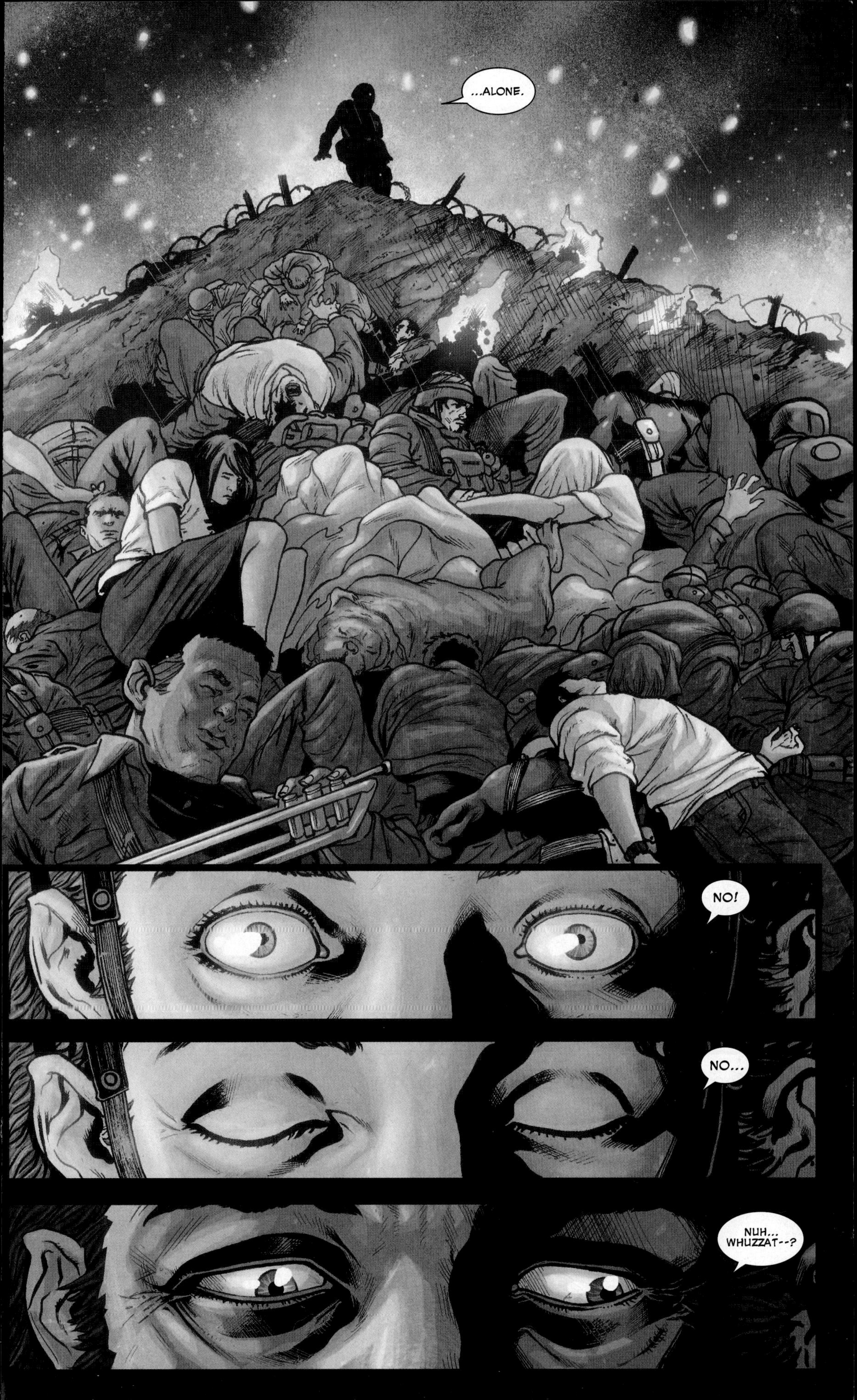
...ALONE.
NO!
NO...
NUH... WHUZZAT--?

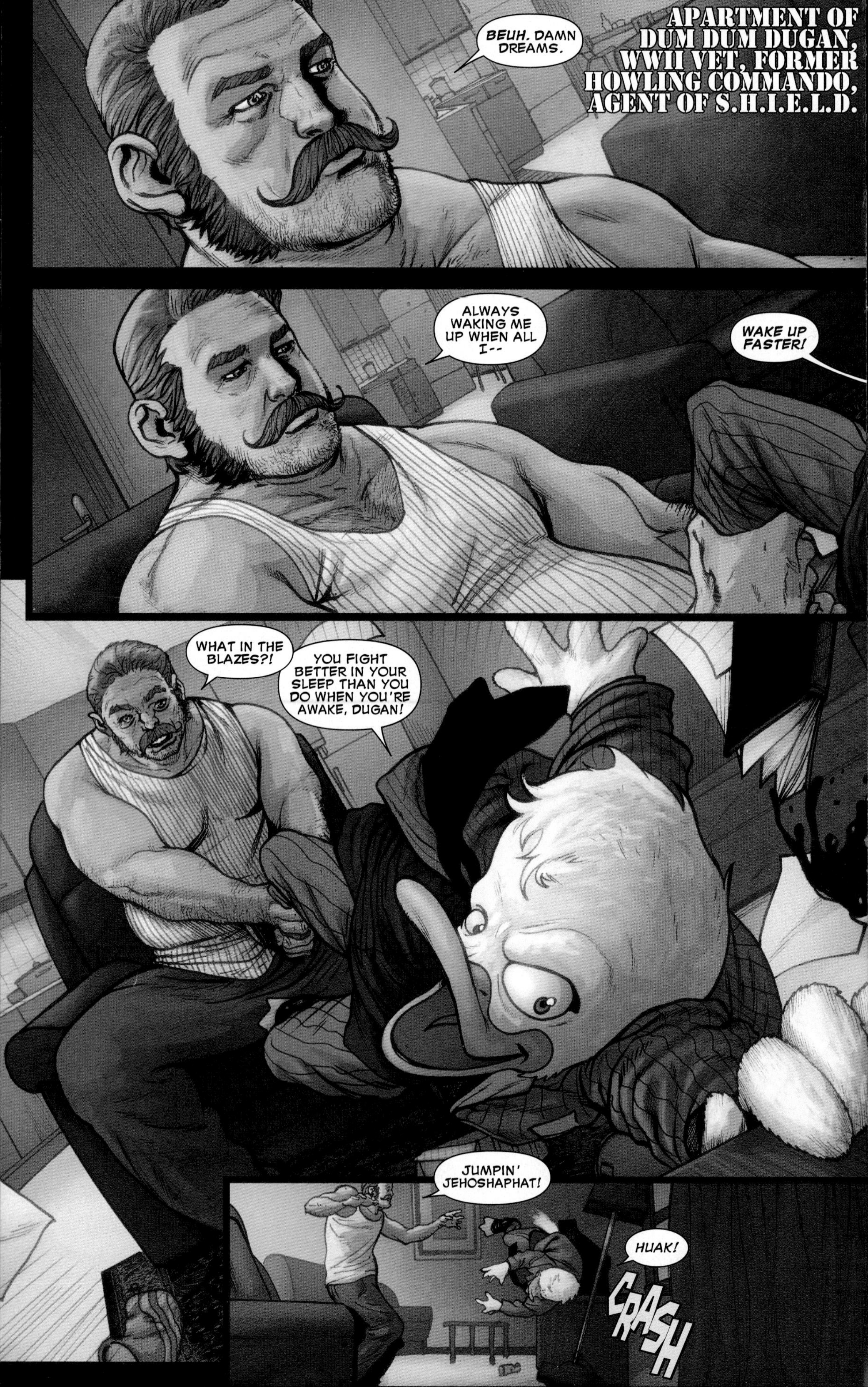
APARTMENT OF DUM DUM DUGAN, WWII VET, FORMER HOWLING COMMANDO, AGENT OF S.H.I.E.L.D.
BEUH. DAMN DREAMS.
ALWAYS WAKING ME UP WHEN ALL I--
WAKE UP FASTER!
WHAT IN THE BLAZES?!
YOU FIGHT BETTER IN YOUR SLEEP THAN YOU DO WHEN YOU'RE AWAKE, DUGAN!
JUMPIN' JEHOSHAPHAT!
HUAK!
CRASH

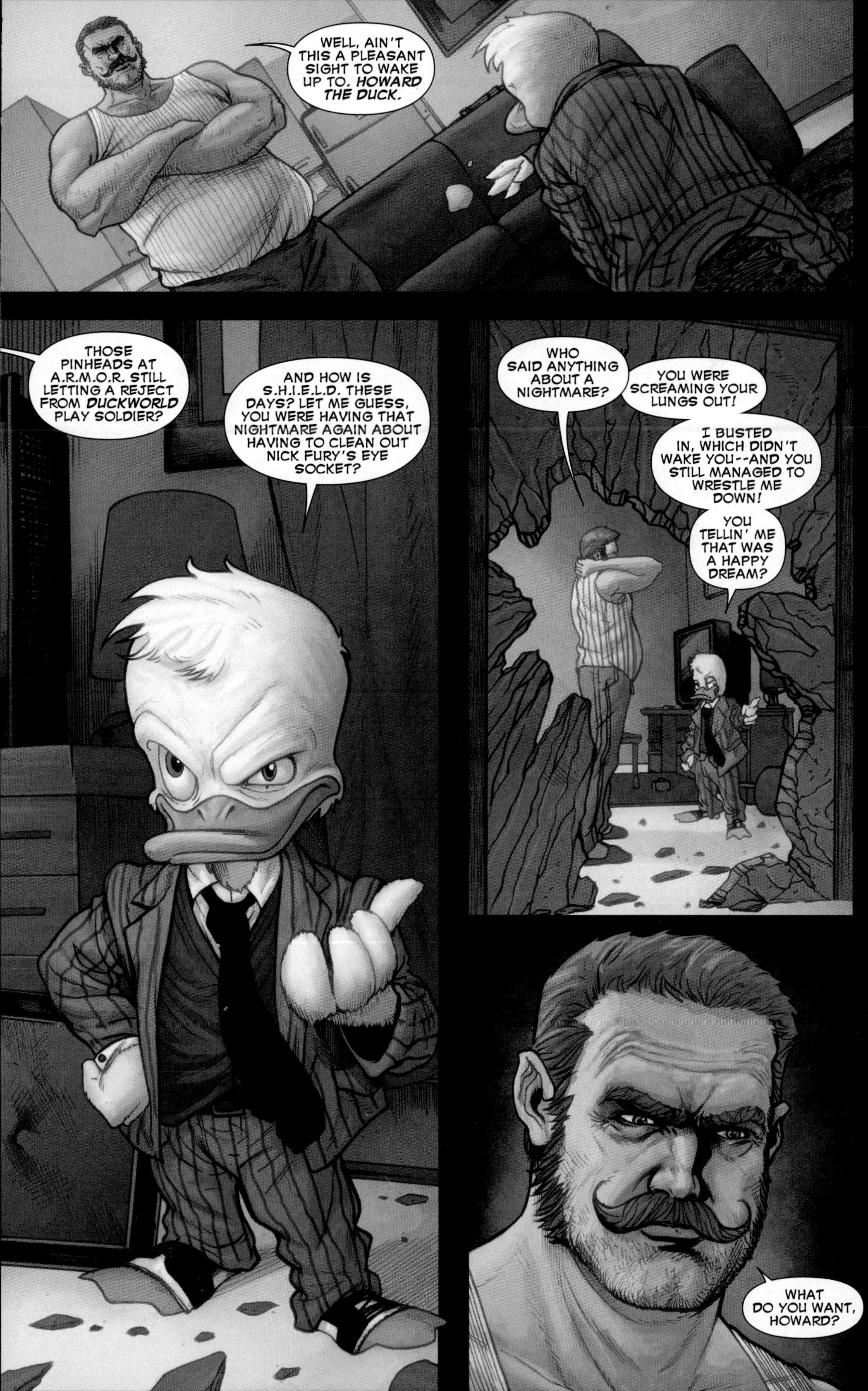
WELL, AIN'T THIS A PLEASANT SIGHT TO WAKE UP TO. HOWARD THE DUCK.
THOSE PINHEADS AT A.R.M.O.R. STILL LETTING A REJECT FROM DUCKWORLD PLAY SOLDIER?
AND HOW IS S.H.I.E.L.D. THESE DAYS? LET ME GUESS, YOU WERE HAVING THAT NIGHTMARE AGAIN ABOUT HAVING TO CLEAN OUT NICK FURY'S EYE SOCKET?
WHO SAID ANYTHING ABOUT A NIGHTMARE?
YOU WERE SCREAMING YOUR LUNGS OUT!
I BUSTED IN, WHICH DIDN'T WAKE YOU--AND YOU STILL MANAGED TO WRESTLE ME DOWN!
YOU TELLIN' ME THAT WAS A HAPPY DREAM?
WHAT DO YOU WANT, HOWARD?

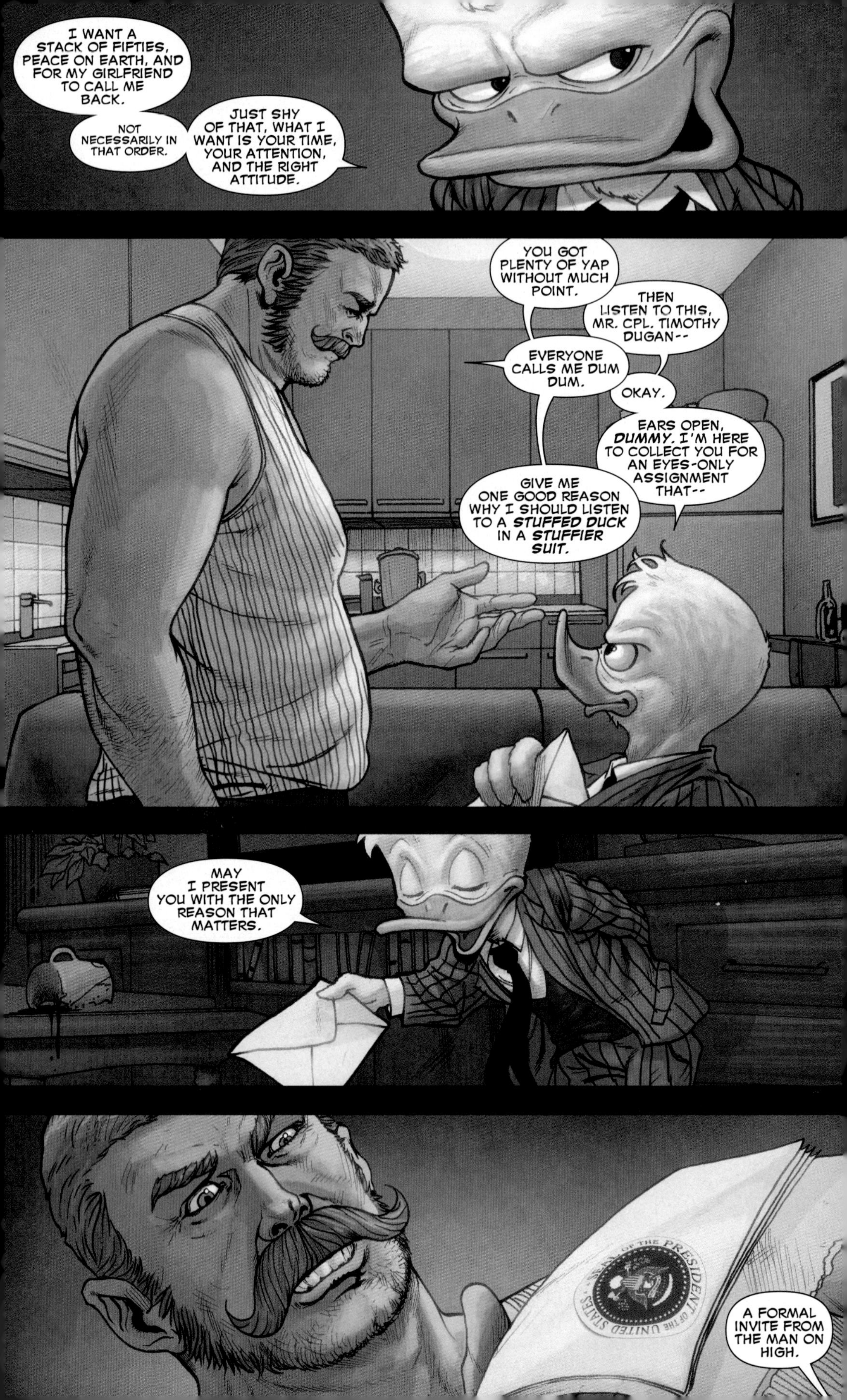
I WANT A STACK OF FIFTIES, PEACE ON EARTH, AND FOR MY GIRLFRIEND TO CALL ME BACK.
NOT NECESSARILY IN THAT ORDER.
JUST SHY OF THAT, WHAT I WANT IS YOUR TIME, YOUR ATTENTION, AND THE RIGHT ATTITUDE.
YOU GOT PLENTY OF YAP WITHOUT MUCH POINT.
THEN LISTEN TO THIS, MR. CPL. TIMOTHY DUGAN--
EVERYONE CALLS ME DUM DUM.
OKAY.
EARS OPEN, *DUMMY.* I'M HERE TO COLLECT YOU FOR AN EYES-ONLY ASSIGNMENT THAT--
GIVE ME ONE GOOD REASON WHY I SHOULD LISTEN TO A *STUFFED DUCK* IN A *STUFFIER SUIT.*
MAY I PRESENT YOU WITH THE ONLY REASON THAT MATTERS.
SEAL OF THE PRESIDENT OF THE UNITED STATES
A FORMAL INVITE FROM THE MAN ON HIGH.

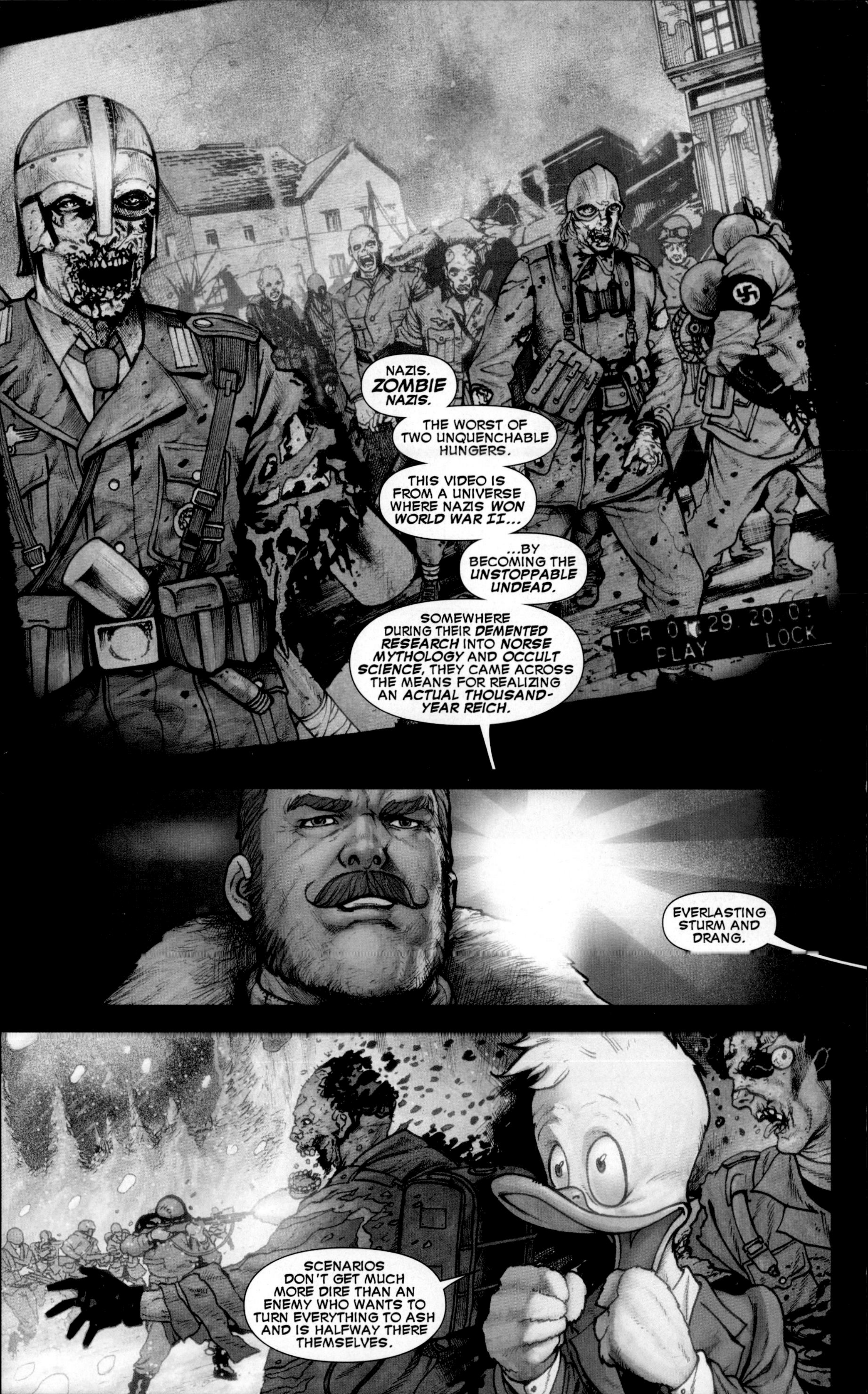
NAZIS. ZOMBIE NAZIS.
THE WORST OF TWO UNQUENCHABLE HUNGERS.
THIS VIDEO IS FROM A UNIVERSE WHERE NAZIS WON WORLD WAR II...
...BY BECOMING THE UNSTOPPABLE UNDEAD.
SOMEWHERE DURING THEIR DEMENTED RESEARCH INTO NORSE MYTHOLOGY AND OCCULT SCIENCE, THEY CAME ACROSS THE MEANS FOR REALIZING AN ACTUAL THOUSAND-YEAR REICH.
PLAY
LOCK
EVERLASTING STURM AND DRANG.
SCENARIOS DON'T GET MUCH MORE DIRE THAN AN ENEMY WHO WANTS TO TURN EVERYTHING TO ASH AND IS HALFWAY THERE THEMSELVES.

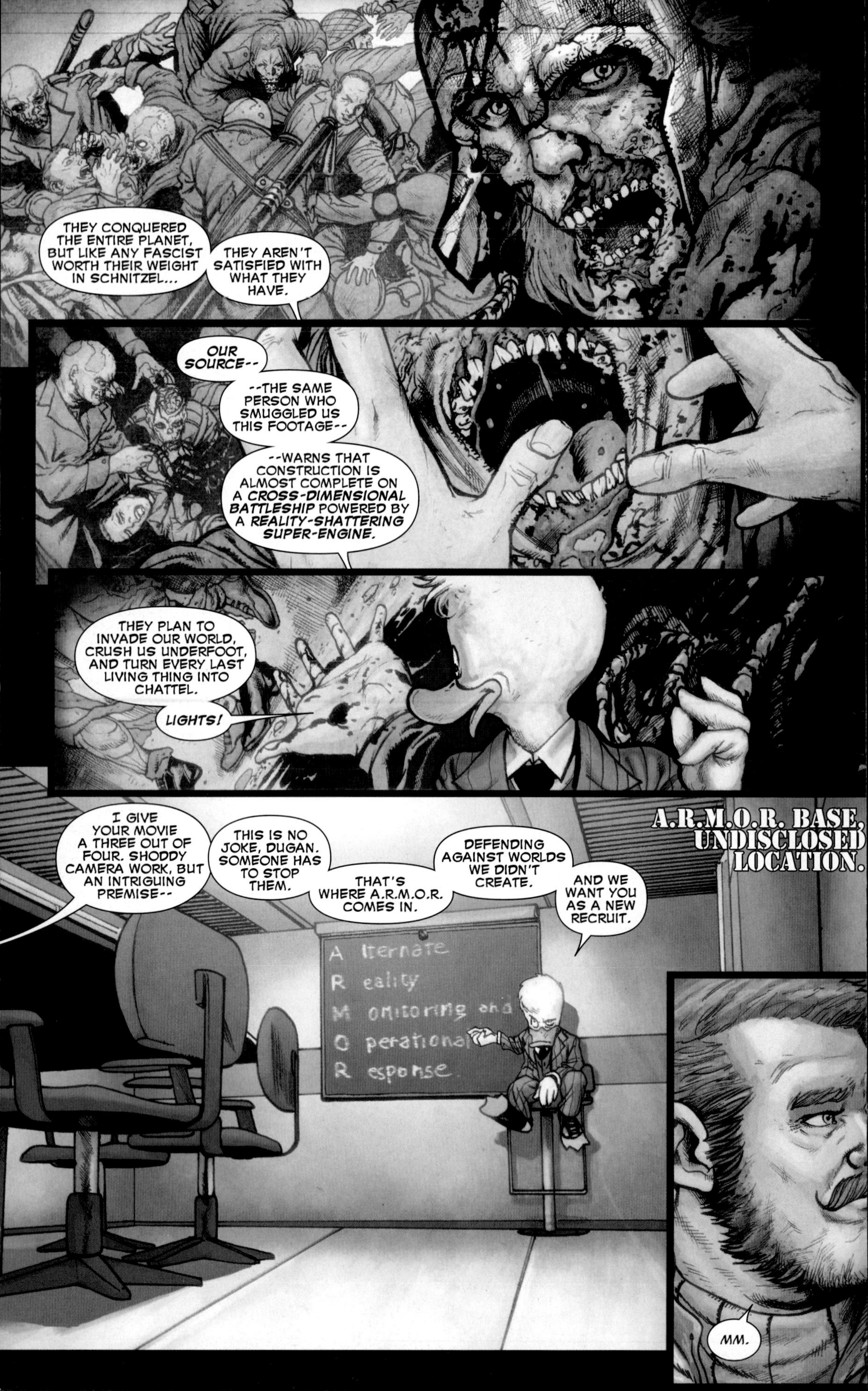
THEY CONQUERED THE ENTIRE PLANET, BUT LIKE ANY FASCIST WORTH THEIR WEIGHT IN SCHNITZEL...
THEY AREN'T SATISFIED WITH WHAT THEY HAVE.
OUR SOURCE--
--THE SAME PERSON WHO SMUGGLED US THIS FOOTAGE--
--WARNS THAT CONSTRUCTION IS ALMOST COMPLETE ON A CROSS-DIMENSIONAL BATTLESHIP POWERED BY A REALITY-SHATTERING SUPER-ENGINE.
THEY PLAN TO INVADE OUR WORLD, CRUSH US UNDERFOOT, AND TURN EVERY LAST LIVING THING INTO CHATTEL.
LIGHTS!
A.R.M.O.R. BASE, UNDISCLOSED LOCATION.
I GIVE YOUR MOVIE A THREE OUT OF FOUR. SHODDY CAMERA WORK, BUT AN INTRIGUING PREMISE--
THIS IS NO JOKE, DUGAN. SOMEONE HAS TO STOP THEM.
THAT'S WHERE A.R.M.O.R. COMES IN.
DEFENDING AGAINST WORLDS WE DIDN'T CREATE.
AND WE WANT YOU AS A NEW RECRUIT.
A lternate
R eality
M onitoring and
O perational
R esponse.
MM.

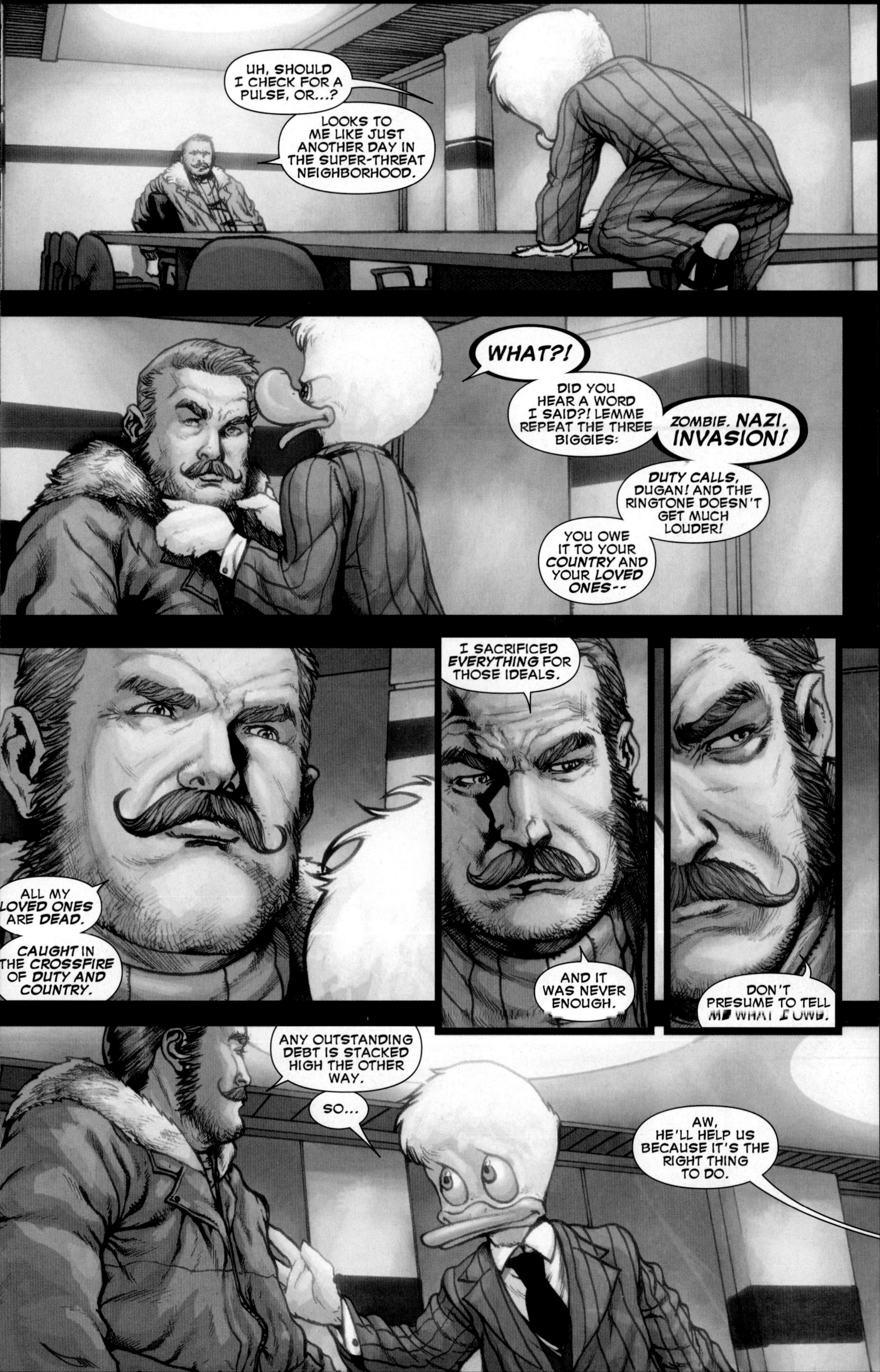
UH, SHOULD I CHECK FOR A PULSE, OR...?
LOOKS TO ME LIKE JUST ANOTHER DAY IN THE SUPER-THREAT NEIGHBORHOOD.
WHAT?!
DID YOU HEAR A WORD I SAID?! LEMME REPEAT THE THREE BIGGIES:
ZOMBIE. NAZI. INVASION!
DUTY CALLS, DUGAN! AND THE RINGTONE DOESN'T GET MUCH LOUDER!
YOU OWE IT TO YOUR COUNTRY AND YOUR LOVED ONES--
ALL MY LOVED ONES ARE DEAD.
CAUGHT IN THE CROSSFIRE OF DUTY AND COUNTRY.
I SACRIFICED EVERYTHING FOR THOSE IDEALS.
AND IT WAS NEVER ENOUGH.
DON'T PRESUME TO TELL
ANY OUTSTANDING DEBT IS STACKED HIGH THE OTHER WAY.
SO...
AW, HE'LL HELP US BECAUSE IT'S THE RIGHT THING TO DO.

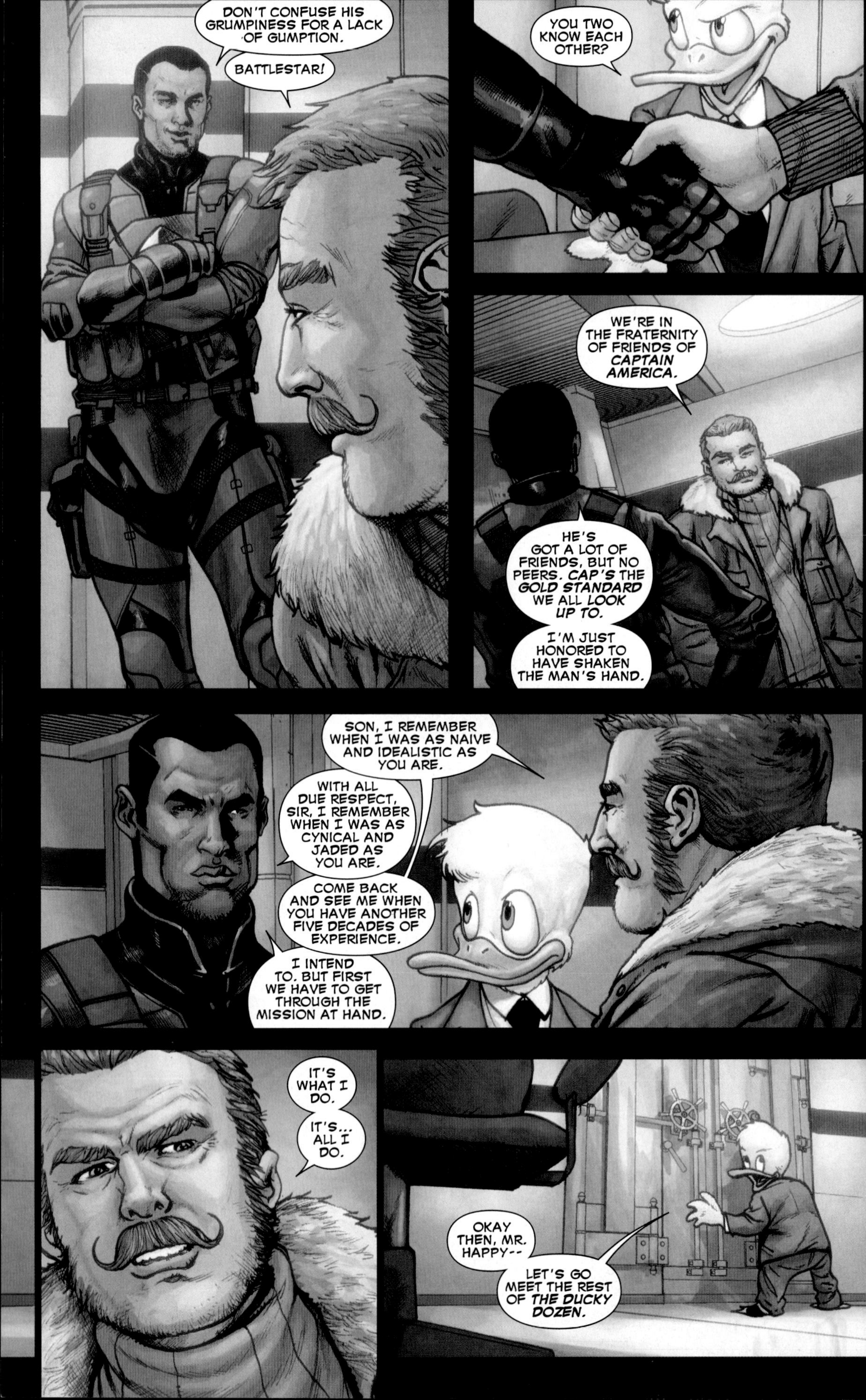
DON'T CONFUSE HIS GRUMPINESS FOR A LACK OF GUMPTION.
BATTLESTAR!
YOU TWO KNOW EACH OTHER?
WE'RE IN THE FRATERNITY OF FRIENDS OF CAPTAIN AMERICA.
HE'S GOT A LOT OF FRIENDS, BUT NO PEERS. CAP'S THE GOLD STANDARD WE ALL LOOK UP TO.
I'M JUST HONORED TO HAVE SHAKEN THE MAN'S HAND.
SON, I REMEMBER WHEN I WAS AS NAIVE AND IDEALISTIC AS YOU ARE.
WITH ALL DUE RESPECT, SIR, I REMEMBER WHEN I WAS AS CYNICAL AND JADED AS YOU ARE.
COME BACK AND SEE ME WHEN YOU HAVE ANOTHER FIVE DECADES OF EXPERIENCE.
I INTEND TO. BUT FIRST WE HAVE TO GET THROUGH THE MISSION AT HAND.
IT'S WHAT I DO.
IT'S... ALL I DO.
OKAY THEN, MR. HAPPY--
LET'S GO MEET THE REST OF THE DUCKY DOZEN.

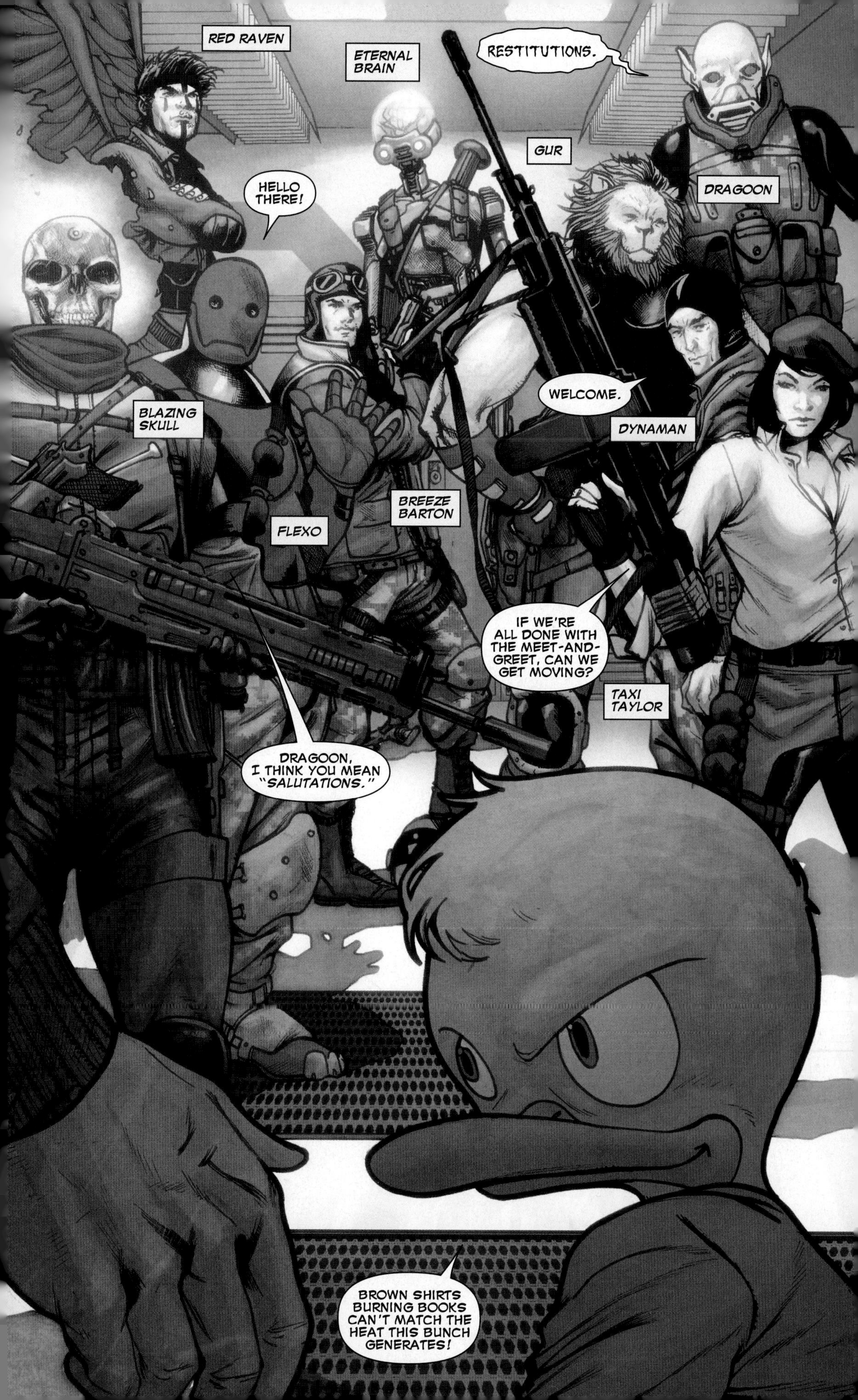
RED RAVEN
ETERNAL BRAIN
RESTITUTIONS.
GUR
DRAGOON
HELLO THERE!
WELCOME.
BLAZING SKULL
DYNAMAN
BREEZE BARTON
FLEXO
IF WE'RE ALL DONE WITH THE MEET-AND-GREET, CAN WE GET MOVING?
TAXI TAYLOR
DRAGOON, I THINK YOU MEAN "SALUTATIONS."
BROWN SHIRTS BURNING BOOKS CAN'T MATCH THE HEAT THIS BUNCH GENERATES!

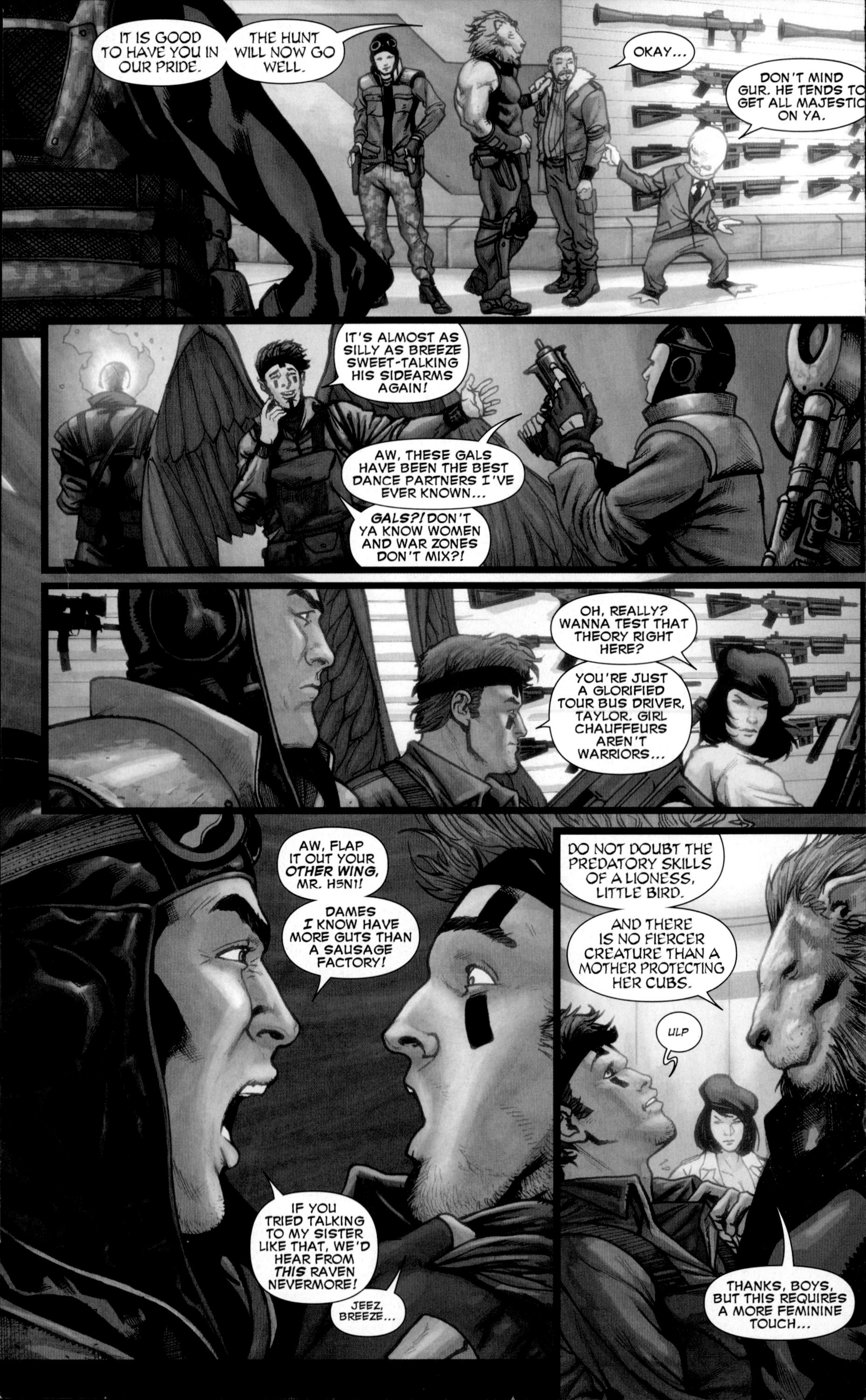
IT IS GOOD TO HAVE YOU IN OUR PRIDE.
THE HUNT WILL NOW GO WELL.
OKAY...
DON'T MIND GUR. HE TENDS TO GET ALL MAJESTIC ON YA.
IT'S ALMOST AS SILLY AS BREEZE SWEET-TALKING HIS SIDEARMS AGAIN!
AW, THESE GALS HAVE BEEN THE BEST DANCE PARTNERS I'VE EVER KNOWN...
GALS?! DON'T YA KNOW WOMEN AND WAR ZONES DON'T MIX?!
OH, REALLY? WANNA TEST THAT THEORY RIGHT HERE?
YOU'RE JUST A GLORIFIED TOUR BUS DRIVER, TAYLOR. GIRL CHAUFFEURS AREN'T WARRIORS...
AW, FLAP IT OUT YOUR OTHER WING, MR. H5N1!
DAMES I KNOW HAVE MORE GUTS THAN A SAUSAGE FACTORY!
IF YOU TRIED TALKING TO MY SISTER LIKE THAT, WE'D HEAR FROM THIS RAVEN NEVERMORE!
JEEZ, BREEZE...
DO NOT DOUBT THE PREDATORY SKILLS OF A LIONESS, LITTLE BIRD.
AND THERE IS NO FIERCER CREATURE THAN A MOTHER PROTECTING HER CUBS.
ULP
THANKS, BOYS, BUT THIS REQUIRES A MORE FEMININE TOUCH...

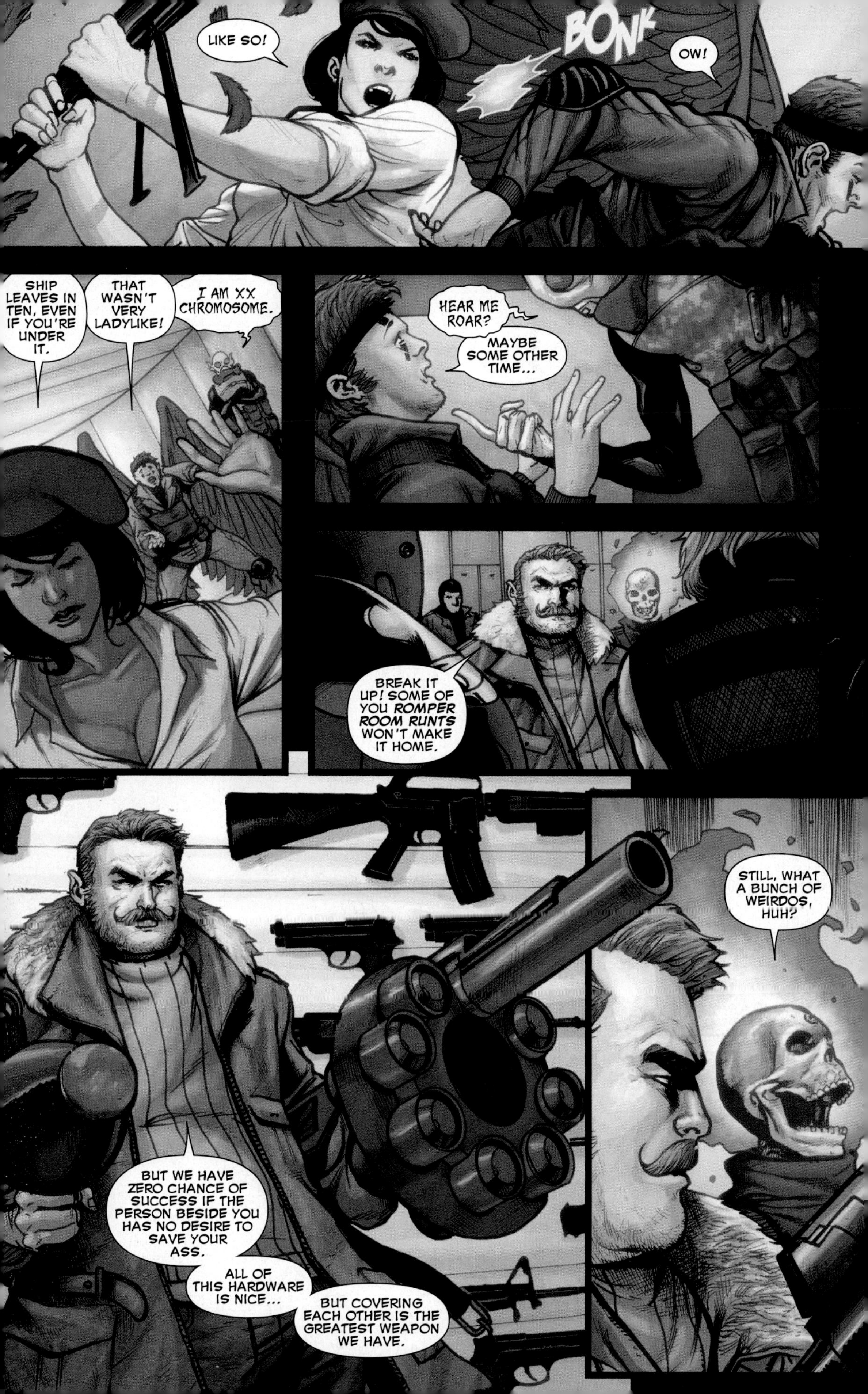
LIKE SO!
BONK
OW!
SHIP LEAVES IN TEN, EVEN IF YOU'RE UNDER IT.
THAT WASN'T VERY LADYLIKE!
I AM XX CHROMOSOME.
HEAR ME ROAR?
MAYBE SOME OTHER TIME...
BREAK IT UP! SOME OF YOU ROMPER ROOM RUNTS WON'T MAKE IT HOME.
BUT WE HAVE ZERO CHANCE OF SUCCESS IF THE PERSON BESIDE YOU HAS NO DESIRE TO SAVE YOUR ASS.
ALL OF THIS HARDWARE IS NICE...
BUT COVERING EACH OTHER IS THE GREATEST WEAPON WE HAVE.
STILL, WHAT A BUNCH OF WEIRDOS, HUH?

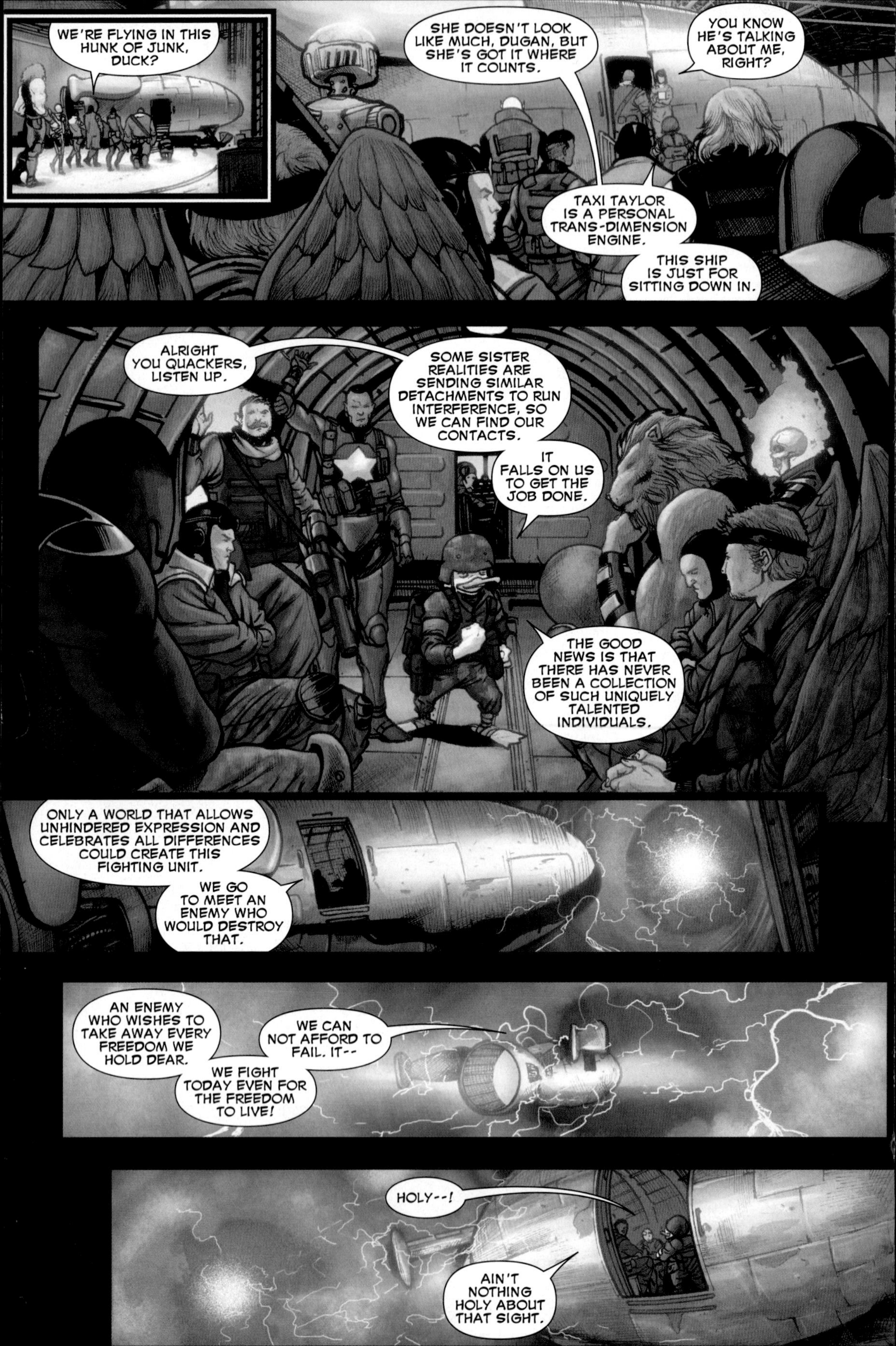

WE'RE FLYING IN THIS HUNK OF JUNK, DUCK?
SHE DOESN'T LOOK LIKE MUCH, DUGAN, BUT SHE'S GOT IT WHERE IT COUNTS.
YOU KNOW HE'S TALKING ABOUT ME, RIGHT?
TAXI TAYLOR IS A PERSONAL TRANS-DIMENSION ENGINE.
THIS SHIP IS JUST FOR SITTING DOWN IN.
ALRIGHT YOU QUACKERS, LISTEN UP.
SOME SISTER REALITIES ARE SENDING SIMILAR DETACHMENTS TO RUN INTERFERENCE, SO WE CAN FIND OUR CONTACTS.
IT FALLS ON US TO GET THE JOB DONE.
THE GOOD NEWS IS THAT THERE HAS NEVER BEEN A COLLECTION OF SUCH UNIQUELY TALENTED INDIVIDUALS.
ONLY A WORLD THAT ALLOWS UNHINDERED EXPRESSION AND CELEBRATES ALL DIFFERENCES COULD CREATE THIS FIGHTING UNIT.
WE GO TO MEET AN ENEMY WHO WOULD DESTROY THAT.
AN ENEMY WHO WISHES TO TAKE AWAY EVERY FREEDOM WE HOLD DEAR.
WE FIGHT TODAY EVEN FOR THE FREEDOM TO LIVE!
WE CAN NOT AFFORD TO FAIL. IT--
HOLY--!
AIN'T NOTHING HOLY ABOUT THAT SIGHT.

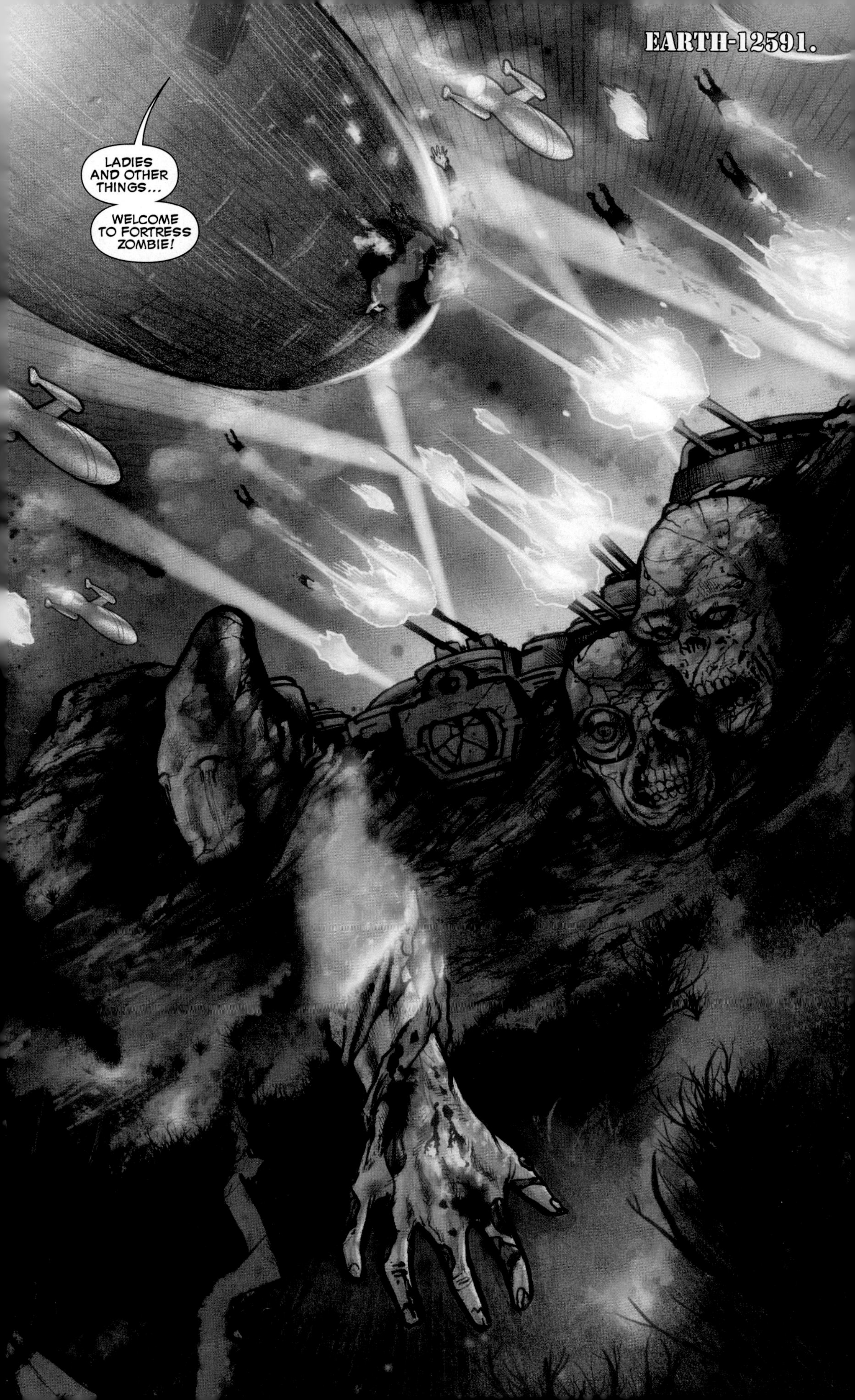
EARTH-12591.
LADIES AND OTHER THINGS...
WELCOME TO FORTRESS ZOMBIE!

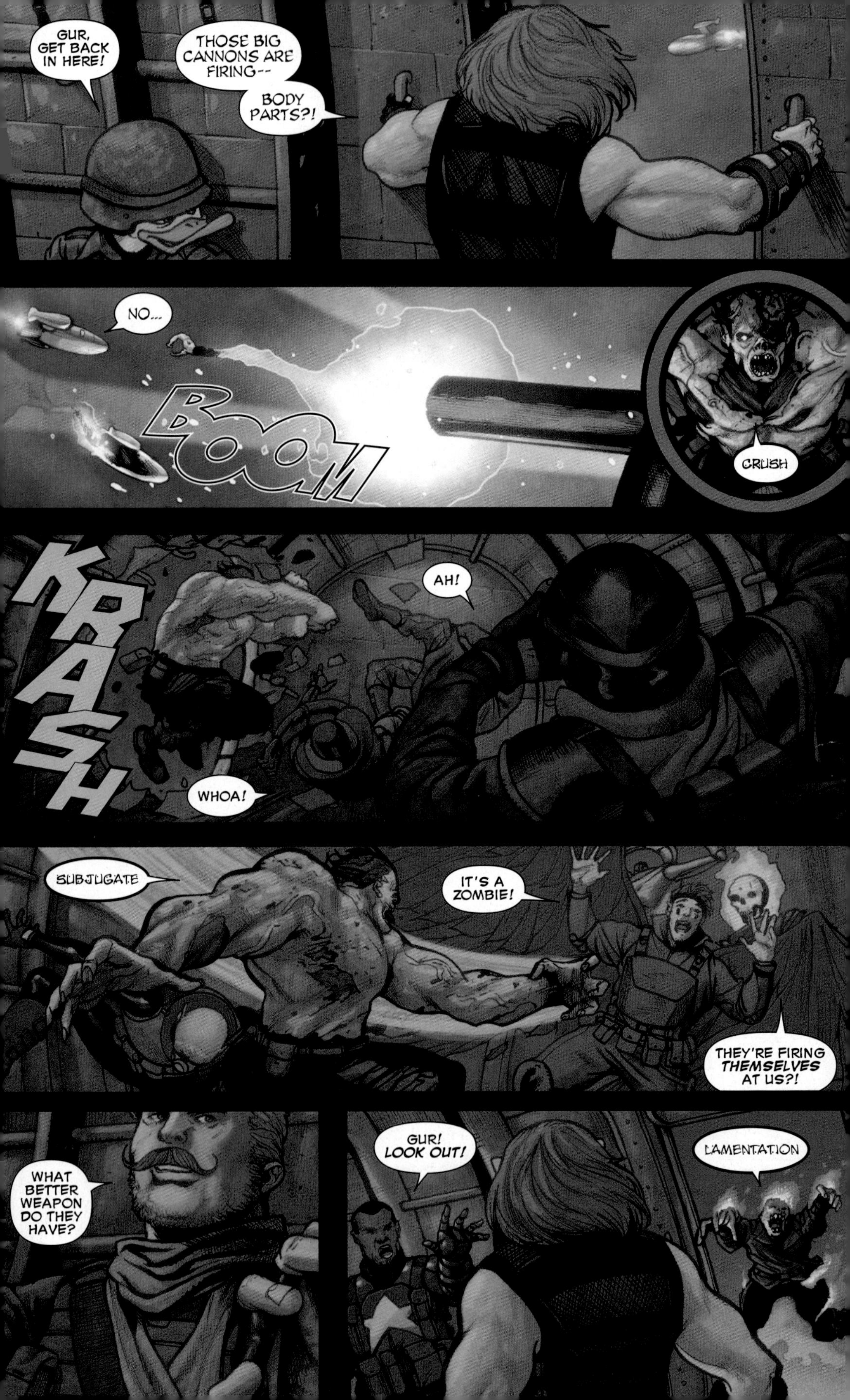
GUR, GET BACK IN HERE!
THOSE BIG CANNONS ARE FIRING--
BODY PARTS?!
NO...
BOOM
CRUSH
KRASH
AH!
WHOA!
SUBJUGATE
IT'S A ZOMBIE!
THEY'RE FIRING *THEMSELVES* AT US?!
WHAT BETTER WEAPON DO THEY HAVE?
GUR! *LOOK OUT!*
LAMENTATION

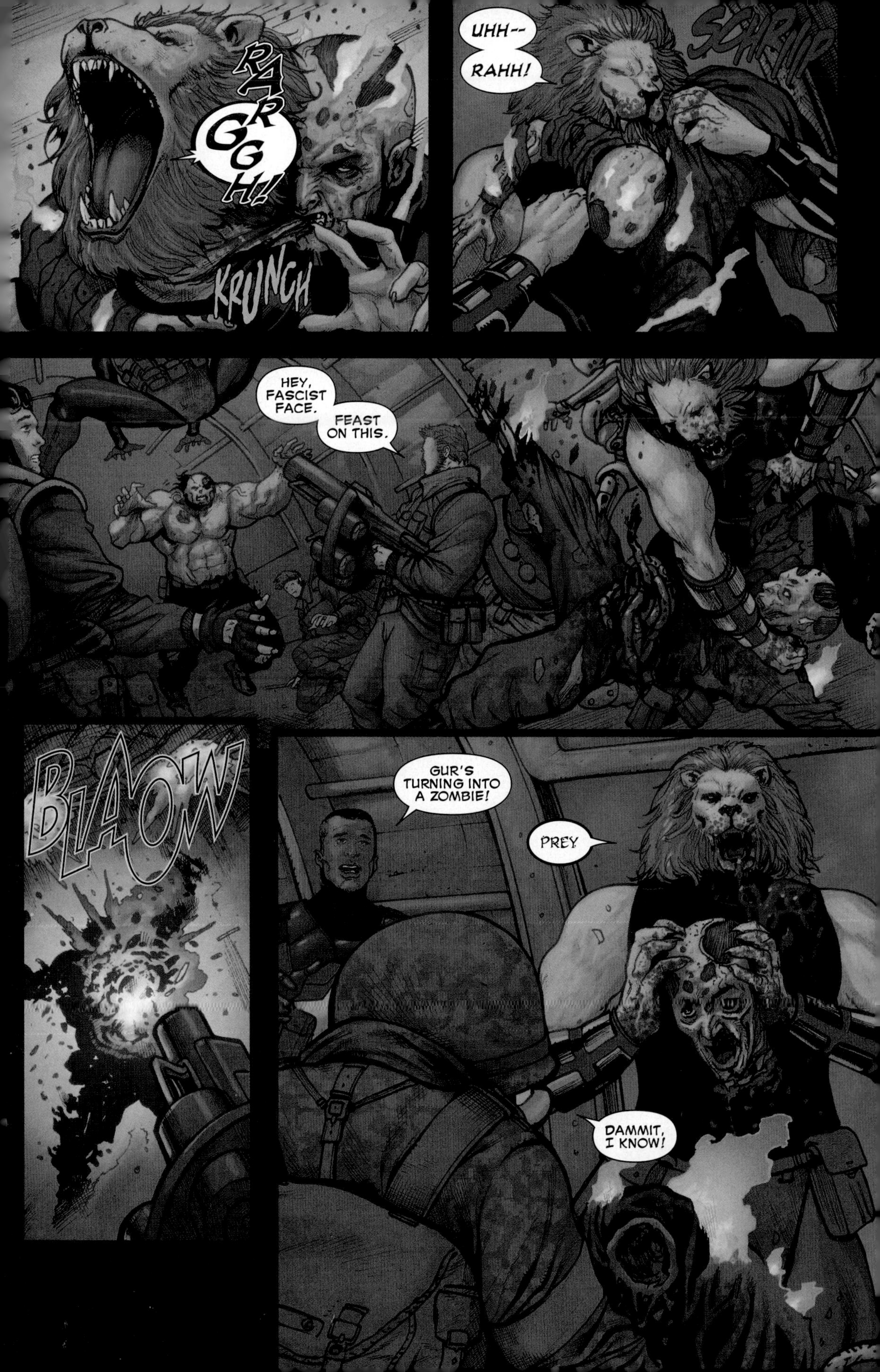
RARGGH!
KRUNCH
UHH--
RAHH!
HEY, FASCIST FACE.
FEAST ON THIS.
BLAOW
GUR'S TURNING INTO A ZOMBIE!
PREY.
DAMMIT, I KNOW!

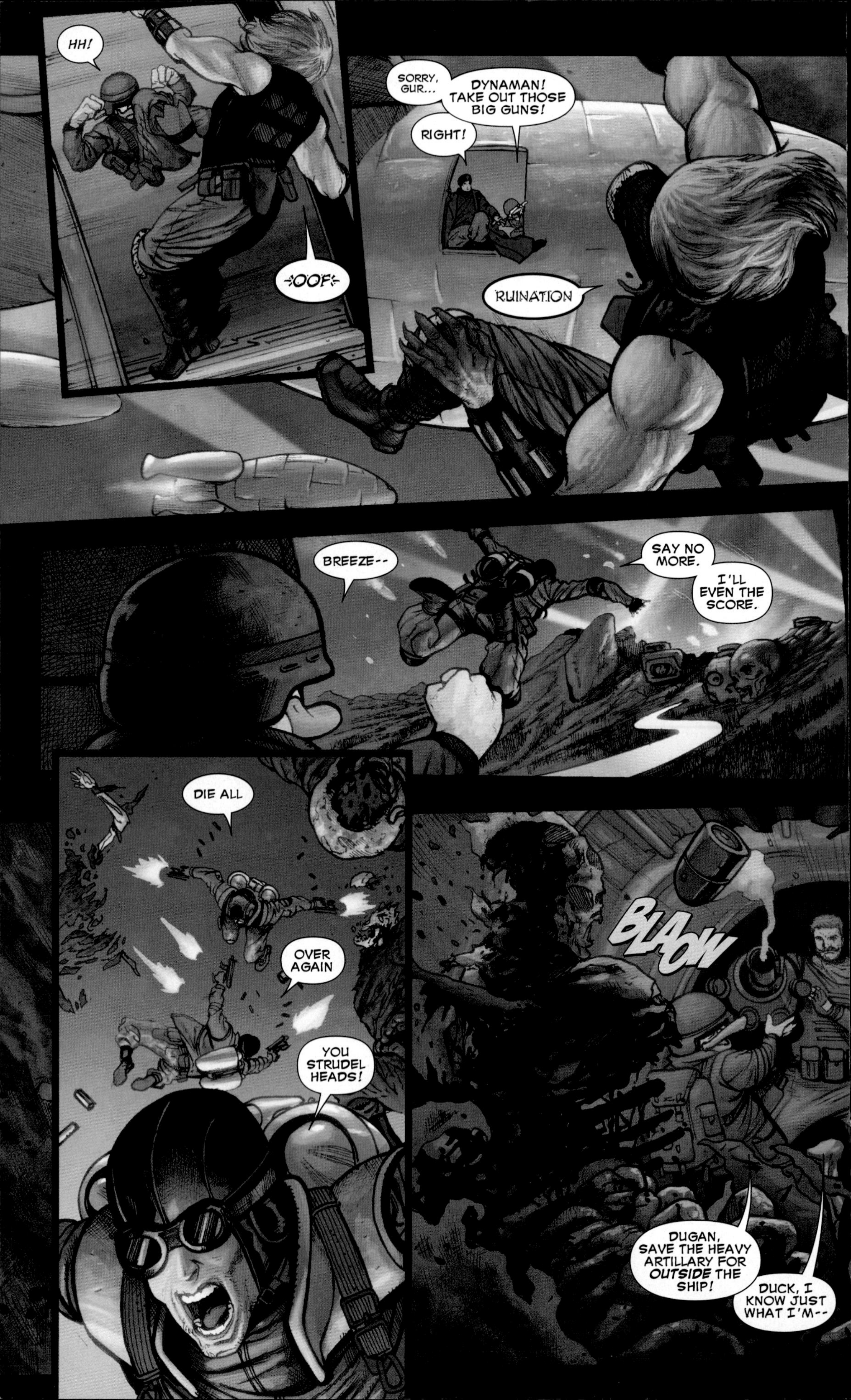
HH!
-OOF-
SORRY, GUR...
DYNAMAN! TAKE OUT THOSE BIG GUNS!
RIGHT!
RUINATION
BREEZE--
SAY NO MORE.
I'LL EVEN THE SCORE.
DIE ALL
OVER AGAIN
YOU STRUDEL HEADS!
BLAOW
DUGAN, SAVE THE HEAVY ARTILLARY FOR *OUTSIDE* THE SHIP!
DUCK, I KNOW JUST WHAT I'M--

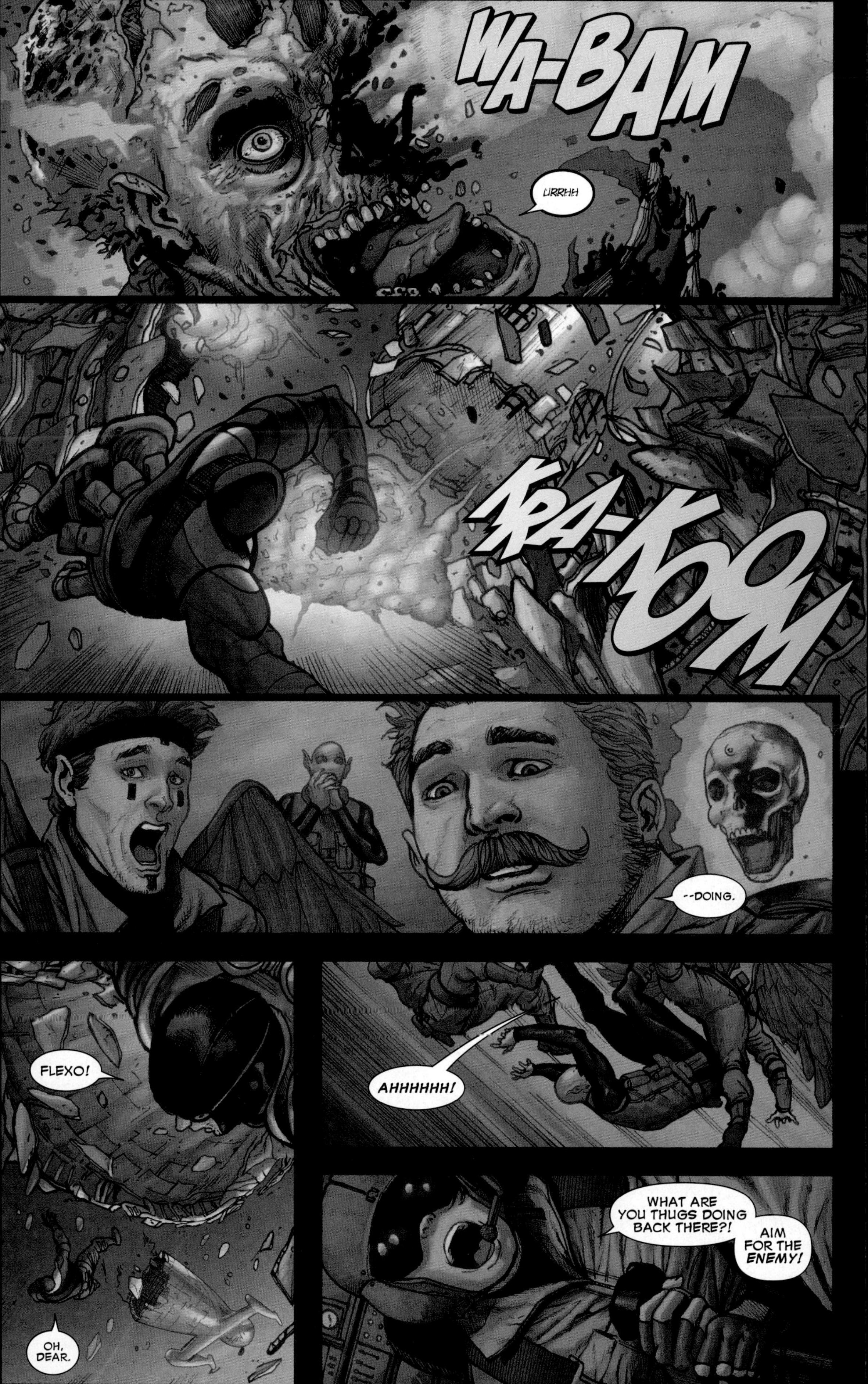
WA-BAM
URRHH
KRA-KOOM
--DOING.
FLEXO!
AHHHHHH!
OH, DEAR.
WHAT ARE YOU THUGS DOING BACK THERE?!
AIM FOR THE ENEMY!

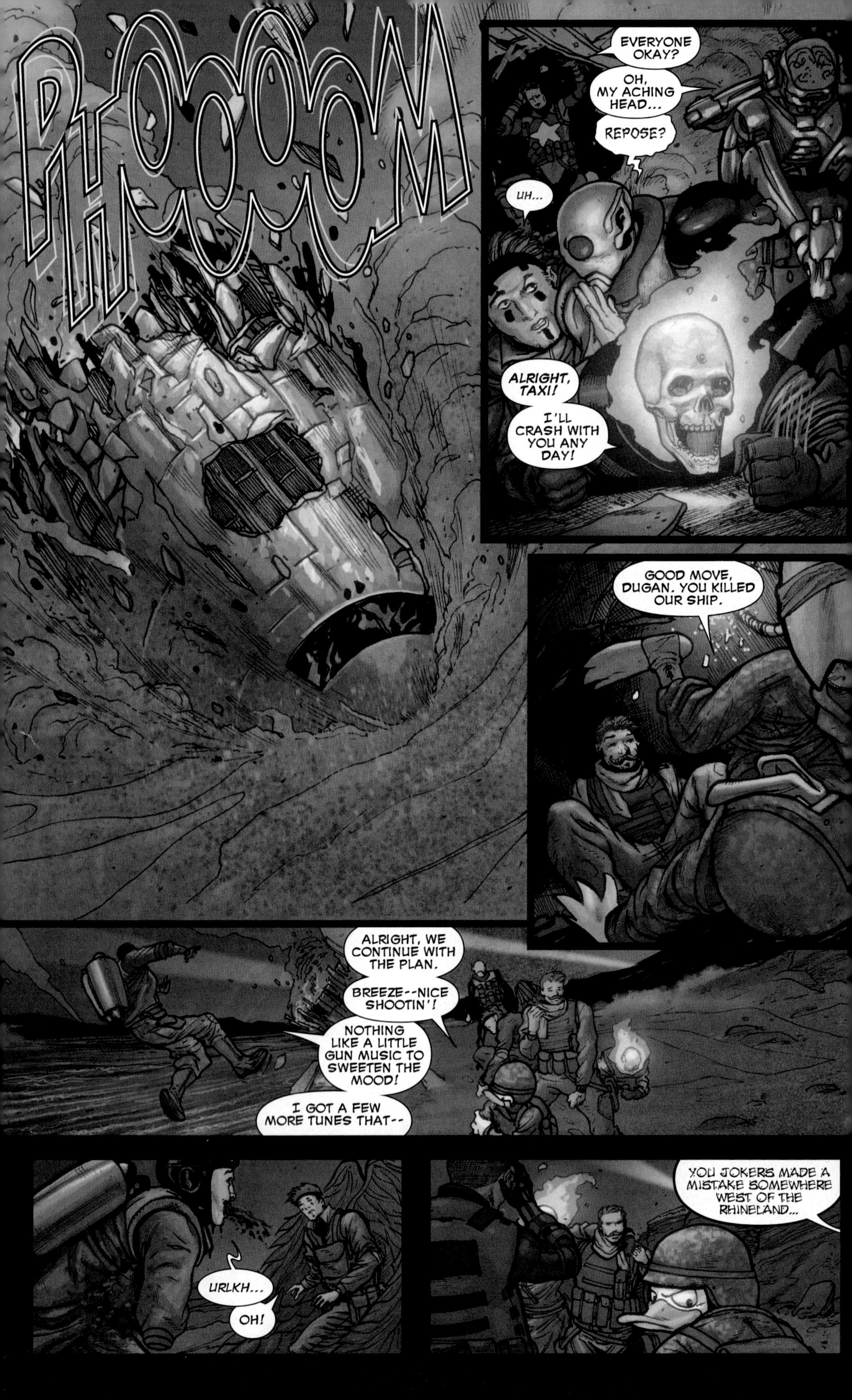
PHOOOOM
EVERYONE OKAY?
OH, MY ACHING HEAD...
REPOSE?
UH...
ALRIGHT, TAXI!
I'LL CRASH WITH YOU ANY DAY!
GOOD MOVE, DUGAN. YOU KILLED OUR SHIP.
ALRIGHT, WE CONTINUE WITH THE PLAN.
BREEZE--NICE SHOOTIN'!
NOTHING LIKE A LITTLE GUN MUSIC TO SWEETEN THE MOOD!
I GOT A FEW MORE TUNES THAT--
URLKH...
OH!
YOU JOKERS MADE A MISTAKE SOMEWHERE WEST OF THE RHINELAND...

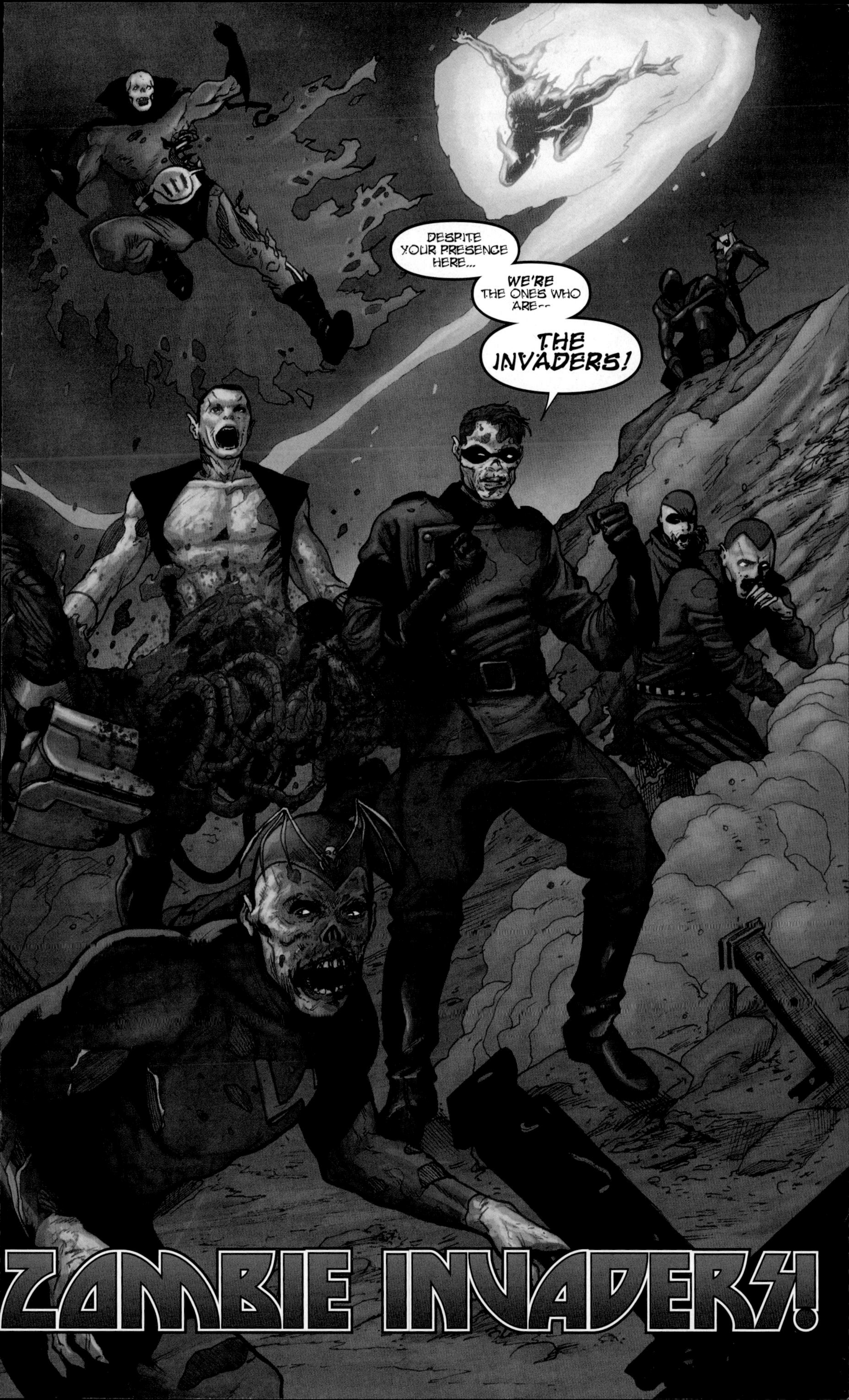
DESPITE YOUR PRESENCE HERE...
WE'RE THE ONES WHO ARE--
THE INVADERS!
ZOMBIE INVADERS!

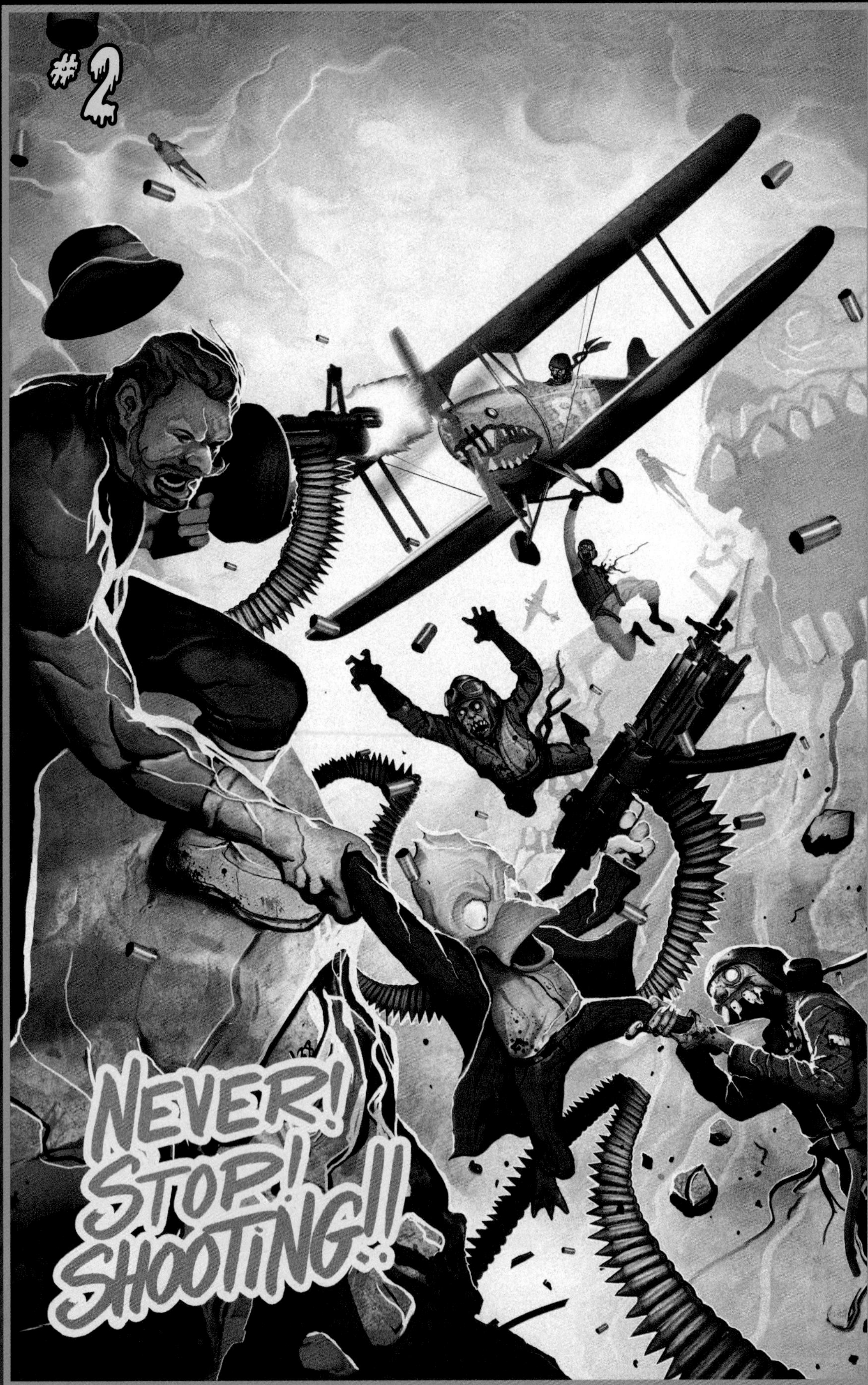

#2
NEVER! STOP! SHOOTING!!

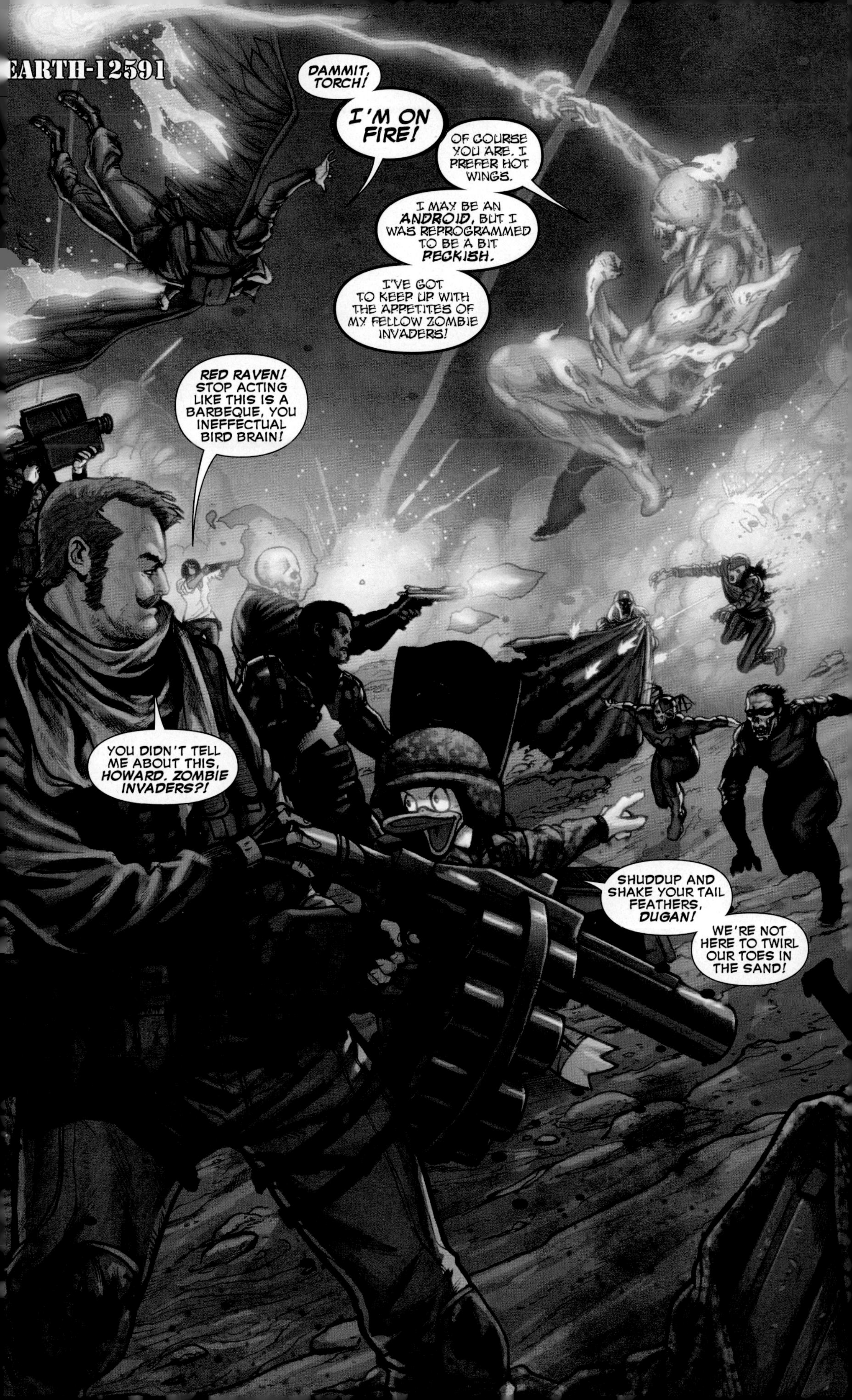
EARTH-12591
DAMMIT, TORCH!
I'M ON FIRE!
OF COURSE YOU ARE. I PREFER HOT WINGS.
I MAY BE AN ANDROID, BUT I WAS REPROGRAMMED TO BE A BIT PECKISH.
I'VE GOT TO KEEP UP WITH THE APPETITES OF MY FELLOW ZOMBIE INVADERS!
RED RAVEN! STOP ACTING LIKE THIS IS A BARBEQUE, YOU INEFFECTUAL BIRD BRAIN!
YOU DIDN'T TELL ME ABOUT THIS, HOWARD. ZOMBIE INVADERS?!
SHUDDUP AND SHAKE YOUR TAIL FEATHERS, DUGAN!
WE'RE NOT HERE TO TWIRL OUR TOES IN THE SAND!

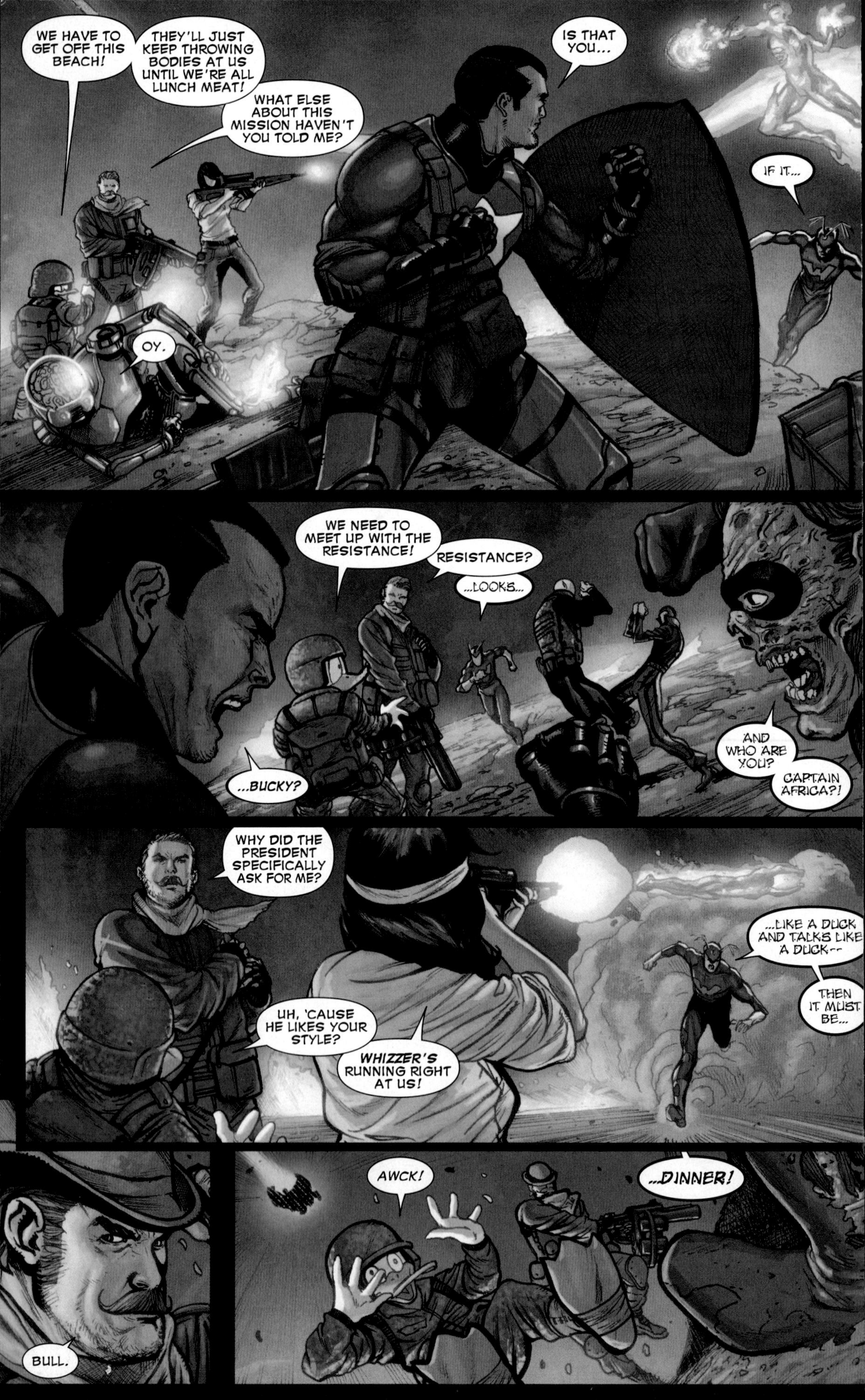
WE HAVE TO GET OFF THIS BEACH!
THEY'LL JUST KEEP THROWING BODIES AT US UNTIL WE'RE ALL LUNCH MEAT!
WHAT ELSE ABOUT THIS MISSION HAVEN'T YOU TOLD ME?
IS THAT YOU...
IF IT...
OY.
WE NEED TO MEET UP WITH THE RESISTANCE!
RESISTANCE?
...LOOKS...
...BUCKY?
AND WHO ARE YOU? CAPTAIN AFRICA?!
WHY DID THE PRESIDENT SPECIFICALLY ASK FOR ME?
UH, 'CAUSE HE LIKES YOUR STYLE?
WHIZZER'S RUNNING RIGHT AT US!
...LIKE A DUCK AND TALKS LIKE A DUCK--
THEN IT MUST BE...
BULL.
AWCK!
...DINNER!

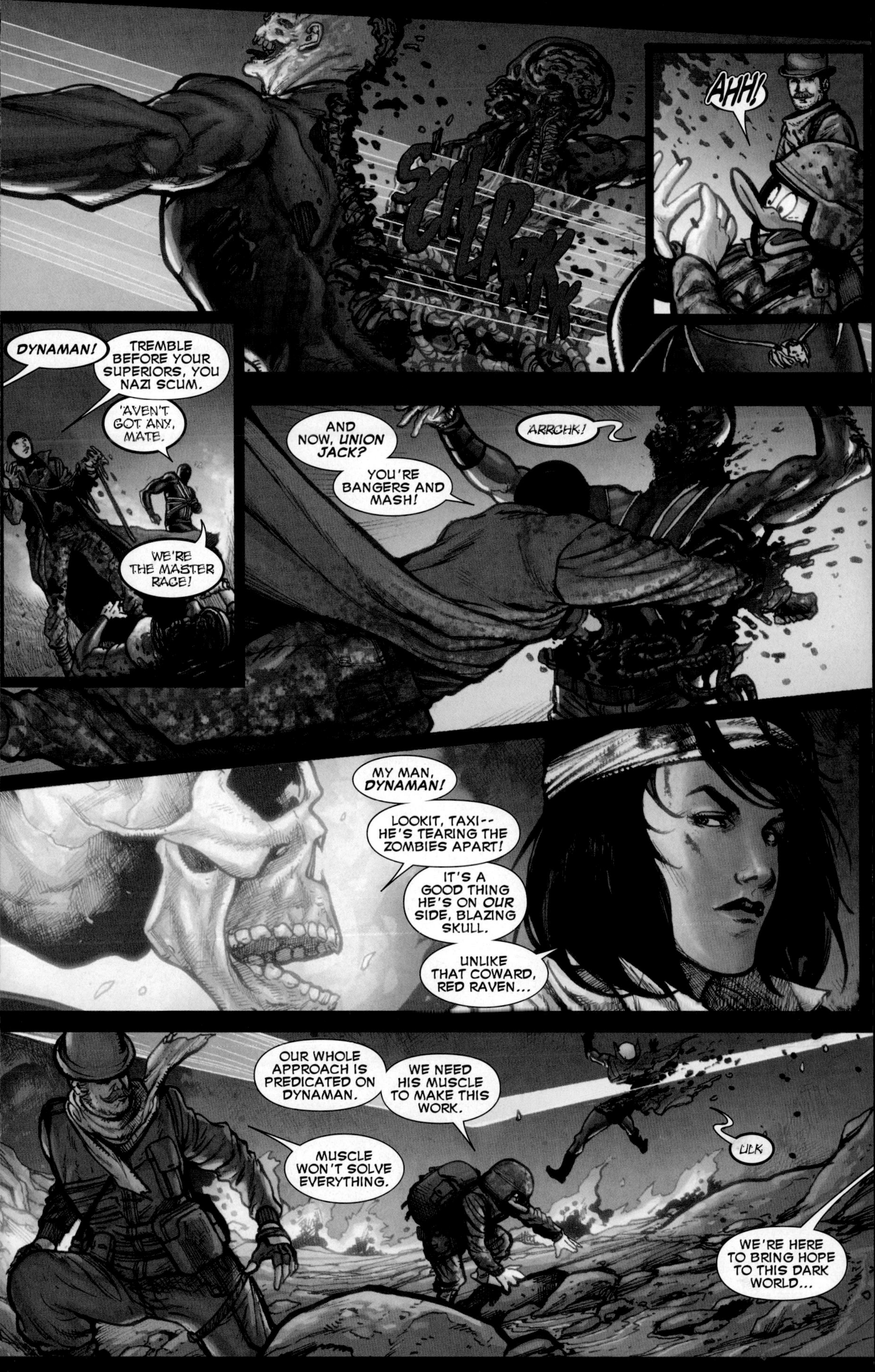
SCHRRKKK
AHH!
DYNAMAN!
TREMBLE BEFORE YOUR SUPERIORS, YOU NAZI SCUM.
'AVEN'T GOT ANY, MATE.
WE'RE THE MASTER RACE!
AND NOW, UNION JACK?
YOU'RE BANGERS AND MASH!
ARRCHK!
MY MAN, DYNAMAN!
LOOKIT, TAXI-- HE'S TEARING THE ZOMBIES APART!
IT'S A GOOD THING HE'S ON OUR SIDE, BLAZING SKULL.
UNLIKE THAT COWARD, RED RAVEN...
OUR WHOLE APPROACH IS PREDICATED ON DYNAMAN.
WE NEED HIS MUSCLE TO MAKE THIS WORK.
MUSCLE WON'T SOLVE EVERYTHING.
ULK
WE'RE HERE TO BRING HOPE TO THIS DARK WORLD...

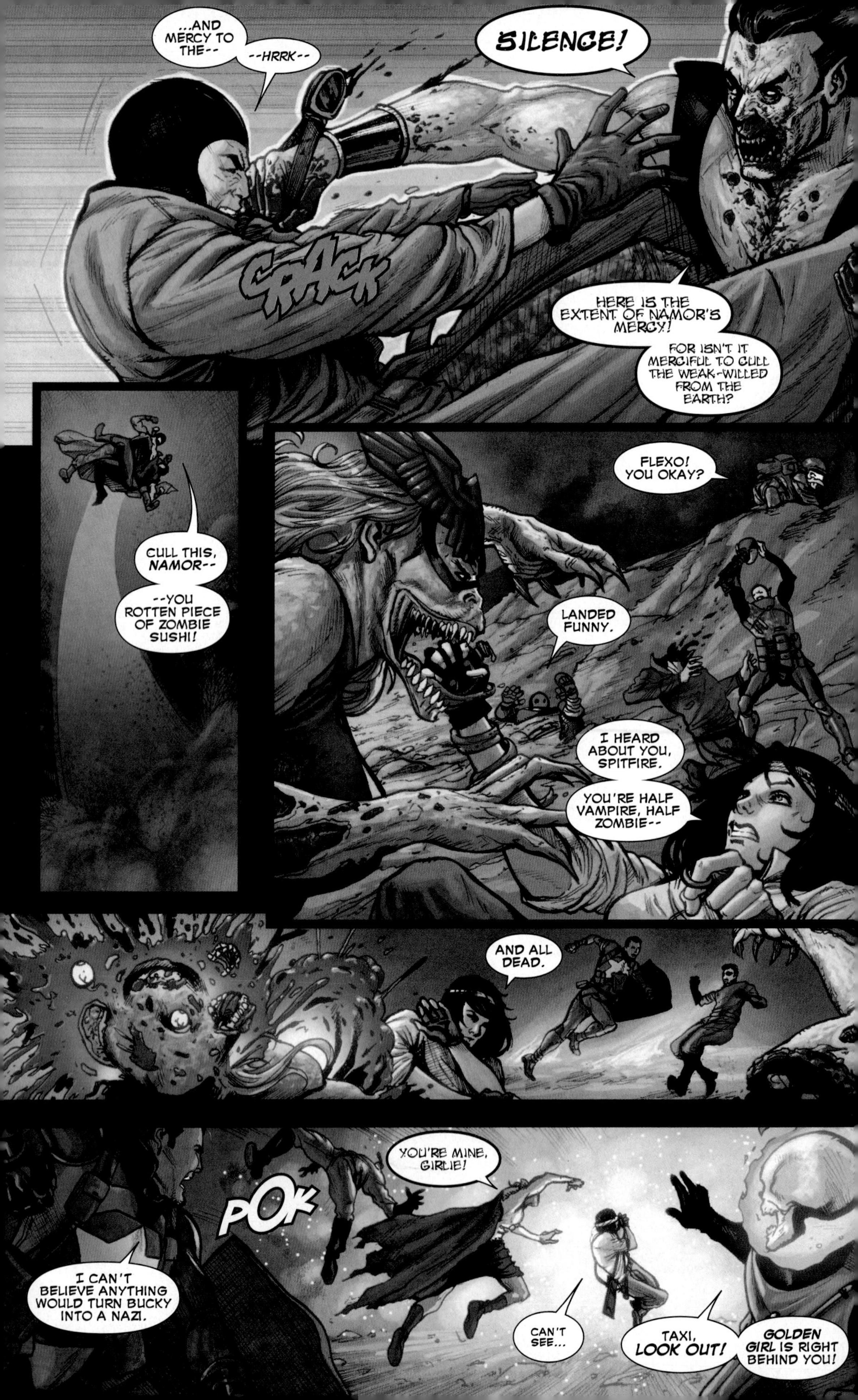
...AND MERCY TO THE--
--HRRK--
SILENCE!
CRACK
HERE IS THE EXTENT OF NAMOR'S MERCY!
FOR ISN'T IT MERCIFUL TO CULL THE WEAK-WILLED FROM THE EARTH?
CULL THIS, NAMOR--
--YOU ROTTEN PIECE OF ZOMBIE SUSHI!
FLEXO! YOU OKAY?
LANDED FUNNY.
I HEARD ABOUT YOU, SPITFIRE.
YOU'RE HALF VAMPIRE, HALF ZOMBIE--
AND ALL DEAD.
YOU'RE MINE, GIRLIE!
POK
I CAN'T BELIEVE ANYTHING WOULD TURN BUCKY INTO A NAZI.
CAN'T SEE...
TAXI, LOOK OUT!
GOLDEN GIRL IS RIGHT BEHIND YOU!

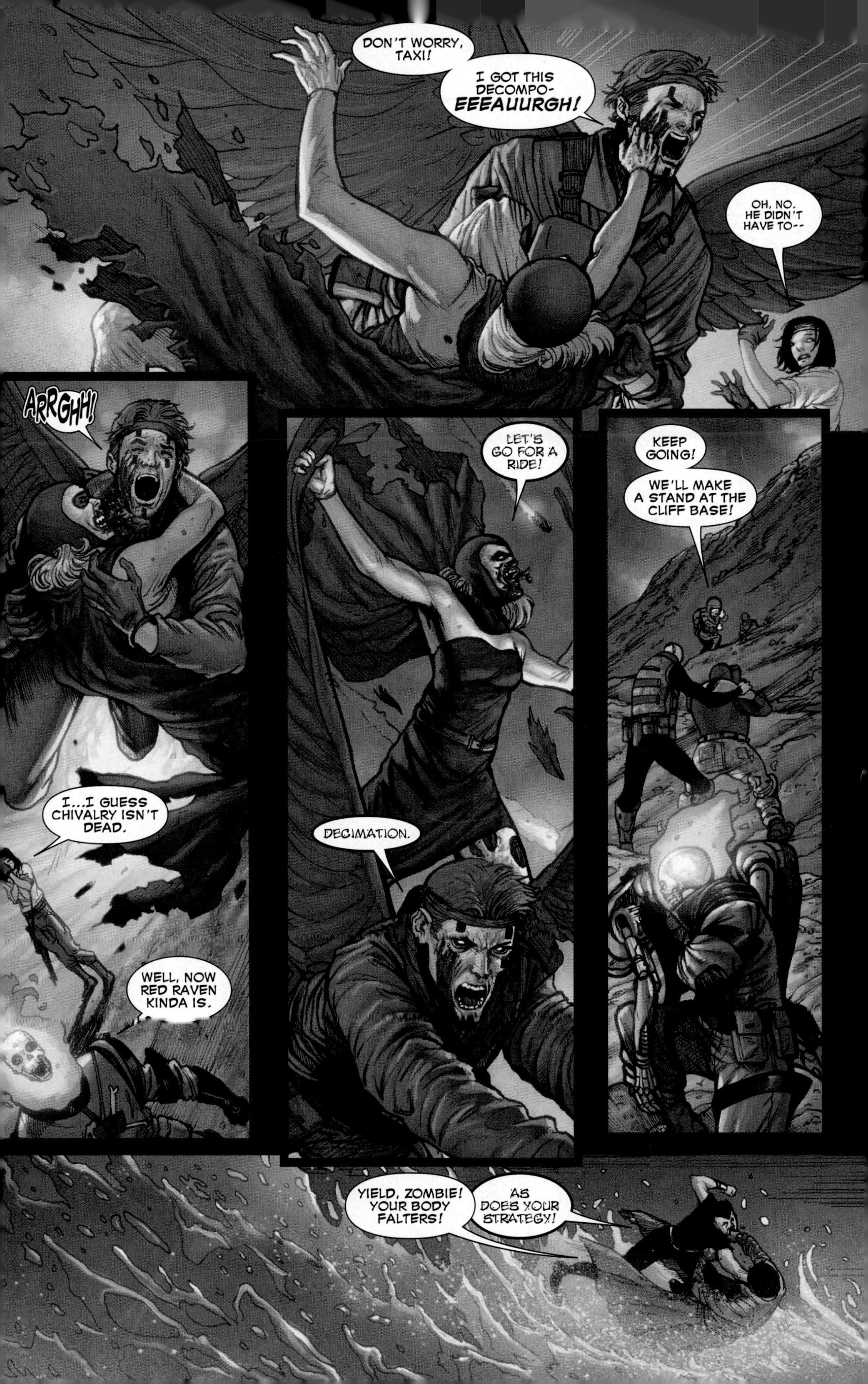
DON'T WORRY, TAXI!
I GOT THIS DECOMPO-EEEAUURGH!
OH, NO. HE DIDN'T HAVE TO--
ARRGHH!
I...I GUESS CHIVALRY ISN'T DEAD.
WELL, NOW RED RAVEN KINDA IS.
LET'S GO FOR A RIDE!
DECIMATION.
KEEP GOING!
WE'LL MAKE A STAND AT THE CLIFF BASE!
YIELD, ZOMBIE! YOUR BODY FALTERS!
AS DOES YOUR STRATEGY!

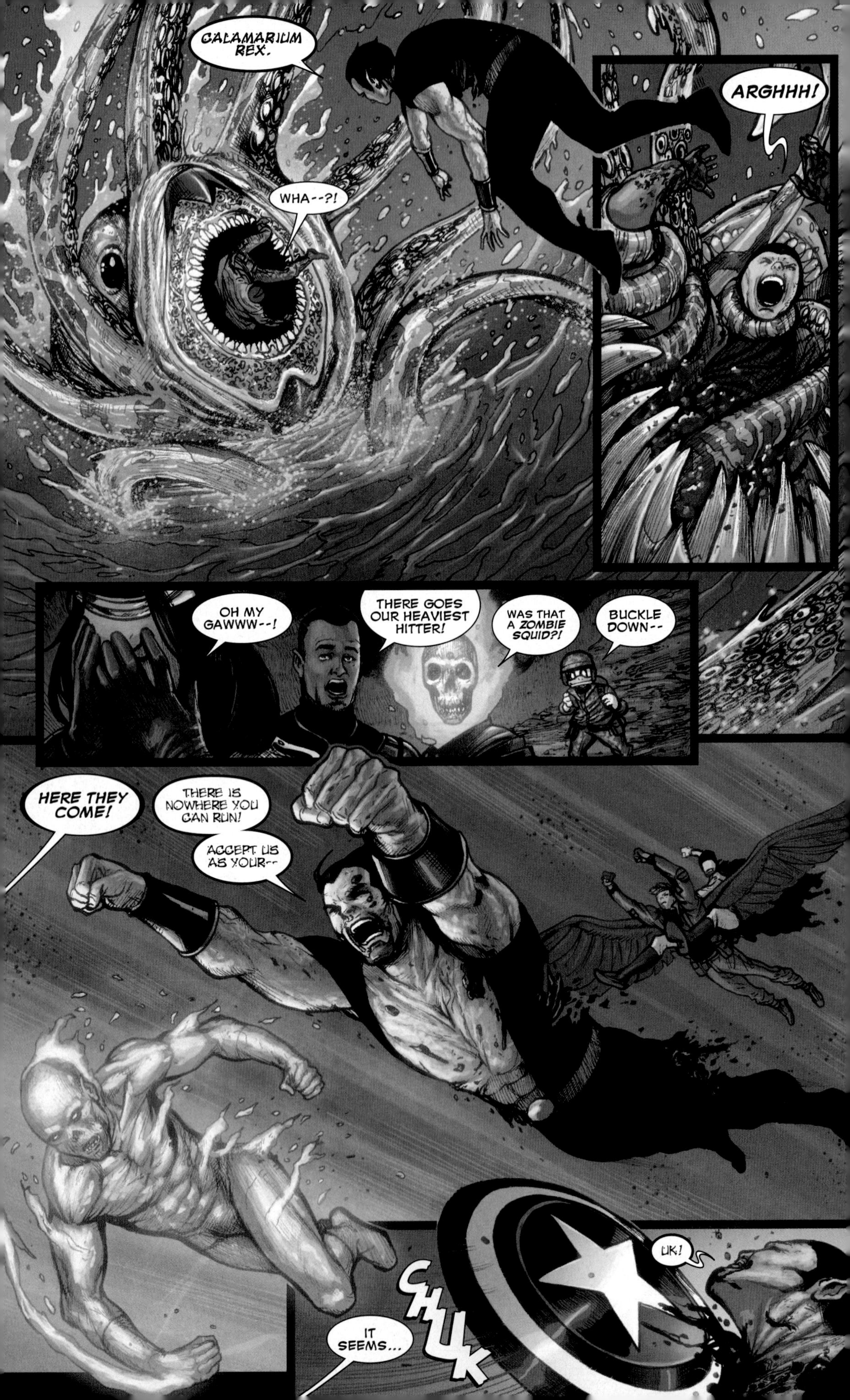
CALAMARIUM REX.
WHA--?!
ARGHHH!
OH MY GAWWW--!
THERE GOES OUR HEAVIEST HITTER!
WAS THAT A ZOMBIE SQUID?!
BUCKLE DOWN--
HERE THEY COME!
THERE IS NOWHERE YOU CAN RUN!
ACCEPT US AS YOUR--
UK!
CHUK
IT SEEMS...

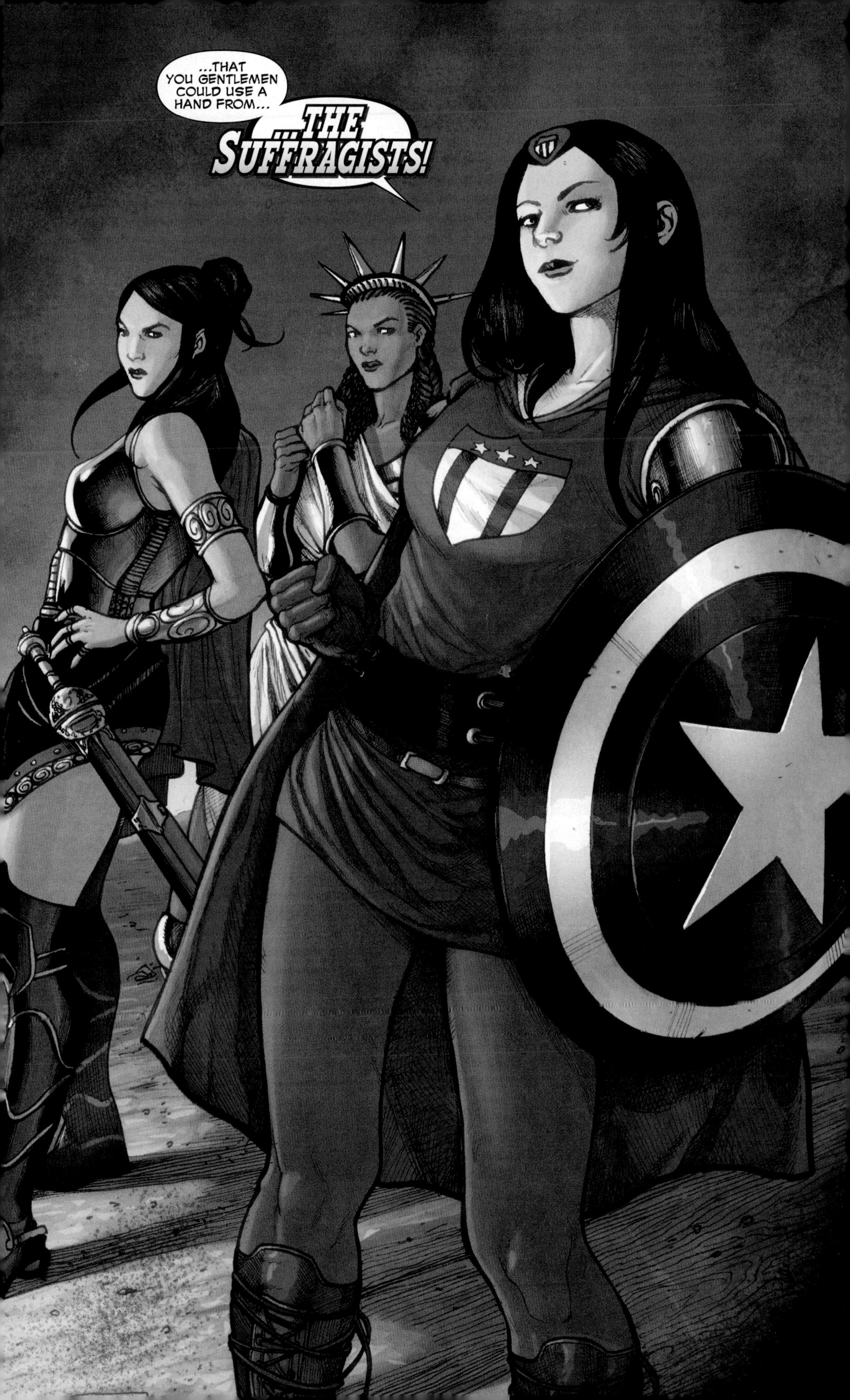
...THAT YOU GENTLEMEN COULD USE A HAND FROM...
...THE SUFFRAGISTS!

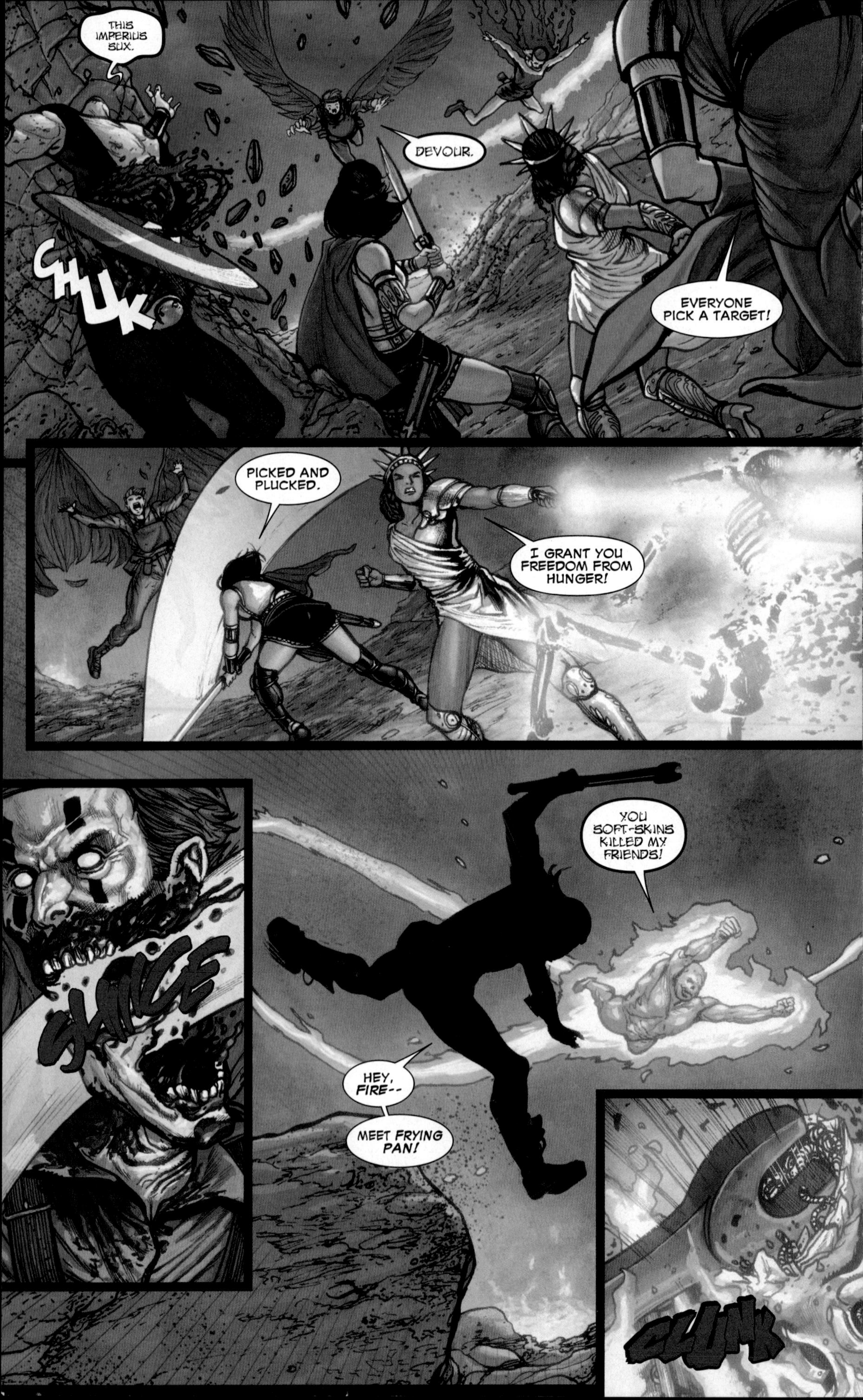
THIS IMPERIUS SUX.
DEVOUR.
CHUK
EVERYONE PICK A TARGET!
PICKED AND PLUCKED.
I GRANT YOU FREEDOM FROM HUNGER!
SHLICE
YOU SOFT-SKINS KILLED MY FRIENDS!
HEY, FIRE--
MEET FRYING PAN!
CLUNK

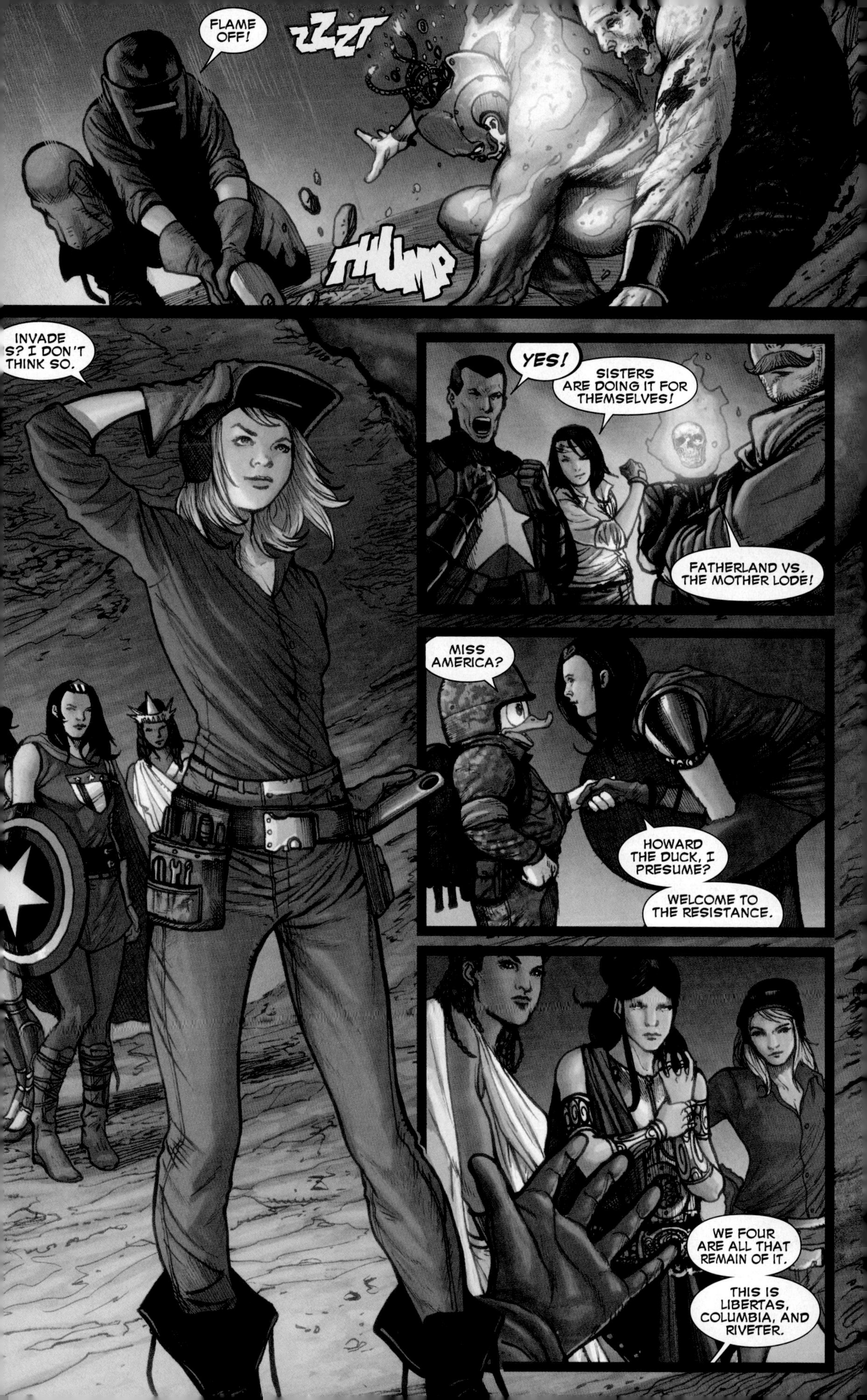
FLAME OFF!
ZZZZT
THUMP
INVADE S? I DON'T THINK SO.
YES!
SISTERS ARE DOING IT FOR THEMSELVES!
FATHERLAND VS. THE MOTHER LODE!
MISS AMERICA?
HOWARD THE DUCK, I PRESUME?
WELCOME TO THE RESISTANCE.
WE FOUR ARE ALL THAT REMAIN OF IT.
THIS IS LIBERTAS, COLUMBIA, AND RIVETER.

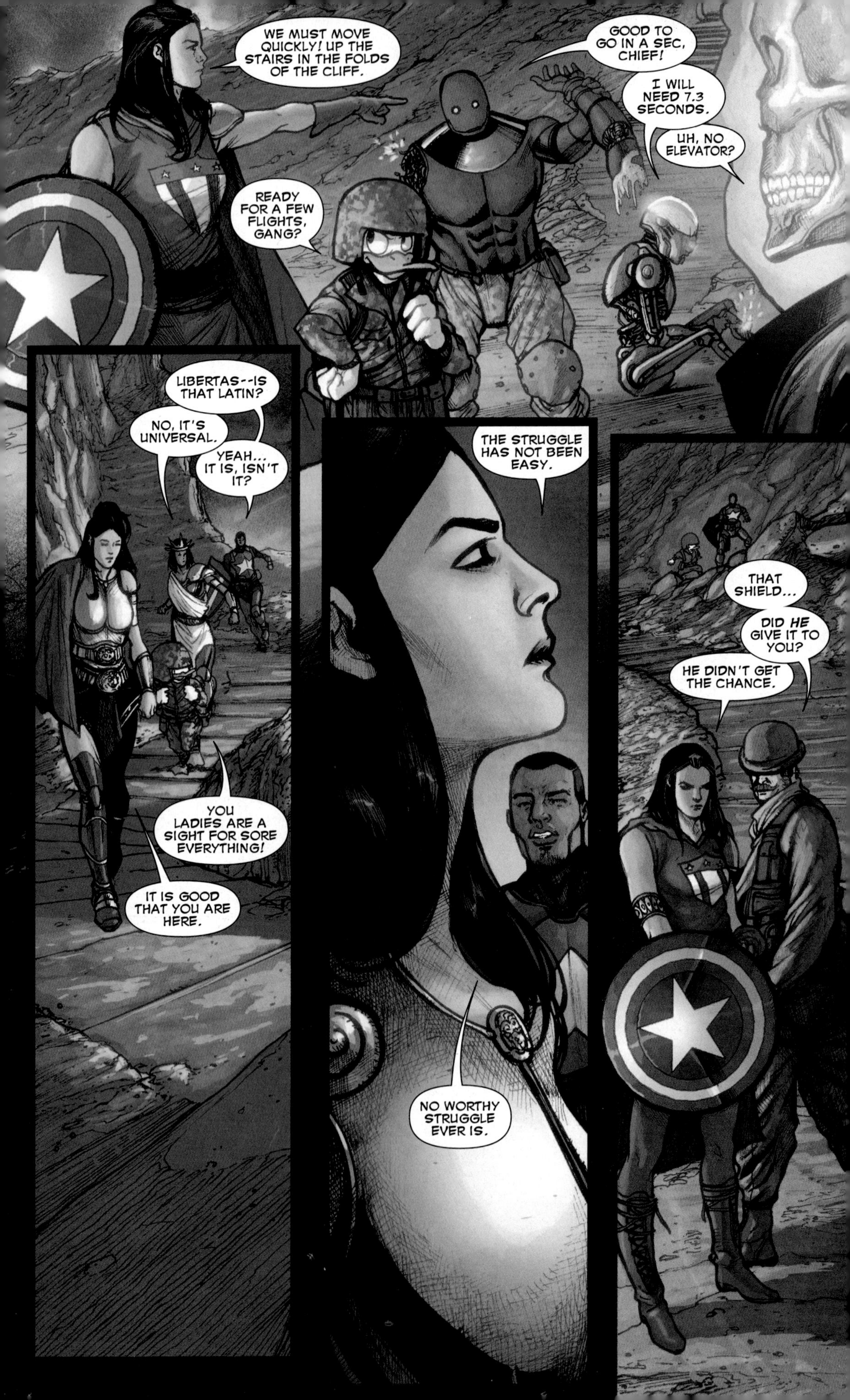
WE MUST MOVE QUICKLY! UP THE STAIRS IN THE FOLDS OF THE CLIFF.
GOOD TO GO IN A SEC, CHIEF!
I WILL NEED 7.3 SECONDS.
UH, NO ELEVATOR?
READY FOR A FEW FLIGHTS, GANG?
LIBERTAS--IS THAT LATIN?
NO, IT'S UNIVERSAL.
YEAH... IT IS, ISN'T IT?
YOU LADIES ARE A SIGHT FOR SORE EVERYTHING!
IT IS GOOD THAT YOU ARE HERE.
THE STRUGGLE HAS NOT BEEN EASY.
NO WORTHY STRUGGLE EVER IS.
THAT SHIELD...
DID HE GIVE IT TO YOU?
HE DIDN'T GET THE CHANCE.

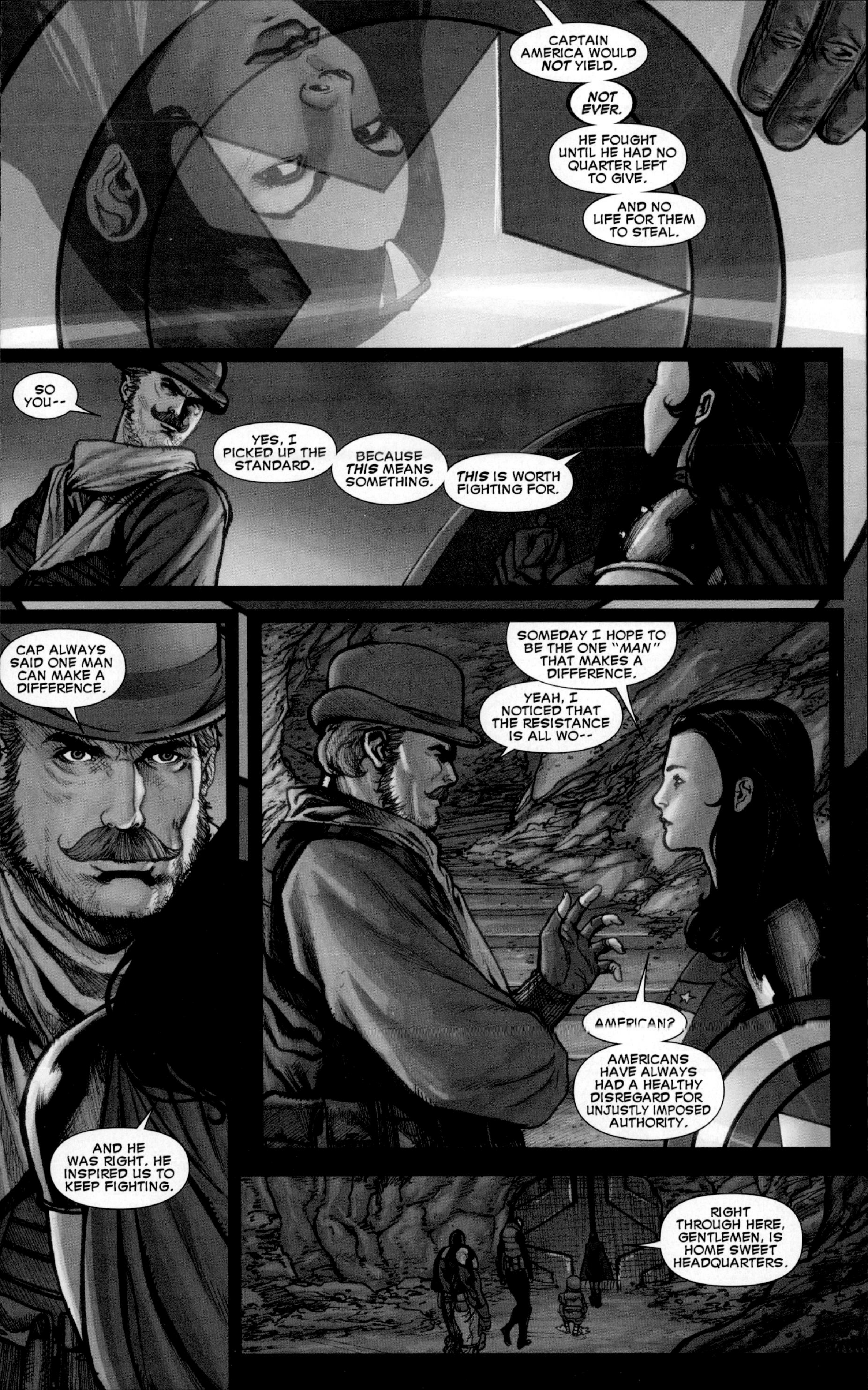
CAPTAIN AMERICA WOULD NOT YIELD.
NOT EVER.
HE FOUGHT UNTIL HE HAD NO QUARTER LEFT TO GIVE.
AND NO LIFE FOR THEM TO STEAL.
SO YOU--
YES, I PICKED UP THE STANDARD.
BECAUSE THIS MEANS SOMETHING.
THIS IS WORTH FIGHTING FOR.
CAP ALWAYS SAID ONE MAN CAN MAKE A DIFFERENCE.
AND HE WAS RIGHT. HE INSPIRED US TO KEEP FIGHTING.
SOMEDAY I HOPE TO BE THE ONE "MAN" THAT MAKES A DIFFERENCE.
YEAH, I NOTICED THAT THE RESISTANCE IS ALL WO--
AMERICAN?
AMERICANS HAVE ALWAYS HAD A HEALTHY DISREGARD FOR UNJUSTLY IMPOSED AUTHORITY.
RIGHT THROUGH HERE, GENTLEMEN, IS HOME SWEET HEADQUARTERS.

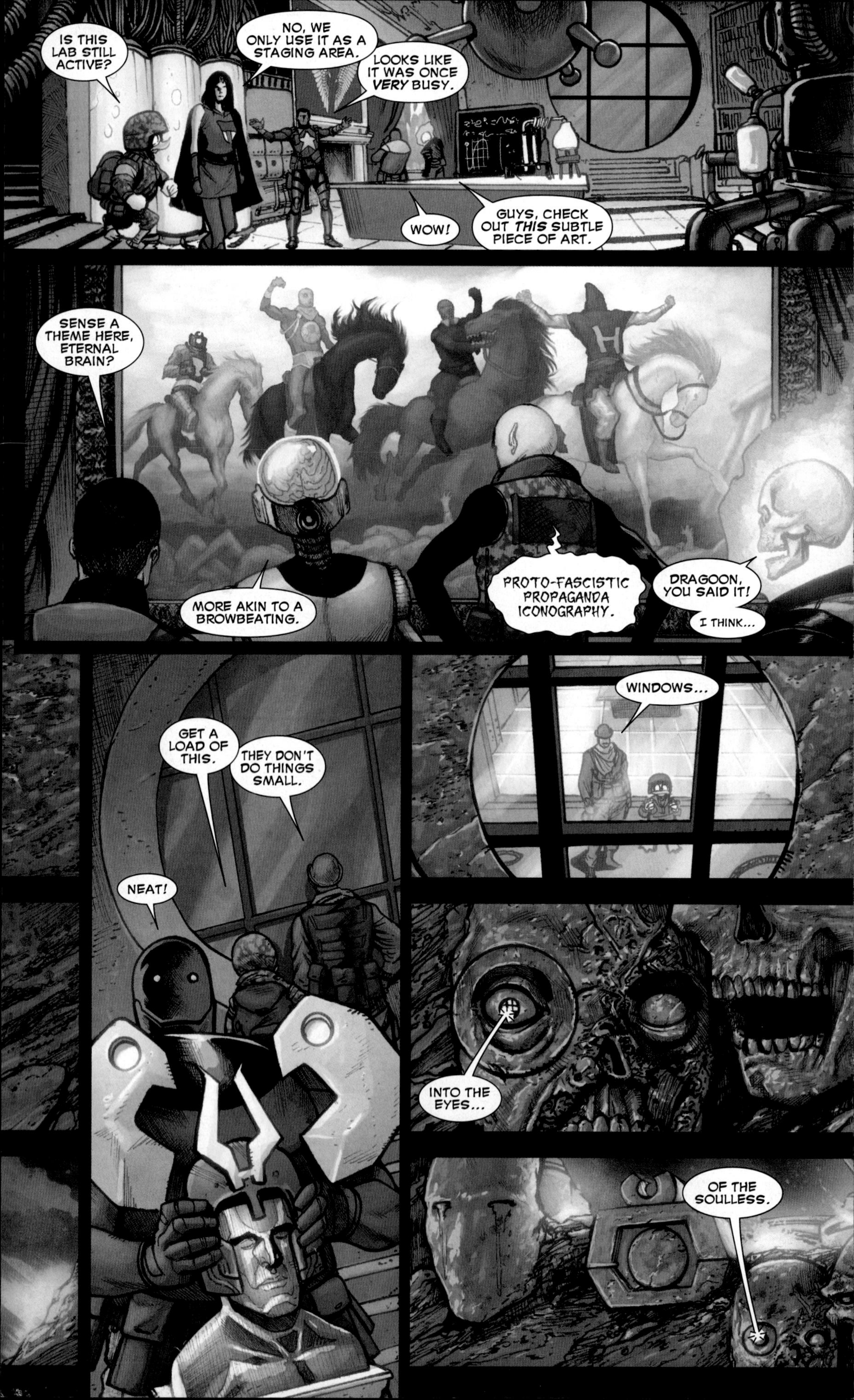
IS THIS LAB STILL ACTIVE?
NO, WE ONLY USE IT AS A STAGING AREA.
LOOKS LIKE IT WAS ONCE VERY BUSY.
WOW!
GUYS, CHECK OUT THIS SUBTLE PIECE OF ART.
SENSE A THEME HERE, ETERNAL BRAIN?
MORE AKIN TO A BROWBEATING.
PROTO-FASCISTIC PROPAGANDA ICONOGRAPHY.
DRAGOON, YOU SAID IT!
I THINK...
GET A LOAD OF THIS.
THEY DON'T DO THINGS SMALL.
NEAT!
WINDOWS...
INTO THE EYES...
OF THE SOULLESS.

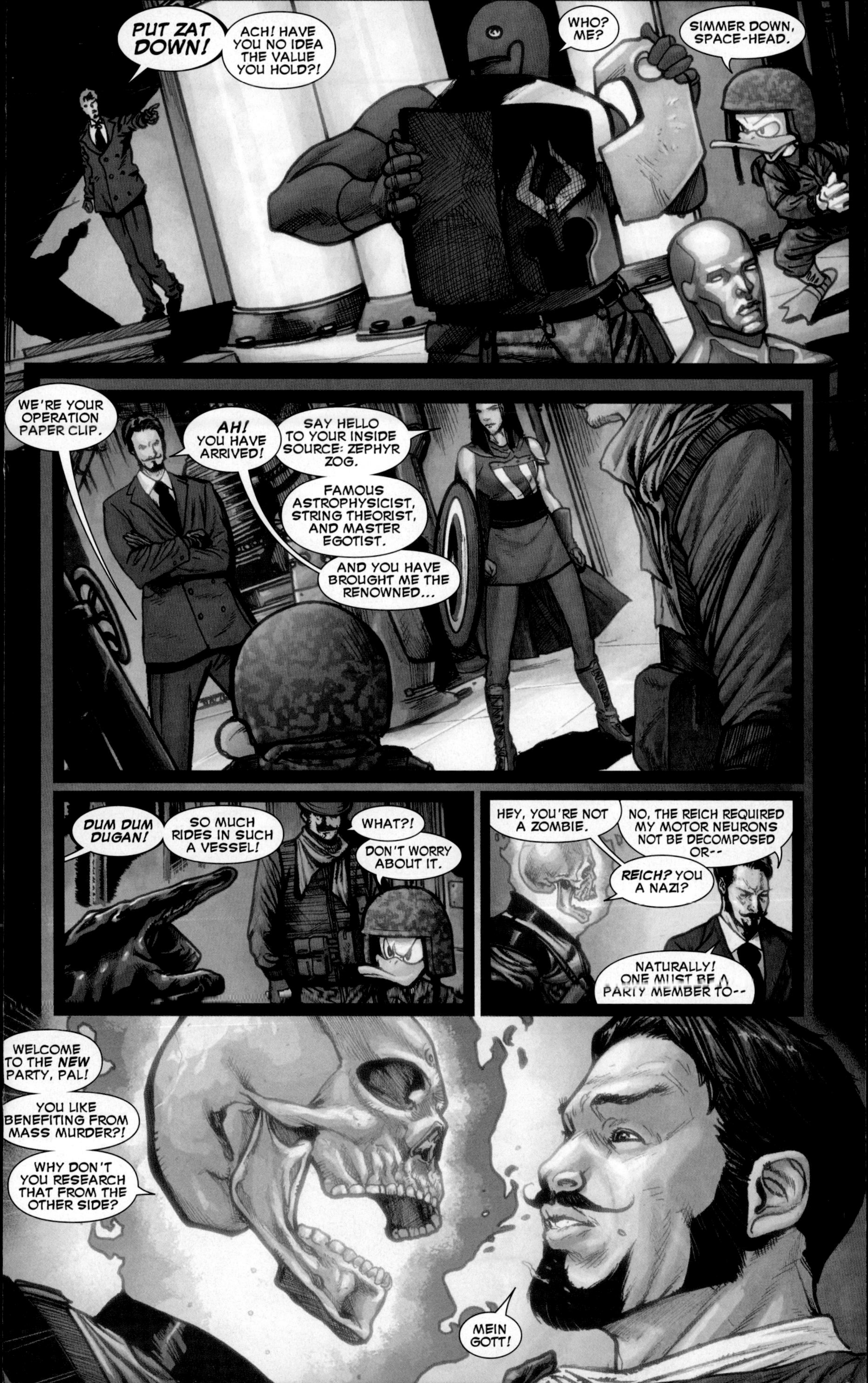
PUT ZAT DOWN!
ACH! HAVE YOU NO IDEA THE VALUE YOU HOLD?!
WHO? ME?
SIMMER DOWN, SPACE-HEAD.
WE'RE YOUR OPERATION PAPER CLIP.
AH! YOU HAVE ARRIVED!
SAY HELLO TO YOUR INSIDE SOURCE: ZEPHYR ZOG.
FAMOUS ASTROPHYSICIST, STRING THEORIST, AND MASTER EGOTIST.
AND YOU HAVE BROUGHT ME THE RENOWNED...
DUM DUM DUGAN!
SO MUCH RIDES IN SUCH A VESSEL!
WHAT?!
DON'T WORRY ABOUT IT.
HEY, YOU'RE NOT A ZOMBIE.
NO, THE REICH REQUIRED MY MOTOR NEURONS NOT BE DECOMPOSED OR--
REICH? YOU A NAZI?
NATURALLY! ONE MUST BE A PARTY MEMBER TO--
WELCOME TO THE NEW PARTY, PAL!
YOU LIKE BENEFITING FROM MASS MURDER?!
WHY DON'T YOU RESEARCH THAT FROM THE OTHER SIDE?
MEIN GOTT!

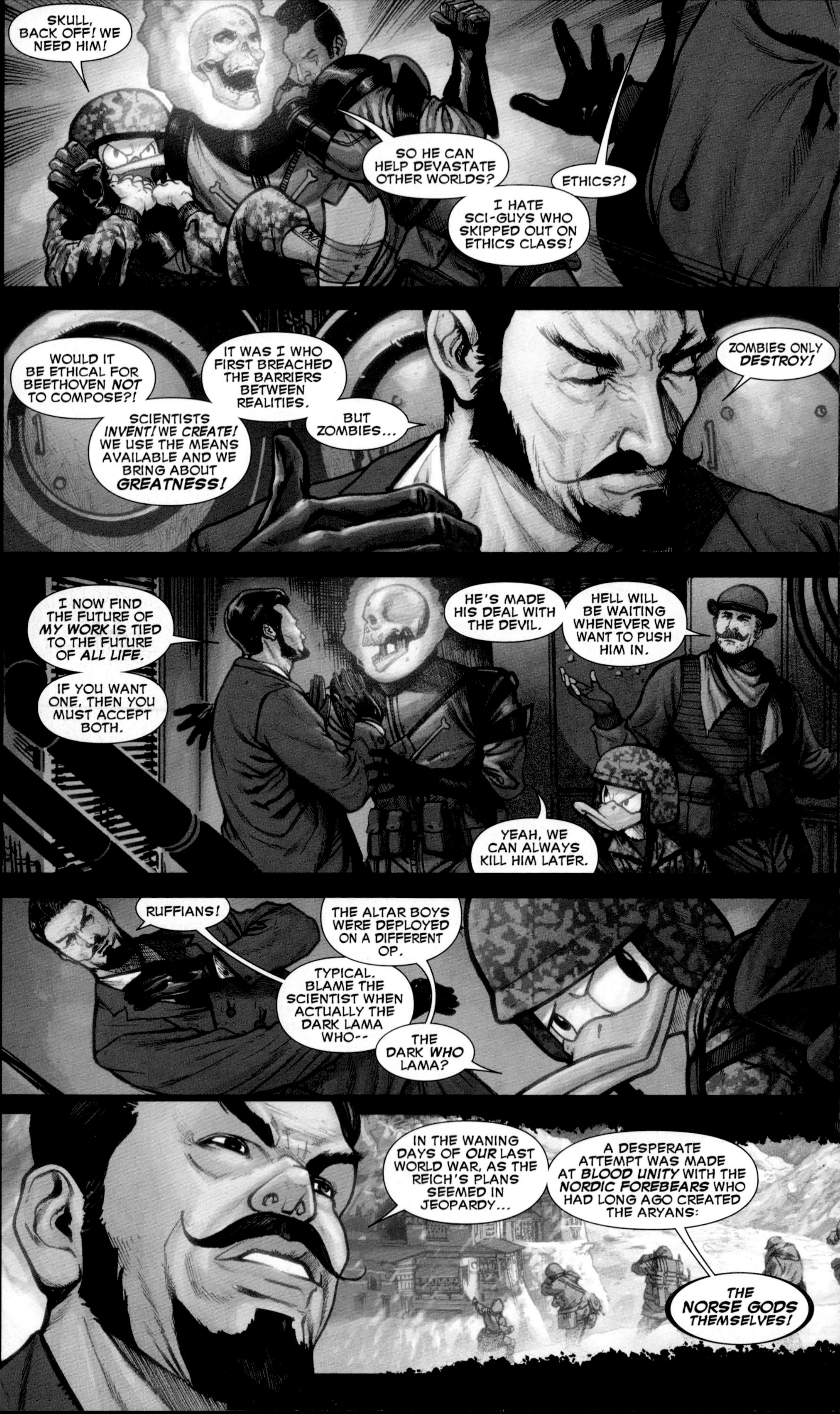
SKULL, BACK OFF! WE NEED HIM!
SO HE CAN HELP DEVASTATE OTHER WORLDS?
ETHICS?!
I HATE SCI-GUYS WHO SKIPPED OUT ON ETHICS CLASS!
WOULD IT BE ETHICAL FOR BEETHOVEN NOT TO COMPOSE?!
SCIENTISTS INVENT! WE CREATE! WE USE THE MEANS AVAILABLE AND WE BRING ABOUT GREATNESS!
IT WAS I WHO FIRST BREACHED THE BARRIERS BETWEEN REALITIES.
BUT ZOMBIES...
ZOMBIES ONLY DESTROY!
I NOW FIND THE FUTURE OF MY WORK IS TIED TO THE FUTURE OF ALL LIFE.
IF YOU WANT ONE, THEN YOU MUST ACCEPT BOTH.
HE'S MADE HIS DEAL WITH THE DEVIL.
HELL WILL BE WAITING WHENEVER WE WANT TO PUSH HIM IN.
YEAH, WE CAN ALWAYS KILL HIM LATER.
RUFFIANS!
THE ALTAR BOYS WERE DEPLOYED ON A DIFFERENT OP.
TYPICAL. BLAME THE SCIENTIST WHEN ACTUALLY THE DARK LAMA WHO--
THE DARK WHO LAMA?
IN THE WANING DAYS OF OUR LAST WORLD WAR, AS THE REICH'S PLANS SEEMED IN JEOPARDY...
A DESPERATE ATTEMPT WAS MADE AT BLOOD UNITY WITH THE NORDIC FOREBEARS WHO HAD LONG AGO CREATED THE ARYANS:
THE NORSE GODS THEMSELVES!

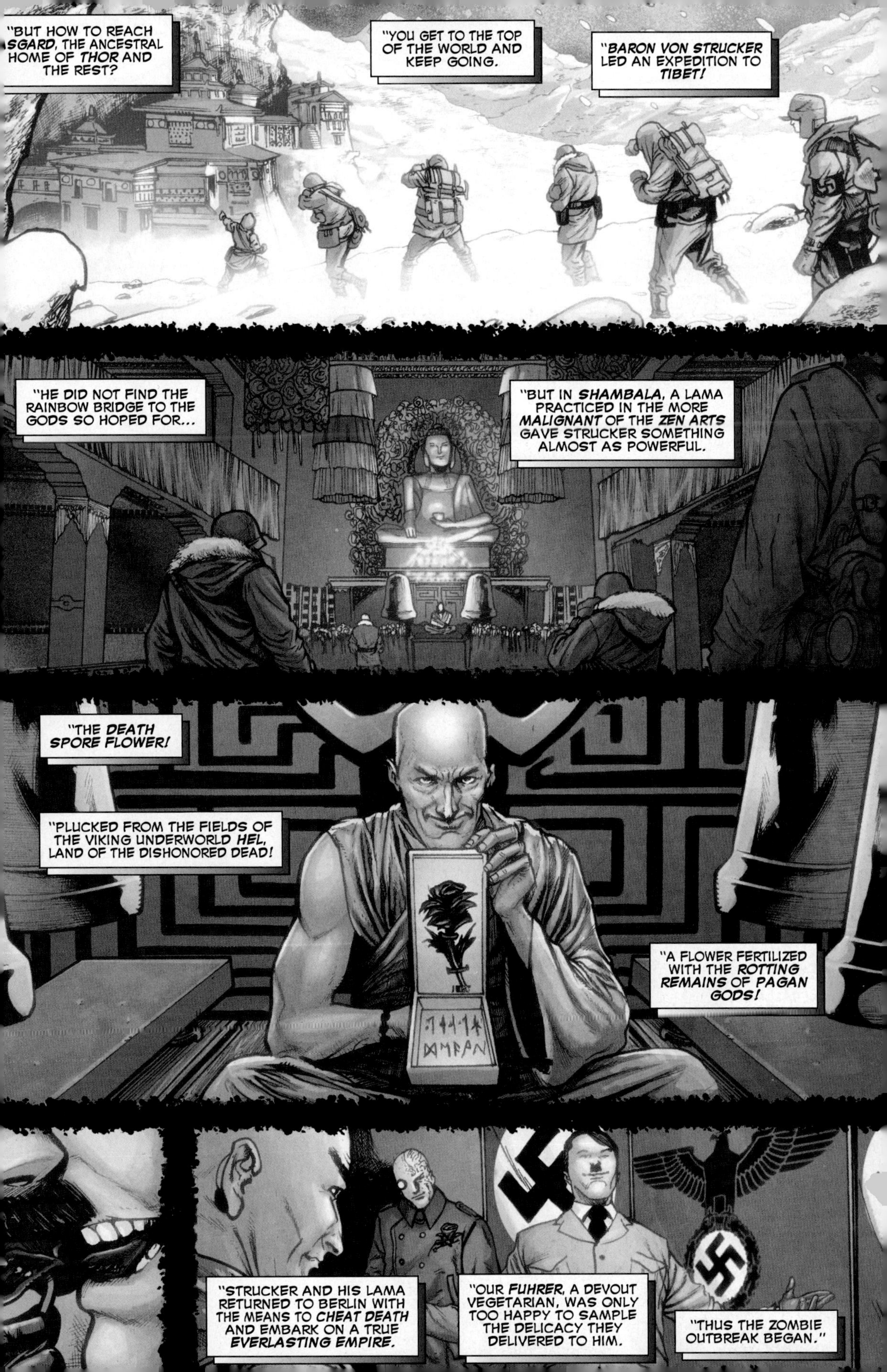
"BUT HOW TO REACH SGARD, THE ANCESTRAL HOME OF THOR AND THE REST?
"YOU GET TO THE TOP OF THE WORLD AND KEEP GOING.
"BARON VON STRUCKER LED AN EXPEDITION TO TIBET!
"HE DID NOT FIND THE RAINBOW BRIDGE TO THE GODS SO HOPED FOR...
"BUT IN SHAMBALA, A LAMA PRACTICED IN THE MORE MALIGNANT OF THE ZEN ARTS GAVE STRUCKER SOMETHING ALMOST AS POWERFUL.
"THE DEATH SPORE FLOWER!
"PLUCKED FROM THE FIELDS OF THE VIKING UNDERWORLD HEL, LAND OF THE DISHONORED DEAD!
"A FLOWER FERTILIZED WITH THE ROTTING REMAINS OF PAGAN GODS!
"STRUCKER AND HIS LAMA RETURNED TO BERLIN WITH THE MEANS TO CHEAT DEATH AND EMBARK ON A TRUE EVERLASTING EMPIRE.
"OUR FUHRER, A DEVOUT VEGETARIAN, WAS ONLY TOO HAPPY TO SAMPLE THE DELICACY THEY DELIVERED TO HIM.
"THUS THE ZOMBIE OUTBREAK BEGAN."

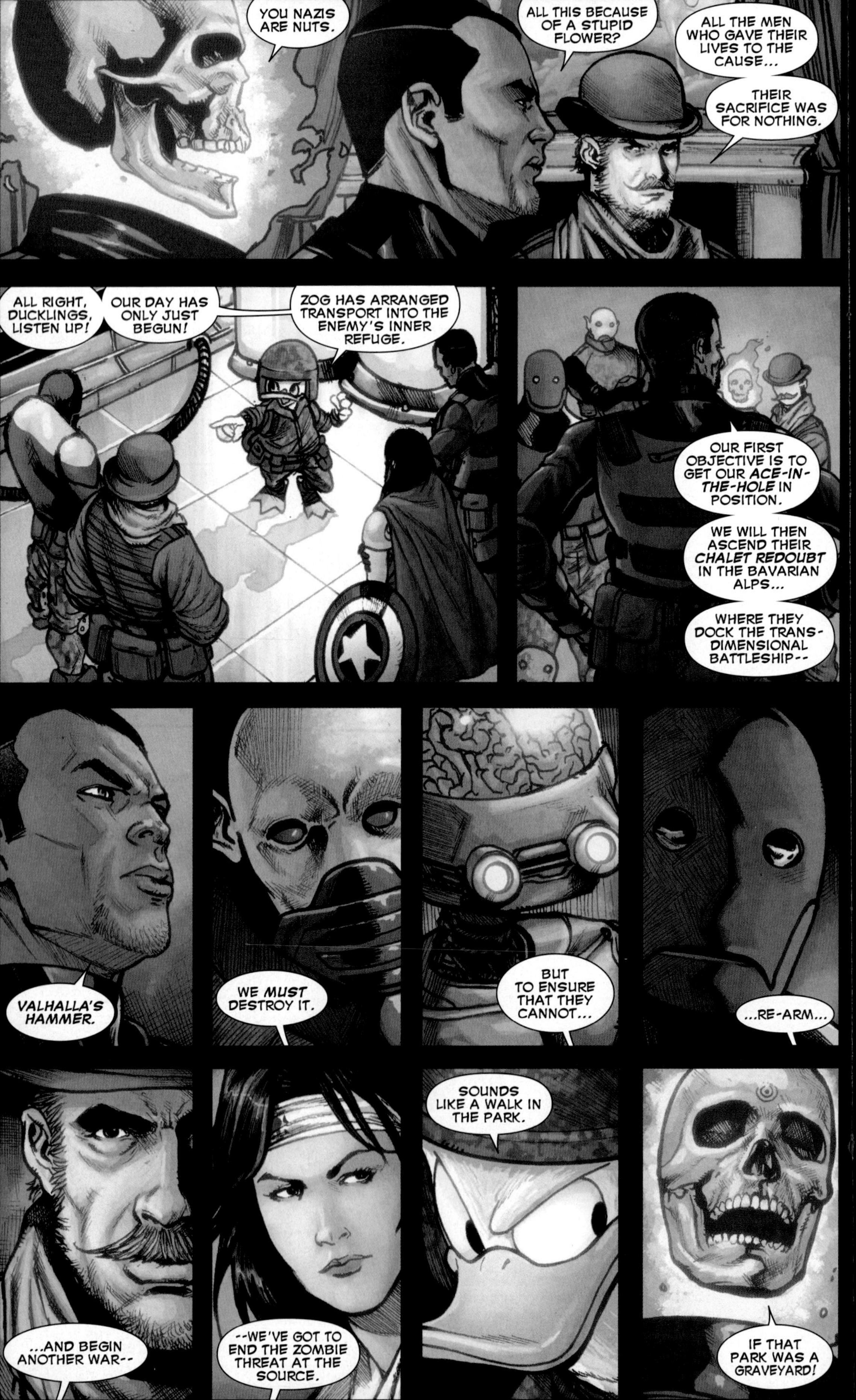
YOU NAZIS ARE NUTS.
ALL THIS BECAUSE OF A STUPID FLOWER?
ALL THE MEN WHO GAVE THEIR LIVES TO THE CAUSE...
THEIR SACRIFICE WAS FOR NOTHING.
ALL RIGHT, DUCKLINGS, LISTEN UP!
OUR DAY HAS ONLY JUST BEGUN!
ZOG HAS ARRANGED TRANSPORT INTO THE ENEMY'S INNER REFUGE.
OUR FIRST OBJECTIVE IS TO GET OUR *ACE-IN-THE-HOLE* IN POSITION.
WE WILL THEN ASCEND THEIR *CHALET REDOUBT* IN THE BAVARIAN ALPS...
WHERE THEY DOCK THE TRANS-DIMENSIONAL BATTLESHIP--
VALHALLA'S HAMMER.
WE *MUST* DESTROY IT.
BUT TO ENSURE THAT THEY CANNOT...
...RE-ARM...
...AND BEGIN ANOTHER WAR--
--WE'VE GOT TO END THE ZOMBIE THREAT AT THE SOURCE.
SOUNDS LIKE A WALK IN THE PARK.
IF THAT PARK WAS A GRAVEYARD!

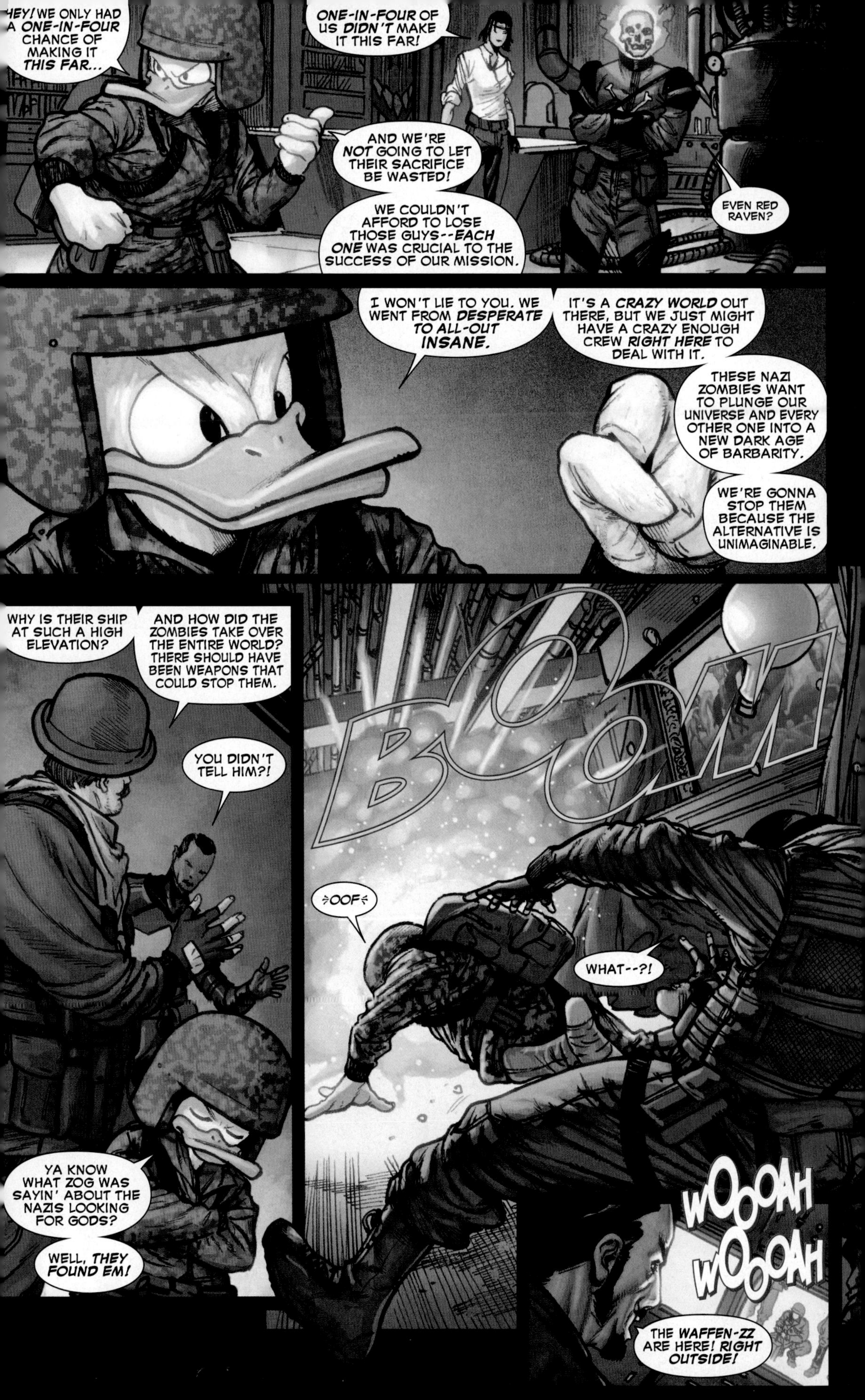
HEY! WE ONLY HAD A ONE-IN-FOUR CHANCE OF MAKING IT THIS FAR...
ONE-IN-FOUR OF US DIDN'T MAKE IT THIS FAR!
AND WE'RE NOT GOING TO LET THEIR SACRIFICE BE WASTED!
WE COULDN'T AFFORD TO LOSE THOSE GUYS--EACH ONE WAS CRUCIAL TO THE SUCCESS OF OUR MISSION.
EVEN RED RAVEN?
I WON'T LIE TO YOU. WE WENT FROM DESPERATE TO ALL-OUT INSANE.
IT'S A CRAZY WORLD OUT THERE, BUT WE JUST MIGHT HAVE A CRAZY ENOUGH CREW RIGHT HERE TO DEAL WITH IT.
THESE NAZI ZOMBIES WANT TO PLUNGE OUR UNIVERSE AND EVERY OTHER ONE INTO A NEW DARK AGE OF BARBARITY.
WE'RE GONNA STOP THEM BECAUSE THE ALTERNATIVE IS UNIMAGINABLE.
WHY IS THEIR SHIP AT SUCH A HIGH ELEVATION?
AND HOW DID THE ZOMBIES TAKE OVER THE ENTIRE WORLD? THERE SHOULD HAVE BEEN WEAPONS THAT COULD STOP THEM.
YOU DIDN'T TELL HIM?!
YA KNOW WHAT ZOG WAS SAYIN' ABOUT THE NAZIS LOOKING FOR GODS?
WELL, THEY FOUND EM!
BOOM
OOF
WHAT--?!
WOOOAH WOOOAH
THE WAFFEN-ZZ ARE HERE! RIGHT OUTSIDE!

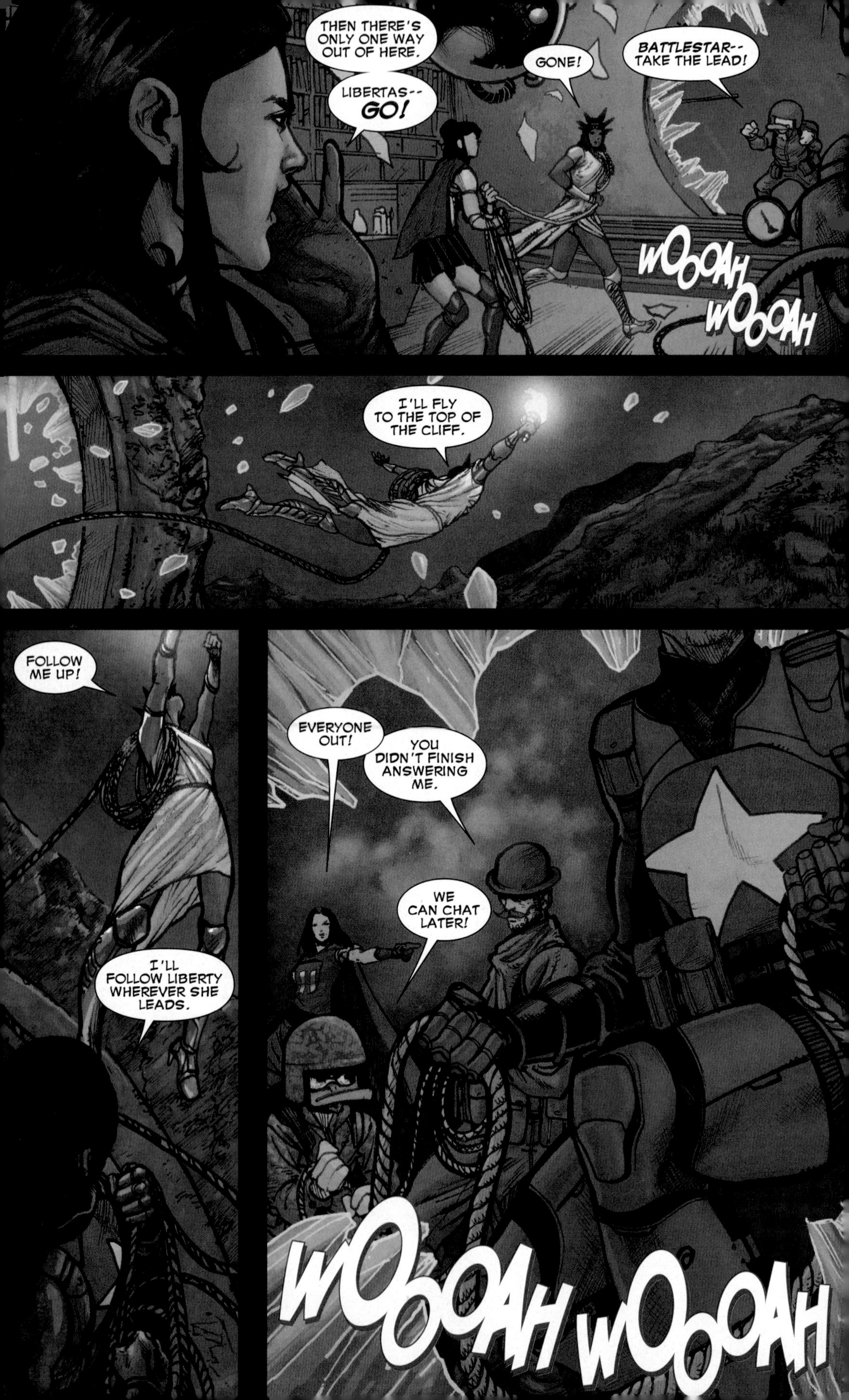
THEN THERE'S ONLY ONE WAY OUT OF HERE.
LIBERTAS-- GO!
GONE!
BATTLESTAR-- TAKE THE LEAD!
WOOOAH WOOOAH
I'LL FLY TO THE TOP OF THE CLIFF.
FOLLOW ME UP!
I'LL FOLLOW LIBERTY WHEREVER SHE LEADS.
EVERYONE OUT!
YOU DIDN'T FINISH ANSWERING ME.
WE CAN CHAT LATER!
WOOOAH WOOOAH

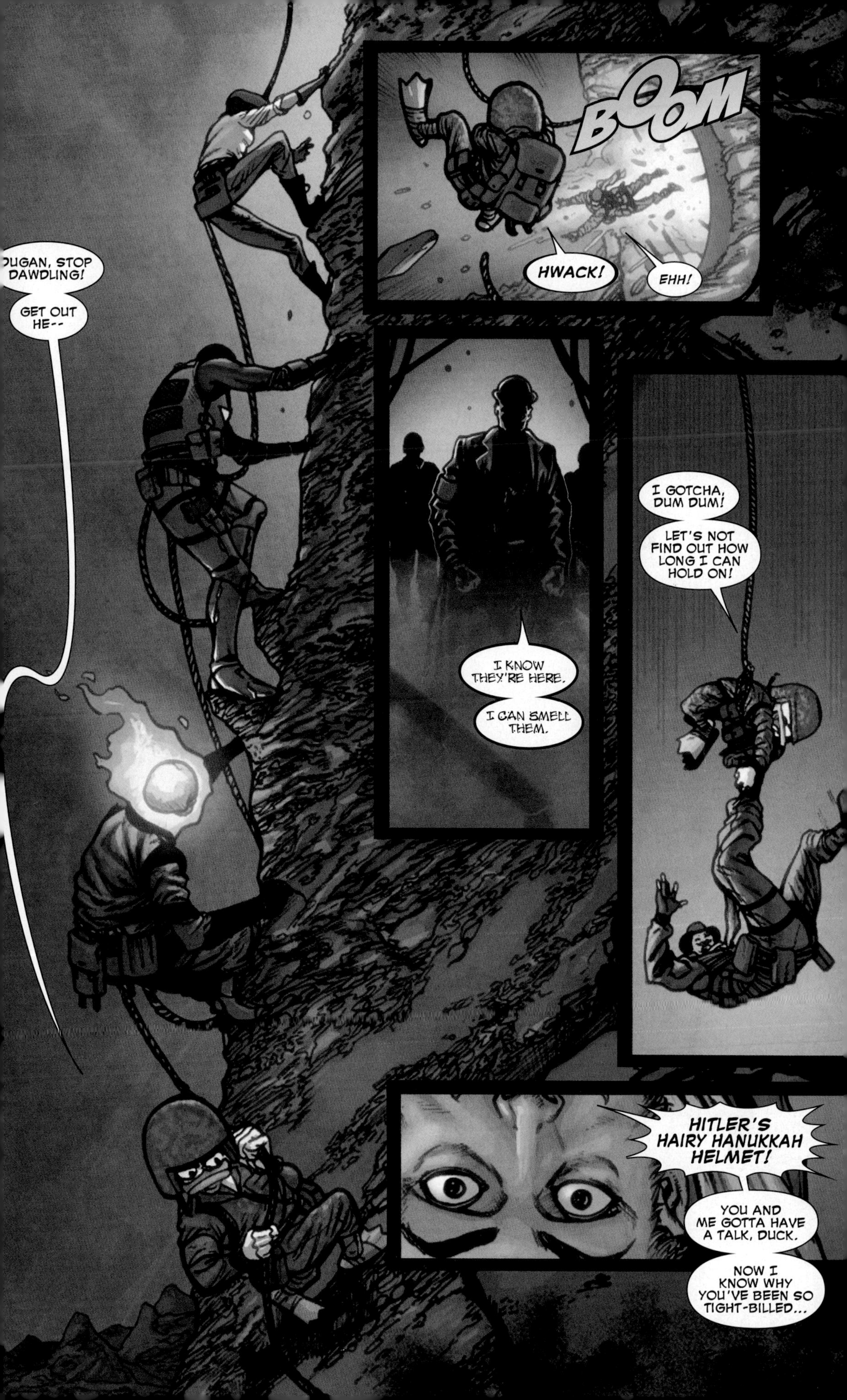

UGAN, STOP DAWDLING!
GET OUT HE--
BOOOM
HWACK!
EHH!
I KNOW THEY'RE HERE.
I CAN SMELL THEM.
I GOTCHA, DUM DUM!
LET'S NOT FIND OUT HOW LONG I CAN HOLD ON!
HITLER'S HAIRY HANUKKAH HELMET!
YOU AND ME GOTTA HAVE A TALK, DUCK.
NOW I KNOW WHY YOU'VE BEEN SO TIGHT-BILLED...

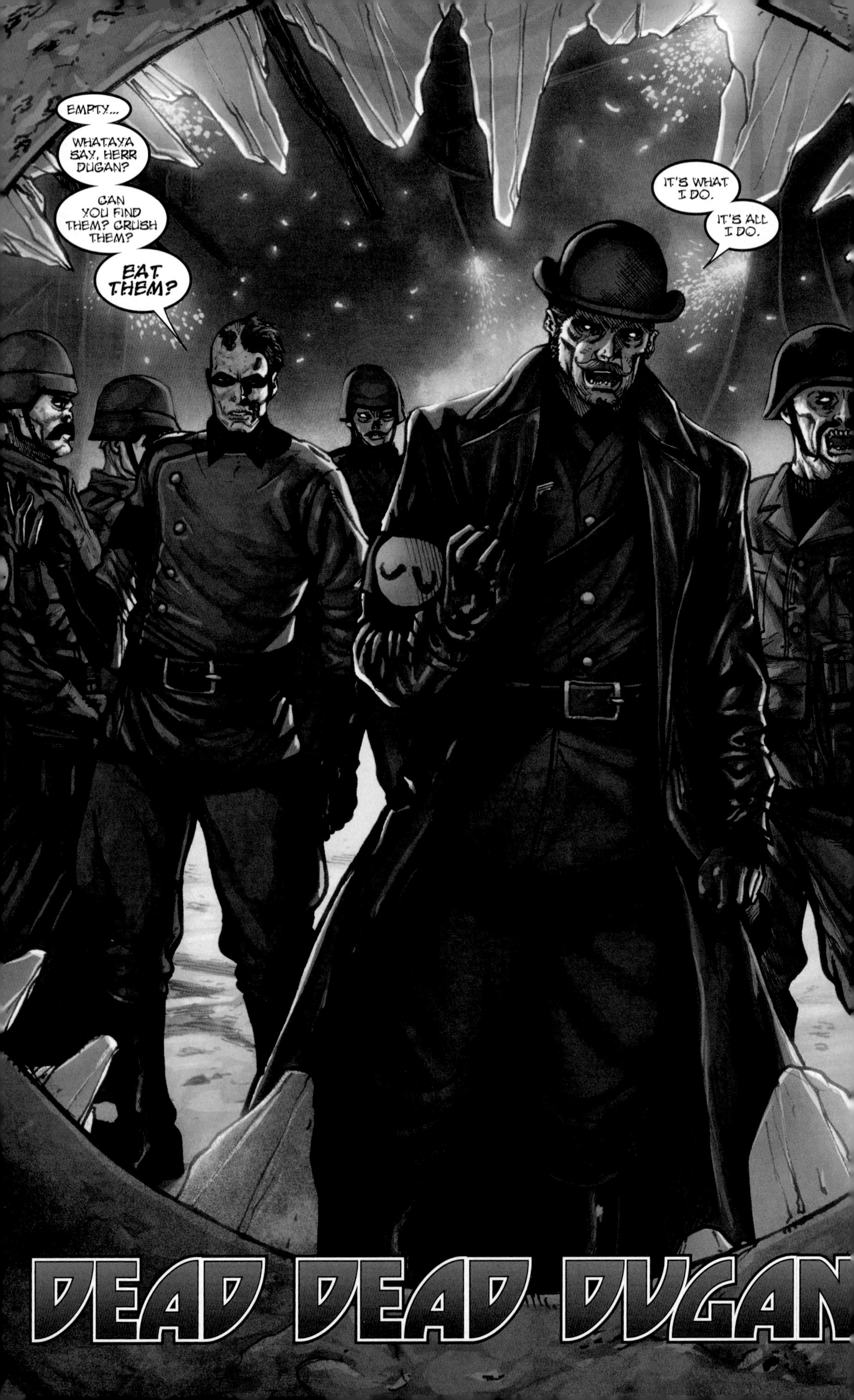
EMPTY...
WHATAYA SAY, HERR DUGAN?
CAN YOU FIND THEM? CRUSH THEM?
EAT THEM?
IT'S WHAT I DO.
IT'S ALL I DO.
DEAD DEAD DUGAN

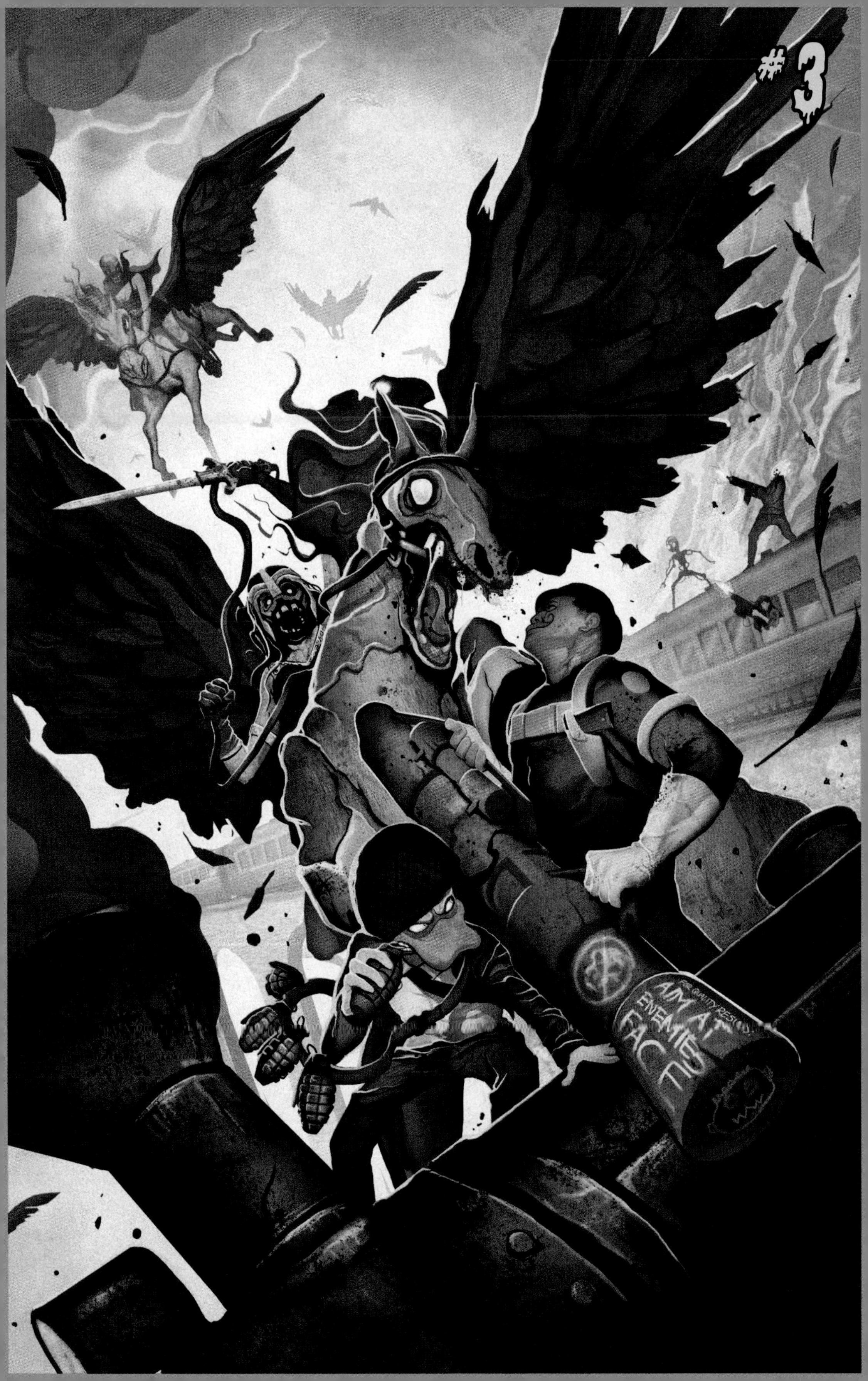
#3
AIM AT
ENEMIES
FACE

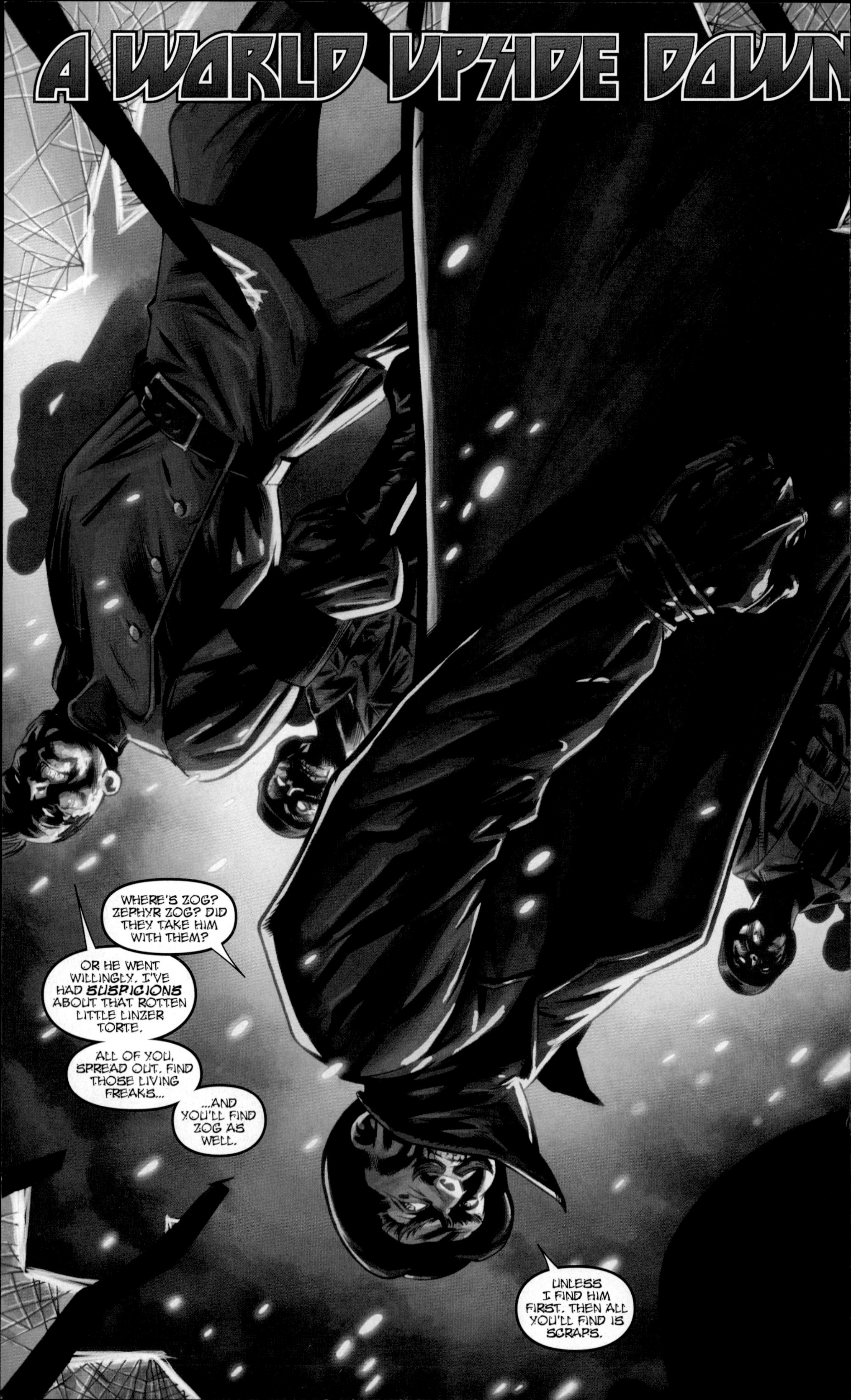
A WORLD UPSIDE DOWN
WHERE'S ZOG? ZEPHYR ZOG? DID THEY TAKE HIM WITH THEM?
OR HE WENT WILLINGLY. I'VE HAD SUSPICIONS ABOUT THAT ROTTEN LITTLE LINZER TORTE.
ALL OF YOU, SPREAD OUT. FIND THOSE LIVING FREAKS...
...AND YOU'LL FIND ZOG AS WELL.
UNLESS I FIND HIM FIRST. THEN ALL YOU'LL FIND IS SCRAPS.

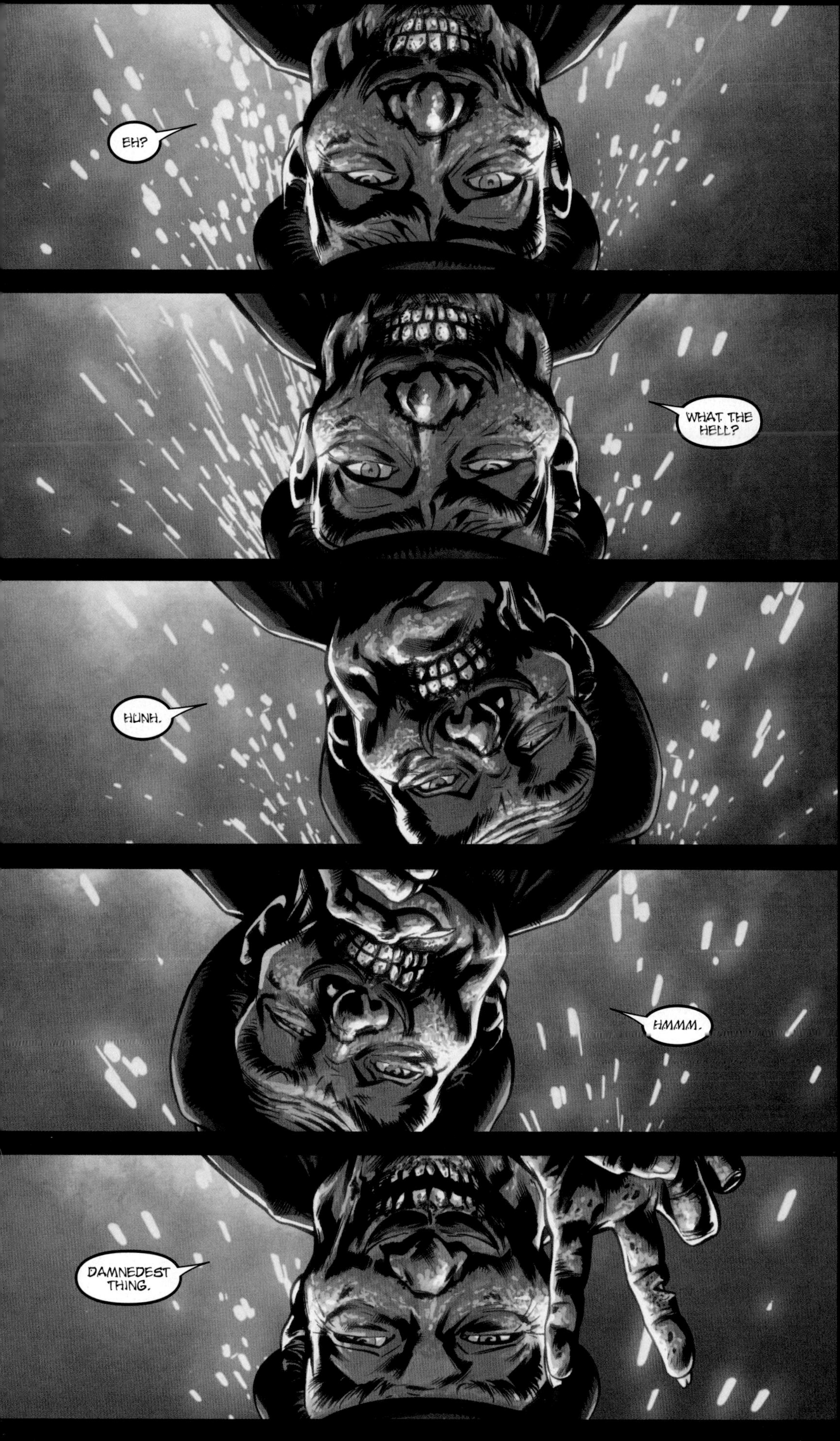
EH?
WHAT THE HELL?
HUNH.
HMMM.
DAMNEDEST THING.

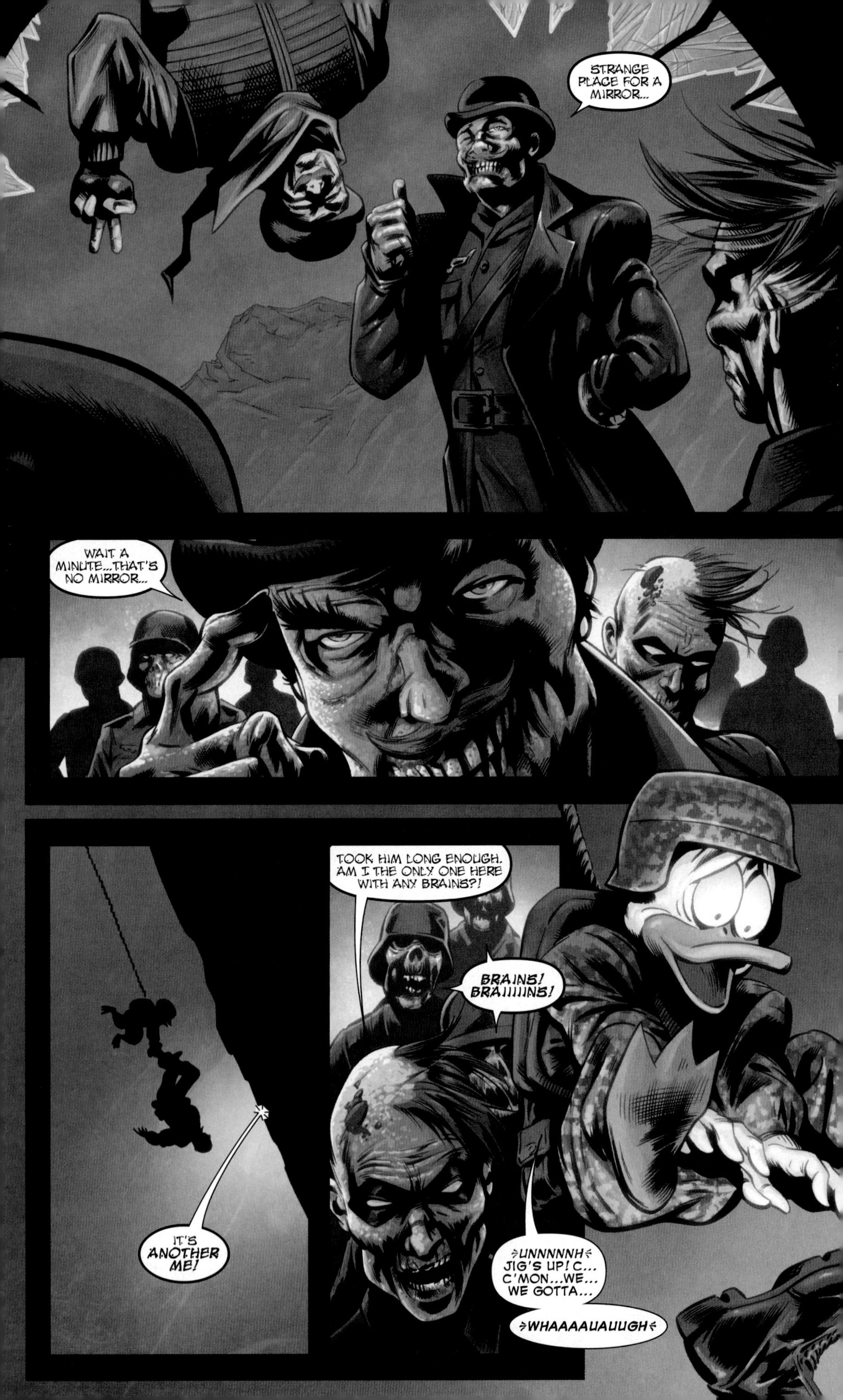
STRANGE PLACE FOR A MIRROR...
WAIT A MINUTE...THAT'S NO MIRROR...
IT'S ANOTHER ME!
TOOK HIM LONG ENOUGH. AM I THE ONLY ONE HERE WITH ANY BRAINS?!
BRAINS! BRAIIIIINS!
UNNNNNH JIG'S UP! C... C'MON...WE... WE GOTTA...
WHAAAAUAUUGH

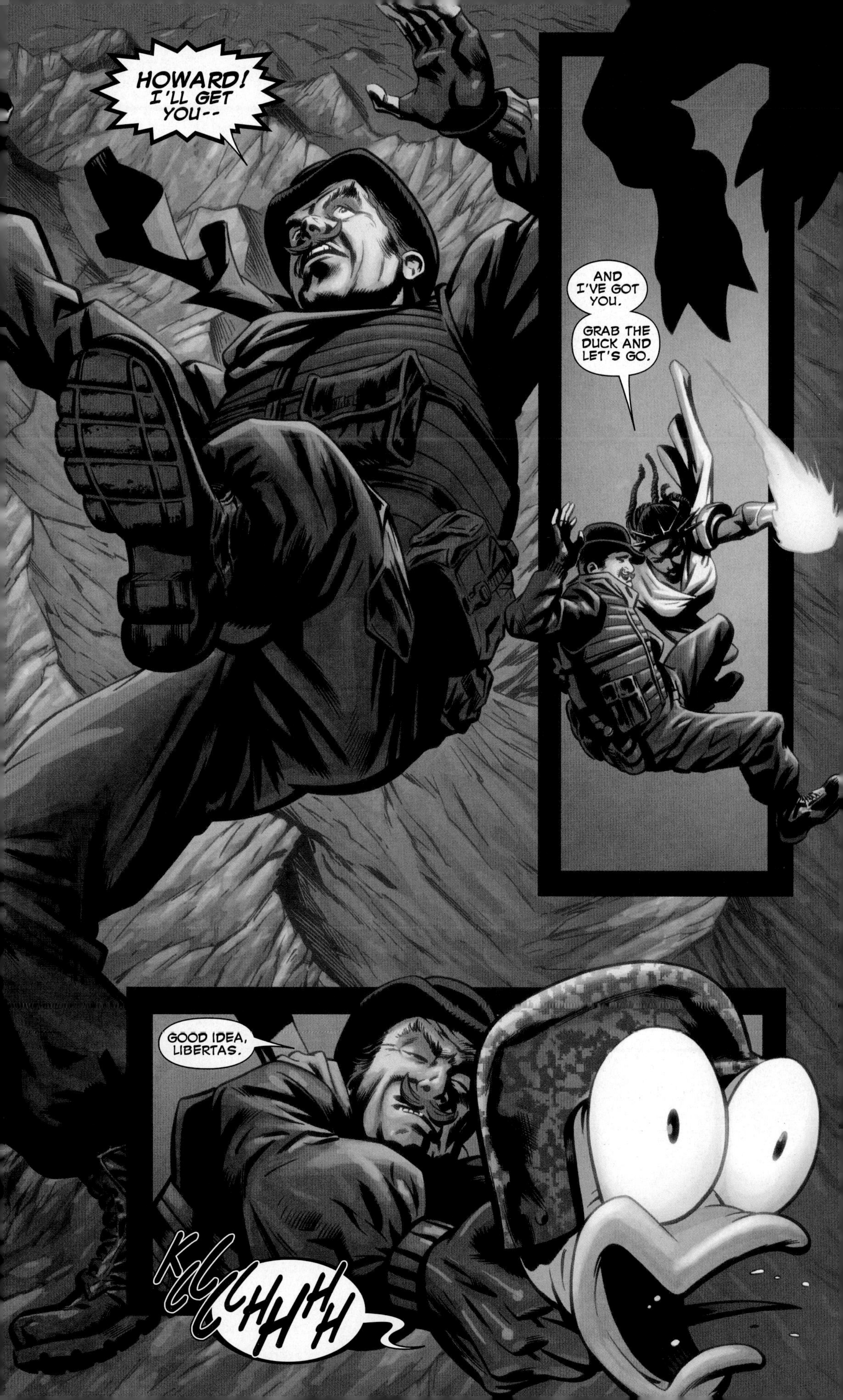
HOWARD! I'LL GET YOU--
AND I'VE GOT YOU.
GRAB THE DUCK AND LET'S GO.
GOOD IDEA, LIBERTAS.
KKKCHHHH

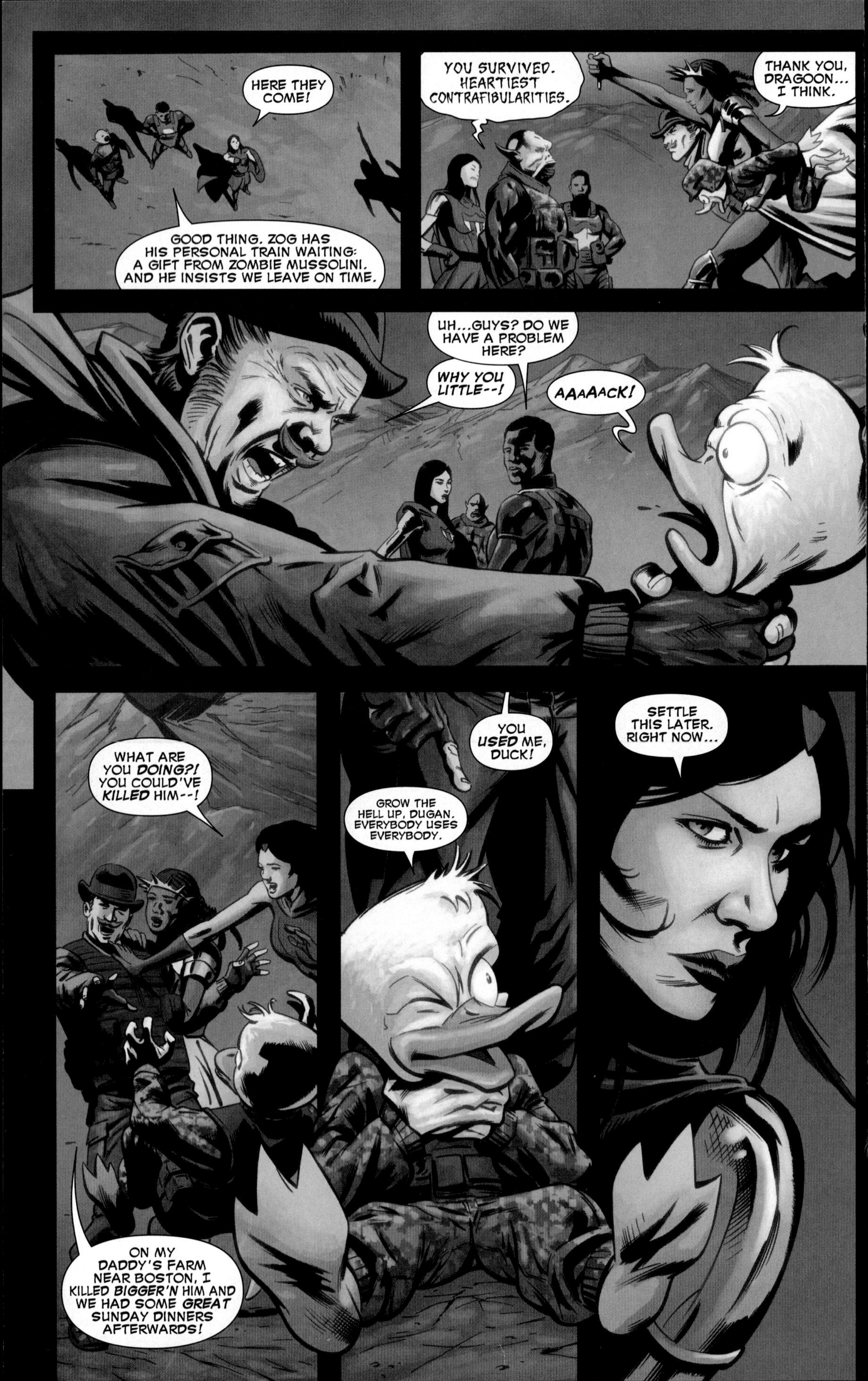
HERE THEY COME!
GOOD THING. ZOG HAS HIS PERSONAL TRAIN WAITING: A GIFT FROM ZOMBIE MUSSOLINI. AND HE INSISTS WE LEAVE ON TIME.
YOU SURVIVED. HEARTIEST CONTRAFIBULARITIES.
THANK YOU, DRAGOON... I THINK.
UH...GUYS? DO WE HAVE A PROBLEM HERE?
WHY YOU LITTLE--!
AAAAACK!
WHAT ARE YOU DOING?! YOU COULD'VE KILLED HIM--!
ON MY DADDY'S FARM NEAR BOSTON, I KILLED BIGGER'N HIM AND WE HAD SOME GREAT SUNDAY DINNERS AFTERWARDS!
YOU USED ME, DUCK!
GROW THE HELL UP, DUGAN. EVERYBODY USES EVERYBODY.
SETTLE THIS LATER. RIGHT NOW...

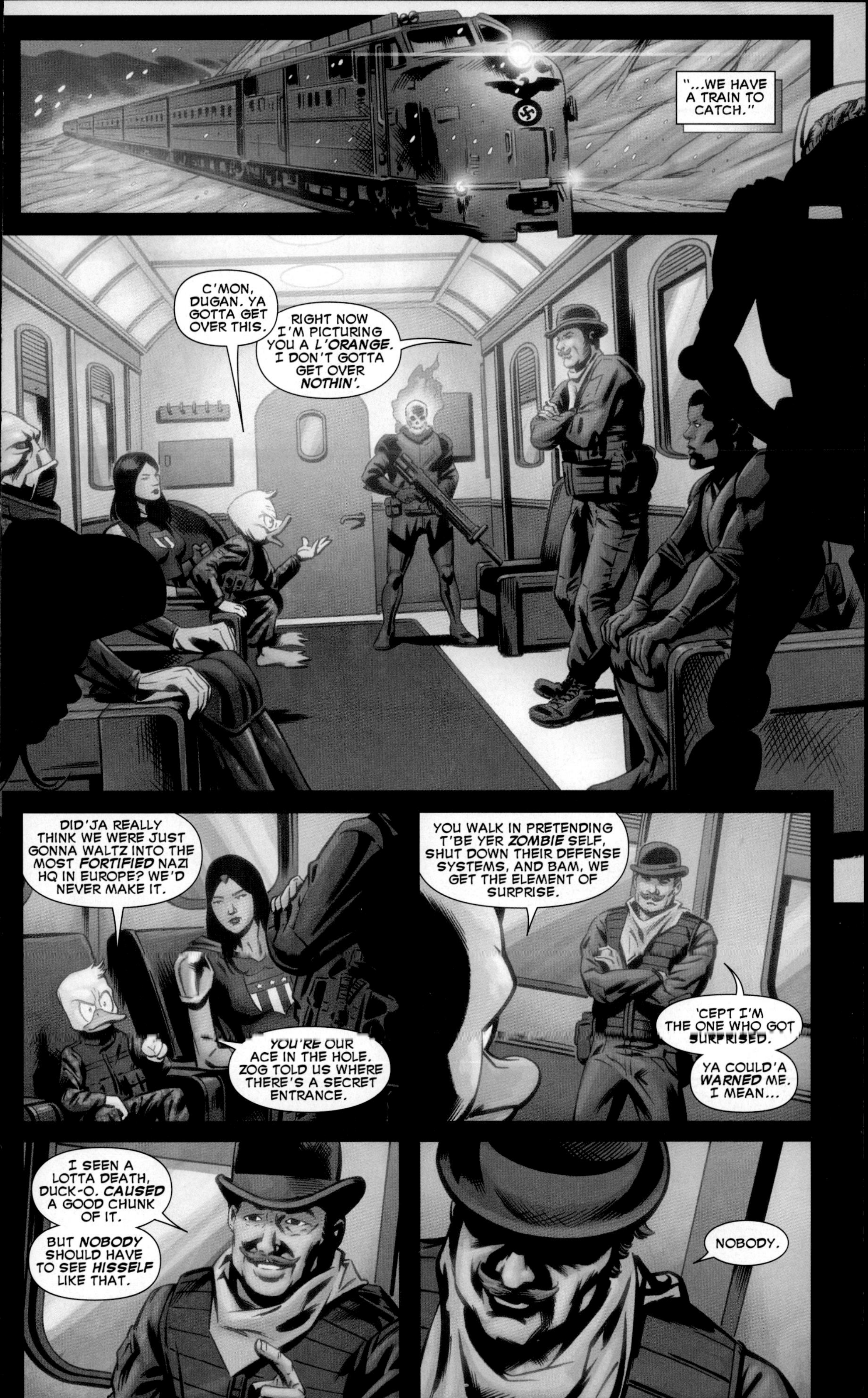
"...WE HAVE A TRAIN TO CATCH."
C'MON, DUGAN. YA GOTTA GET OVER THIS.
RIGHT NOW I'M PICTURING YOU A L'ORANGE. I DON'T GOTTA GET OVER NOTHIN'.
DID'JA REALLY THINK WE WERE JUST GONNA WALTZ INTO THE MOST FORTIFIED NAZI HQ IN EUROPE? WE'D NEVER MAKE IT.
YOU'RE OUR ACE IN THE HOLE. ZOG TOLD US WHERE THERE'S A SECRET ENTRANCE.
YOU WALK IN PRETENDING T'BE YER ZOMBIE SELF, SHUT DOWN THEIR DEFENSE SYSTEMS, AND BAM, WE GET THE ELEMENT OF SURPRISE.
'CEPT I'M THE ONE WHO GOT SURPRISED.
YA COULD'A WARNED ME. I MEAN...
I SEEN A LOTTA DEATH, DUCK-O. CAUSED A GOOD CHUNK OF IT.
BUT NOBODY SHOULD HAVE TO SEE HISSELF LIKE THAT.
NOBODY.

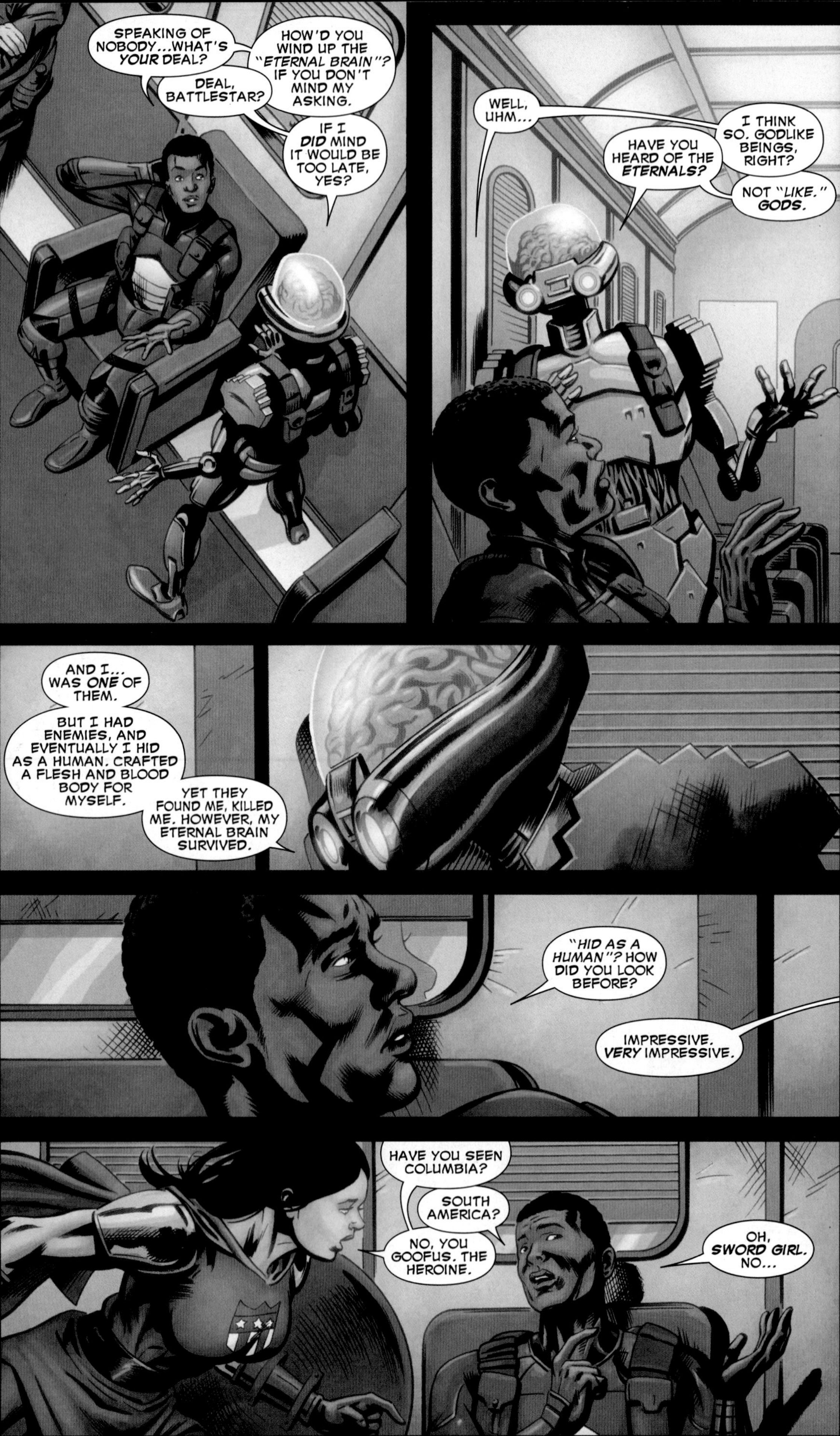
SPEAKING OF NOBODY...WHAT'S *YOUR* DEAL?
DEAL, BATTLESTAR?
HOW'D YOU WIND UP THE "*ETERNAL BRAIN*"? IF YOU DON'T MIND MY ASKING.
IF I *DID* MIND IT WOULD BE TOO LATE, YES?
WELL, UHM...
HAVE YOU HEARD OF THE *ETERNALS?*
I THINK SO. GODLIKE BEINGS, RIGHT?
NOT "*LIKE.*" *GODS.*
AND I... WAS *ONE* OF THEM.
BUT I HAD ENEMIES, AND EVENTUALLY I HID AS A HUMAN. CRAFTED A FLESH AND BLOOD BODY FOR MYSELF.
YET THEY FOUND ME, KILLED ME. HOWEVER, MY ETERNAL BRAIN SURVIVED.
"*HID AS A HUMAN*"? HOW *DID* YOU LOOK BEFORE?
IMPRESSIVE. *VERY* IMPRESSIVE.
HAVE YOU SEEN COLUMBIA?
SOUTH AMERICA?
NO, YOU GOOFUS. THE HEROINE.
OH, *SWORD GIRL.* NO...

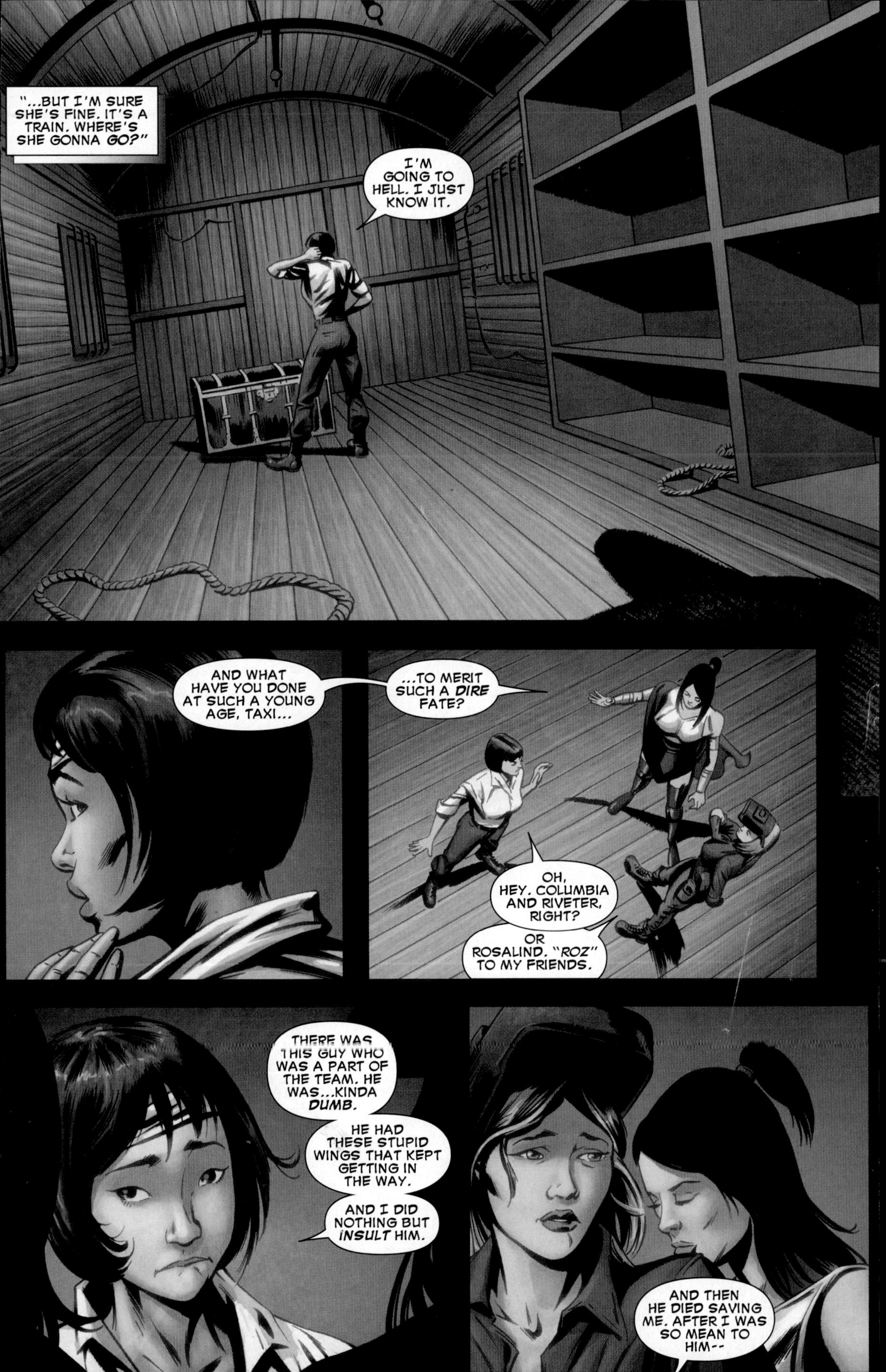
"...BUT I'M SURE SHE'S FINE. IT'S A TRAIN. WHERE'S SHE GONNA GO?"
I'M GOING TO HELL. I JUST KNOW IT.
AND WHAT HAVE YOU DONE AT SUCH A YOUNG AGE, TAXI...
...TO MERIT SUCH A DIRE FATE?
OH, HEY. COLUMBIA AND RIVETER, RIGHT?
OR ROSALIND. "ROZ" TO MY FRIENDS.
THERE WAS THIS GUY WHO WAS A PART OF THE TEAM. HE WAS...KINDA DUMB.
HE HAD THESE STUPID WINGS THAT KEPT GETTING IN THE WAY.
AND I DID NOTHING BUT INSULT HIM.
AND THEN HE DIED SAVING ME. AFTER I WAS SO MEAN TO HIM--

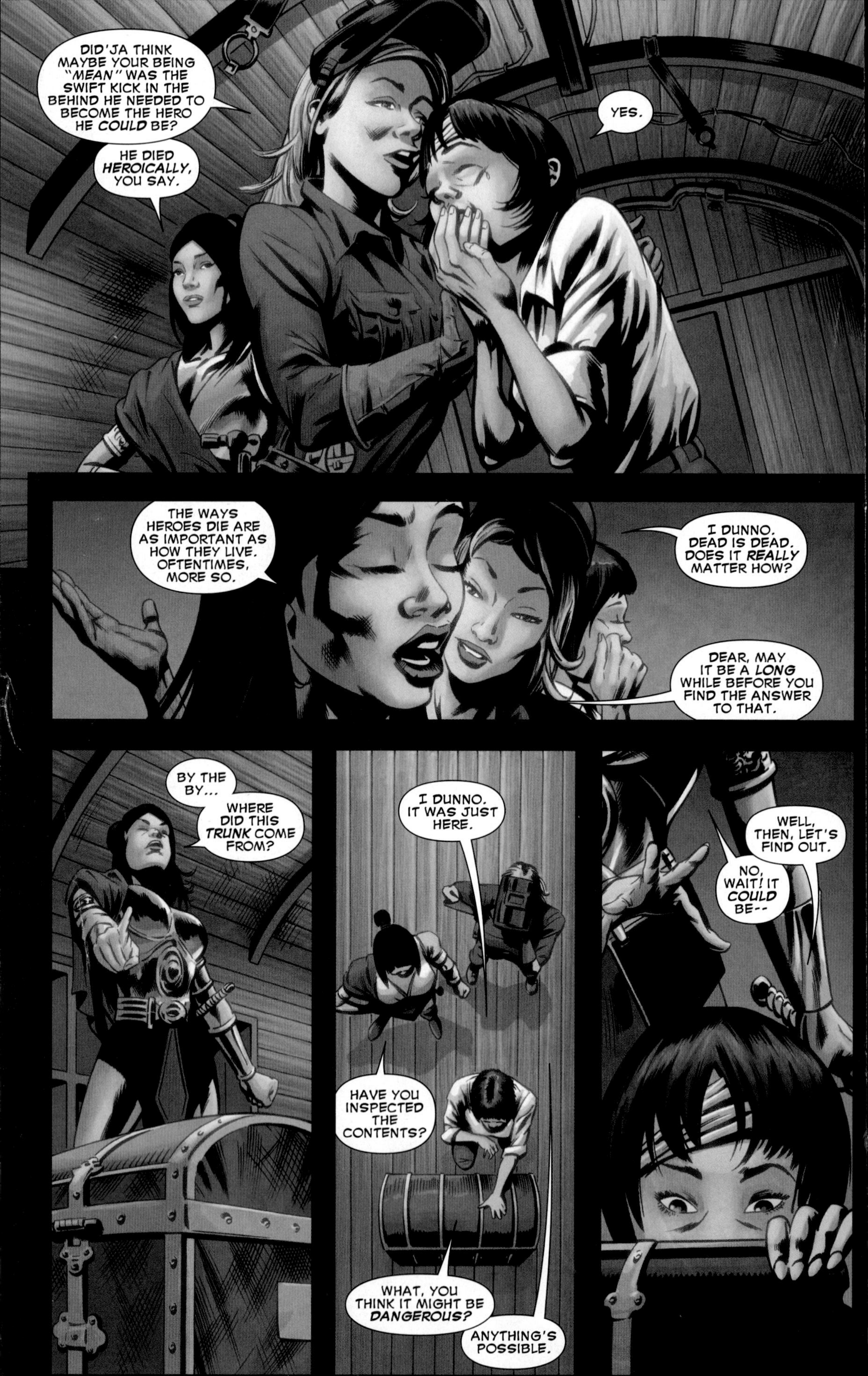
DID'JA THINK MAYBE YOUR BEING "MEAN" WAS THE SWIFT KICK IN THE BEHIND HE NEEDED TO BECOME THE HERO HE COULD BE?
YES.
HE DIED HEROICALLY, YOU SAY.
THE WAYS HEROES DIE ARE AS IMPORTANT AS HOW THEY LIVE. OFTENTIMES, MORE SO.
I DUNNO. DEAD IS DEAD. DOES IT REALLY MATTER HOW?
DEAR, MAY IT BE A LONG WHILE BEFORE YOU FIND THE ANSWER TO THAT.
BY THE BY...
WHERE DID THIS TRUNK COME FROM?
I DUNNO. IT WAS JUST HERE.
HAVE YOU INSPECTED THE CONTENTS?
WHAT, YOU THINK IT MIGHT BE DANGEROUS?
ANYTHING'S POSSIBLE.
WELL, THEN, LET'S FIND OUT.
NO, WAIT! IT COULD BE--

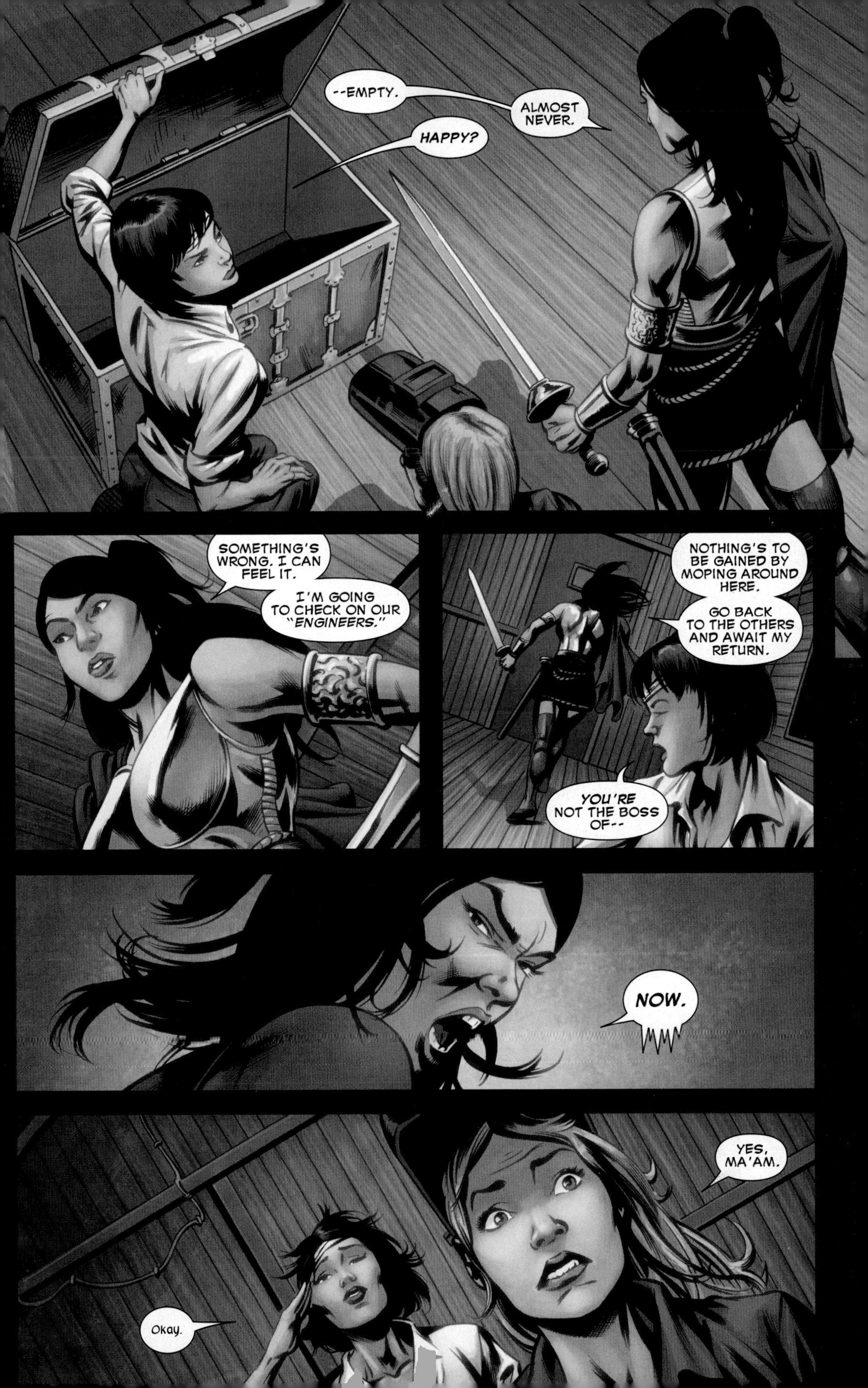
--EMPTY.
HAPPY?
ALMOST NEVER.
SOMETHING'S WRONG. I CAN FEEL IT.
I'M GOING TO CHECK ON OUR "ENGINEERS."
NOTHING'S TO BE GAINED BY MOPING AROUND HERE.
GO BACK TO THE OTHERS AND AWAIT MY RETURN.
YOU'RE NOT THE BOSS OF--
NOW.
YES, MA'AM.
Okay.

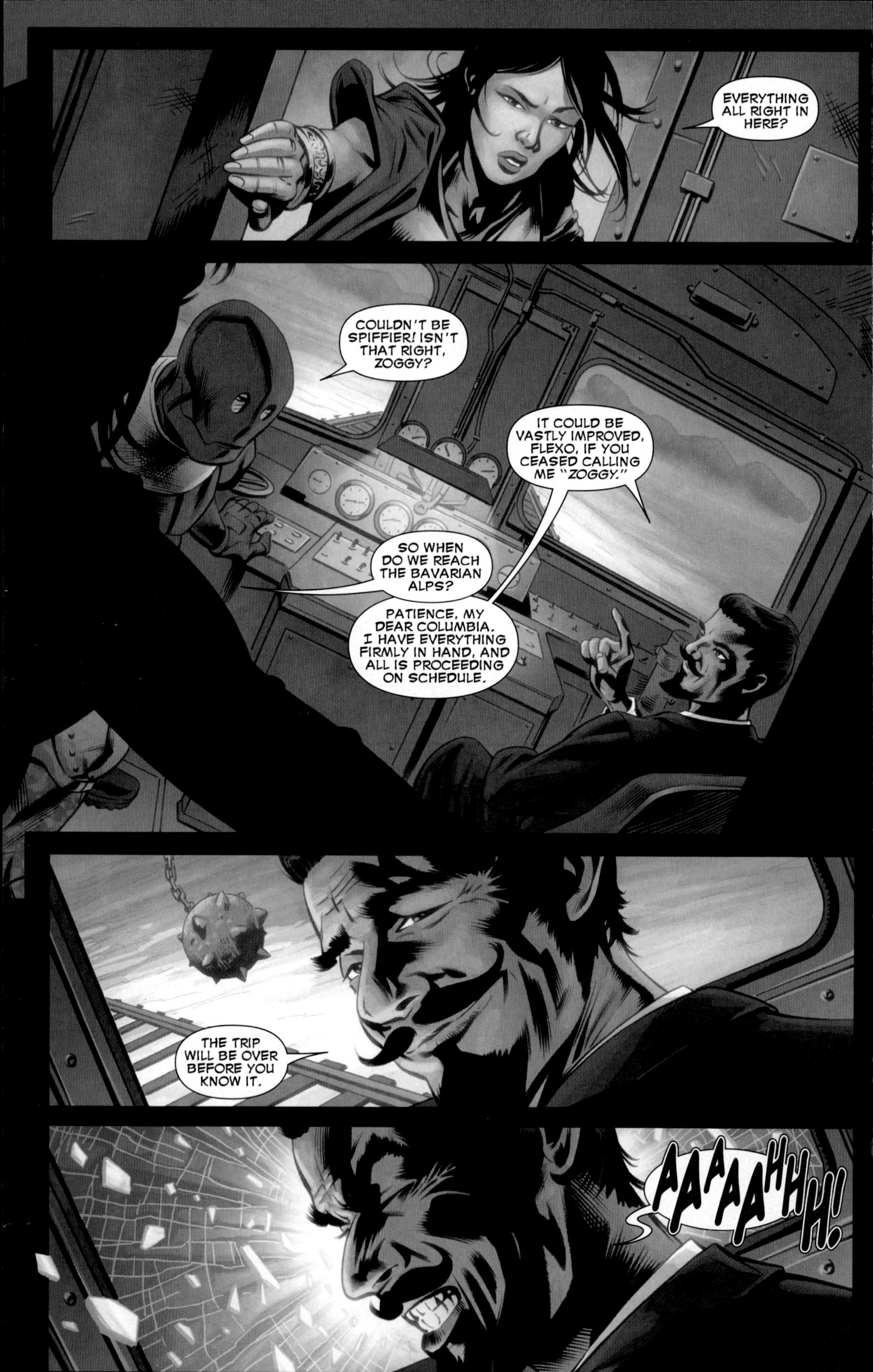
EVERYTHING ALL RIGHT IN HERE?
COULDN'T BE SPIFFIER! ISN'T THAT RIGHT, ZOGGY?
IT COULD BE VASTLY IMPROVED, FLEXO, IF YOU CEASED CALLING ME "ZOGGY."
SO WHEN DO WE REACH THE BAVARIAN ALPS?
PATIENCE, MY DEAR COLUMBIA. I HAVE EVERYTHING FIRMLY IN HAND, AND ALL IS PROCEEDING ON SCHEDULE.
THE TRIP WILL BE OVER BEFORE YOU KNOW IT.
AAAAAHHHH!

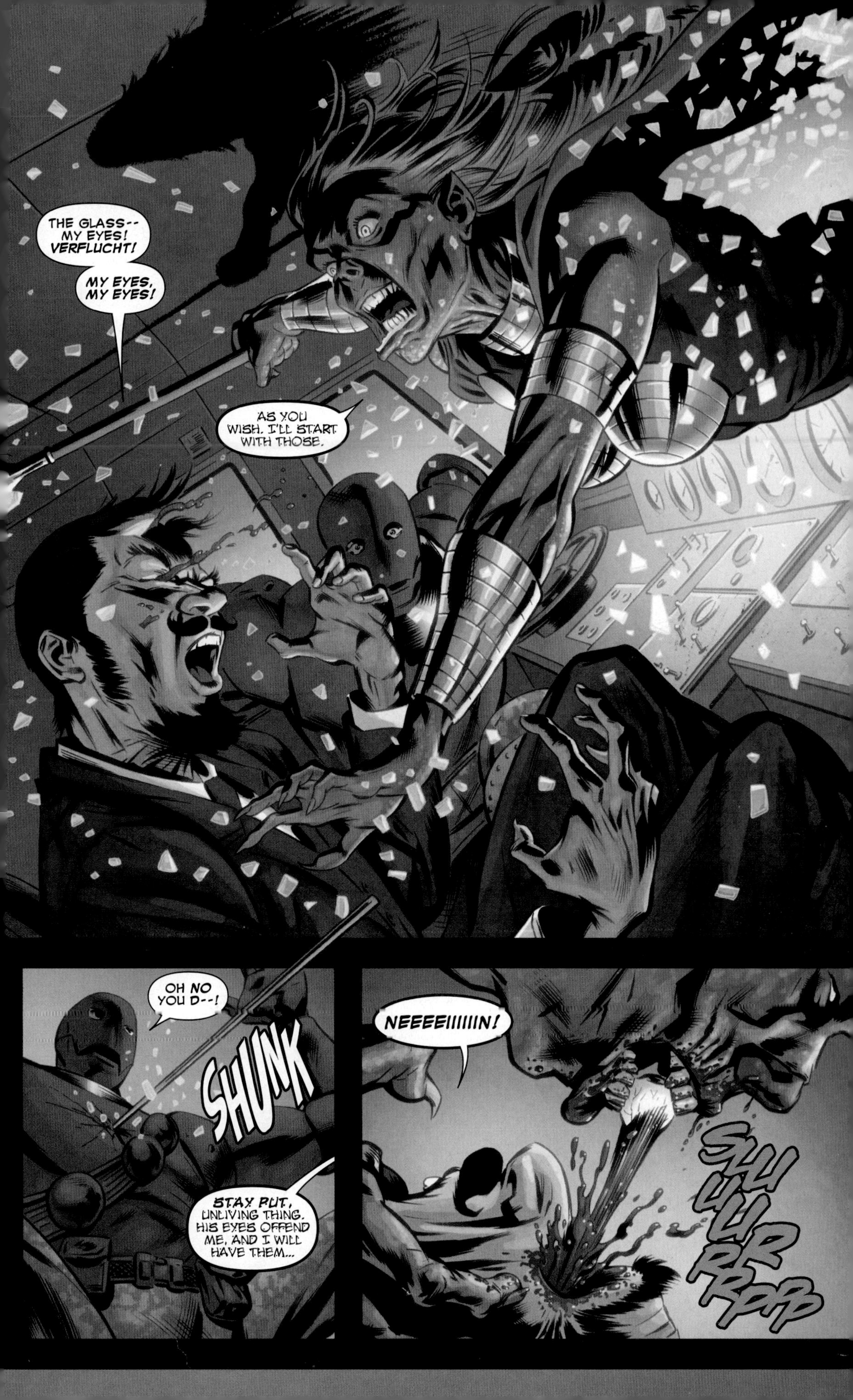
THE GLASS-- MY EYES! VERFLUCHT!
MY EYES, MY EYES!
AS YOU WISH. I'LL START WITH THOSE.
OH NO YOU D--!
SHUNK
STAY PUT, UNLIVING THING. HIS EYES OFFEND ME, AND I WILL HAVE THEM...
NEEEEIIIIIIN!
SHUURRRPP

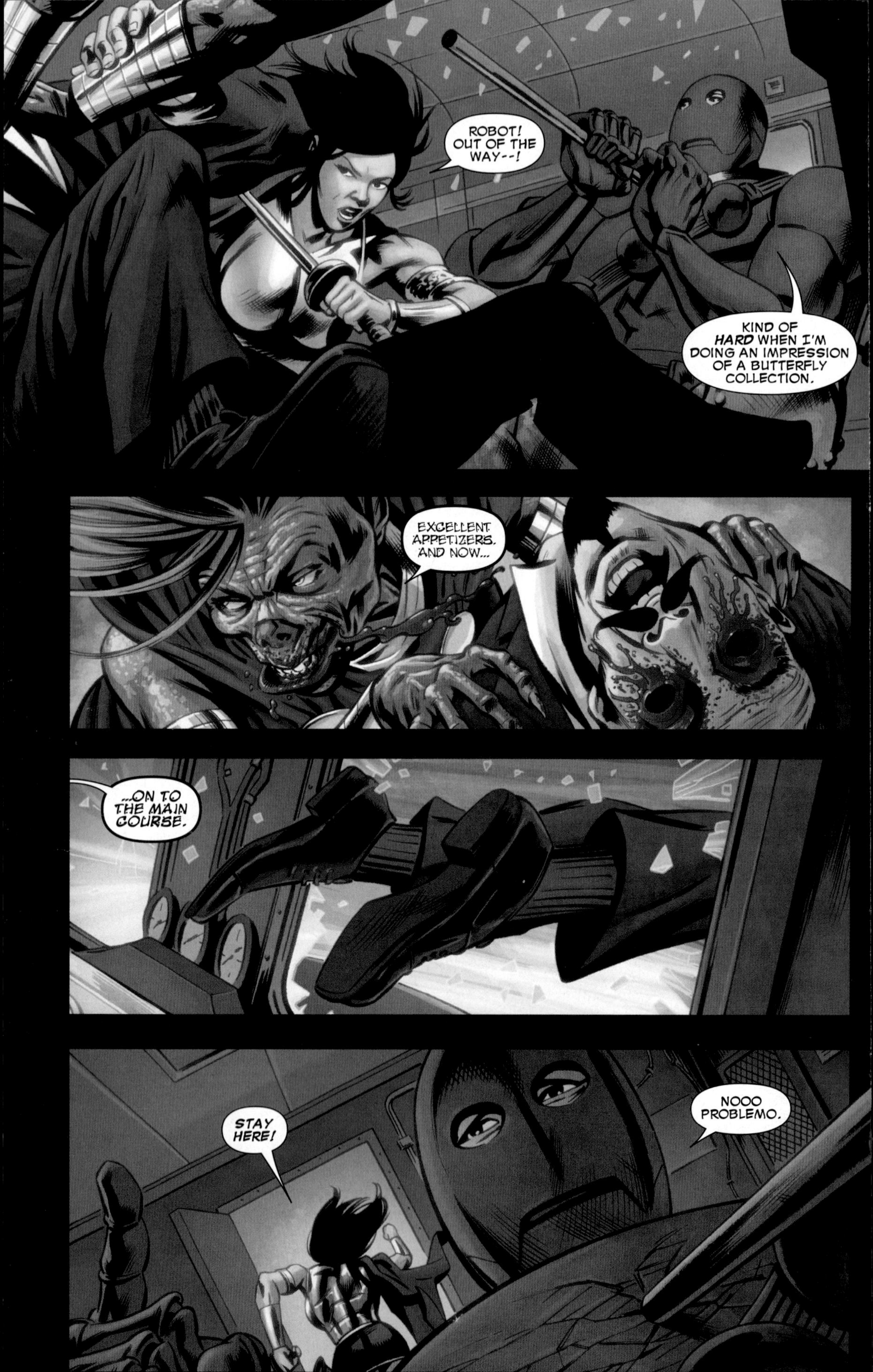
ROBOT! OUT OF THE WAY--!
KIND OF HARD WHEN I'M DOING AN IMPRESSION OF A BUTTERFLY COLLECTION.
EXCELLENT APPETIZERS. AND NOW...
...ON TO THE MAIN COURSE.
STAY HERE!
NOOO PROBLEMO.

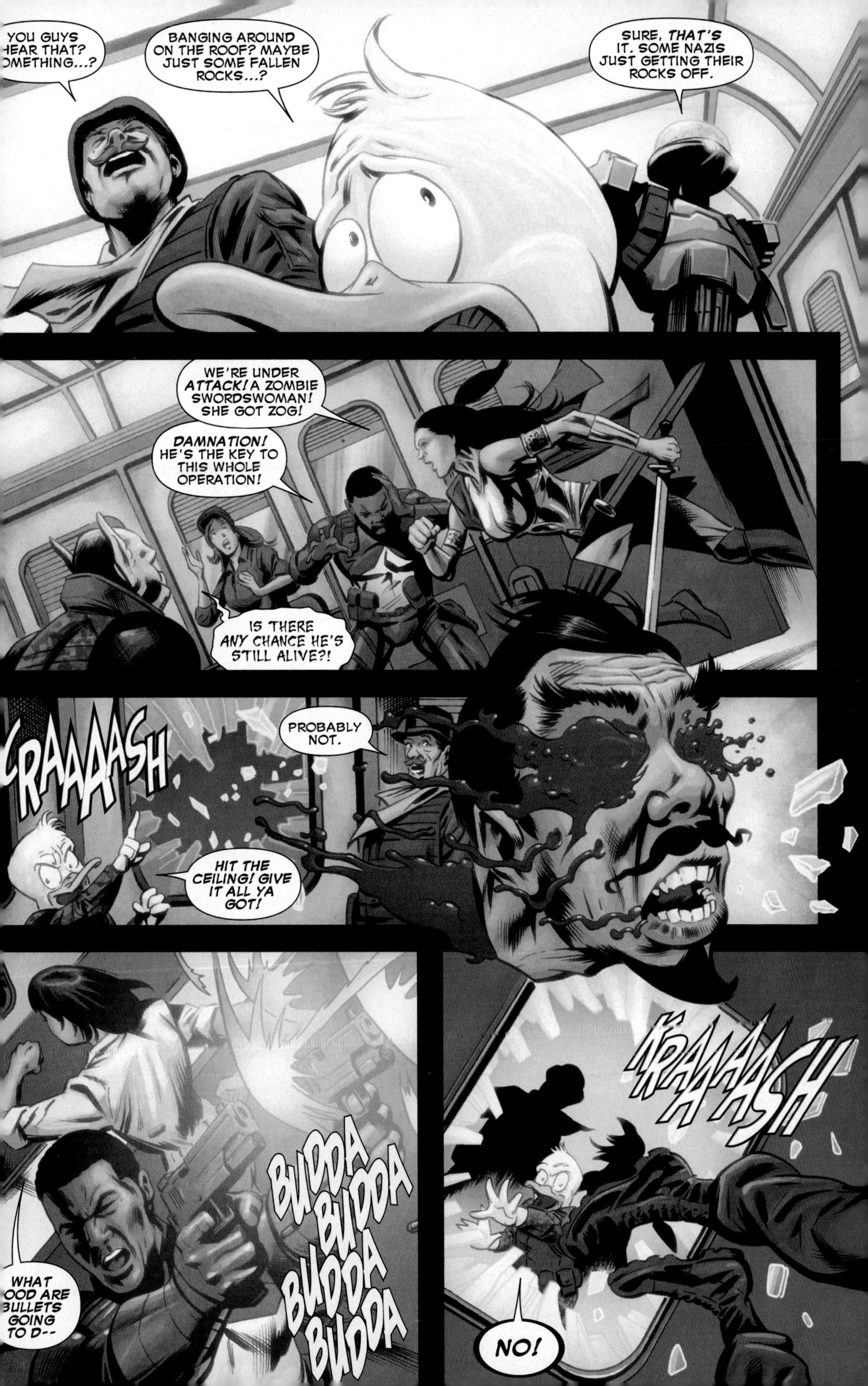

YOU GUYS HEAR THAT? OMETHING...?
BANGING AROUND ON THE ROOF? MAYBE JUST SOME FALLEN ROCKS...?
SURE, THAT'S IT. SOME NAZIS JUST GETTING THEIR ROCKS OFF.
WE'RE UNDER ATTACK! A ZOMBIE SWORDSWOMAN! SHE GOT ZOG!
DAMNATION! HE'S THE KEY TO THIS WHOLE OPERATION!
IS THERE ANY CHANCE HE'S STILL ALIVE?!
CRAAAASH
PROBABLY NOT.
HIT THE CEILING! GIVE IT ALL YA GOT!
WHAT OOD ARE ULLETS GOING TO D--
BUDDA BUDDA BUDDA BUDDA
KRAAAASH
NO!

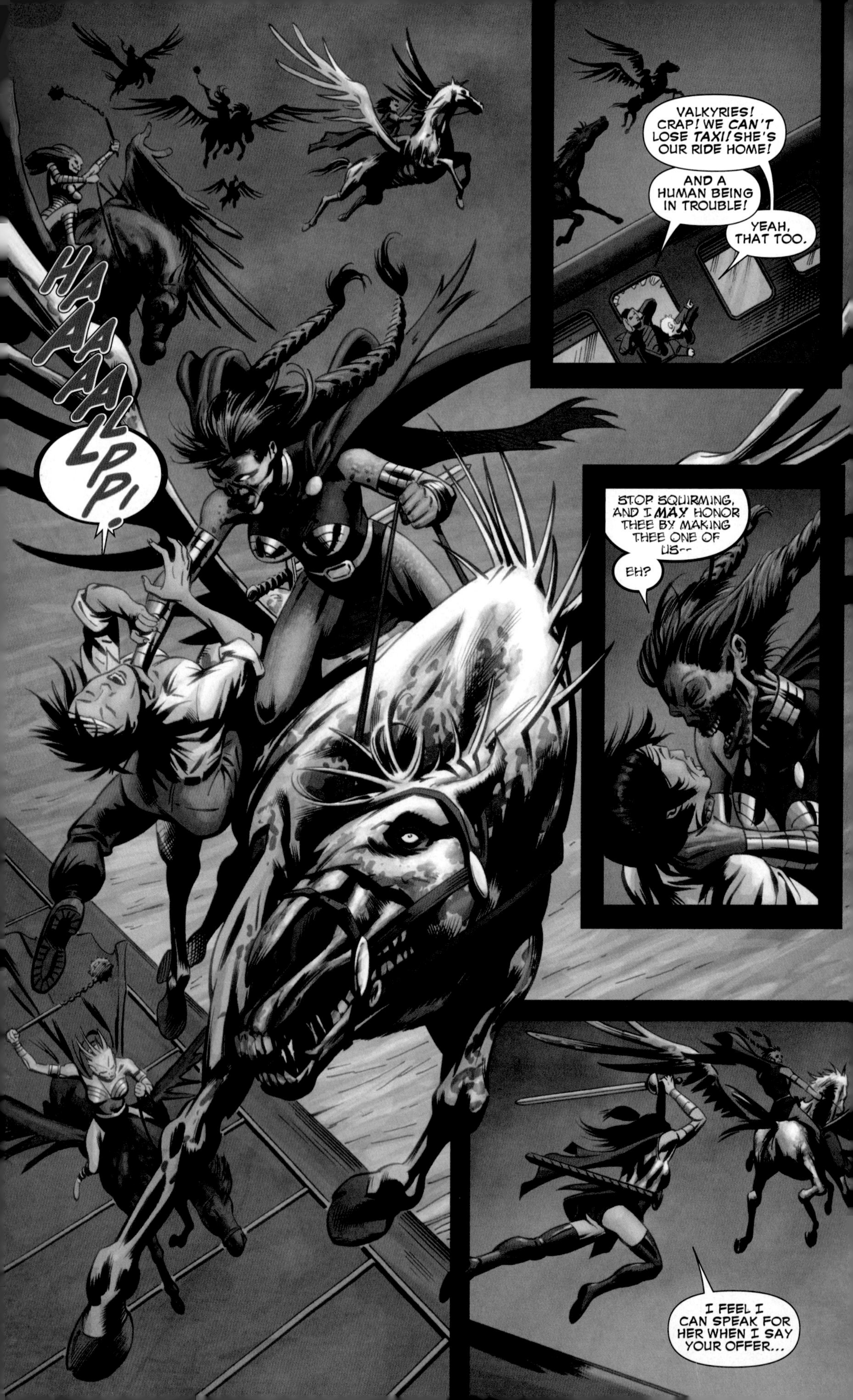
HAAAAALPP!
VALKYRIES! CRAP! WE CAN'T LOSE TAXI! SHE'S OUR RIDE HOME!
AND A HUMAN BEING IN TROUBLE!
YEAH, THAT TOO.
STOP SQUIRMING, AND I MAY HONOR THEE BY MAKING THEE ONE OF US--
EH?
I FEEL I CAN SPEAK FOR HER WHEN I SAY YOUR OFFER...

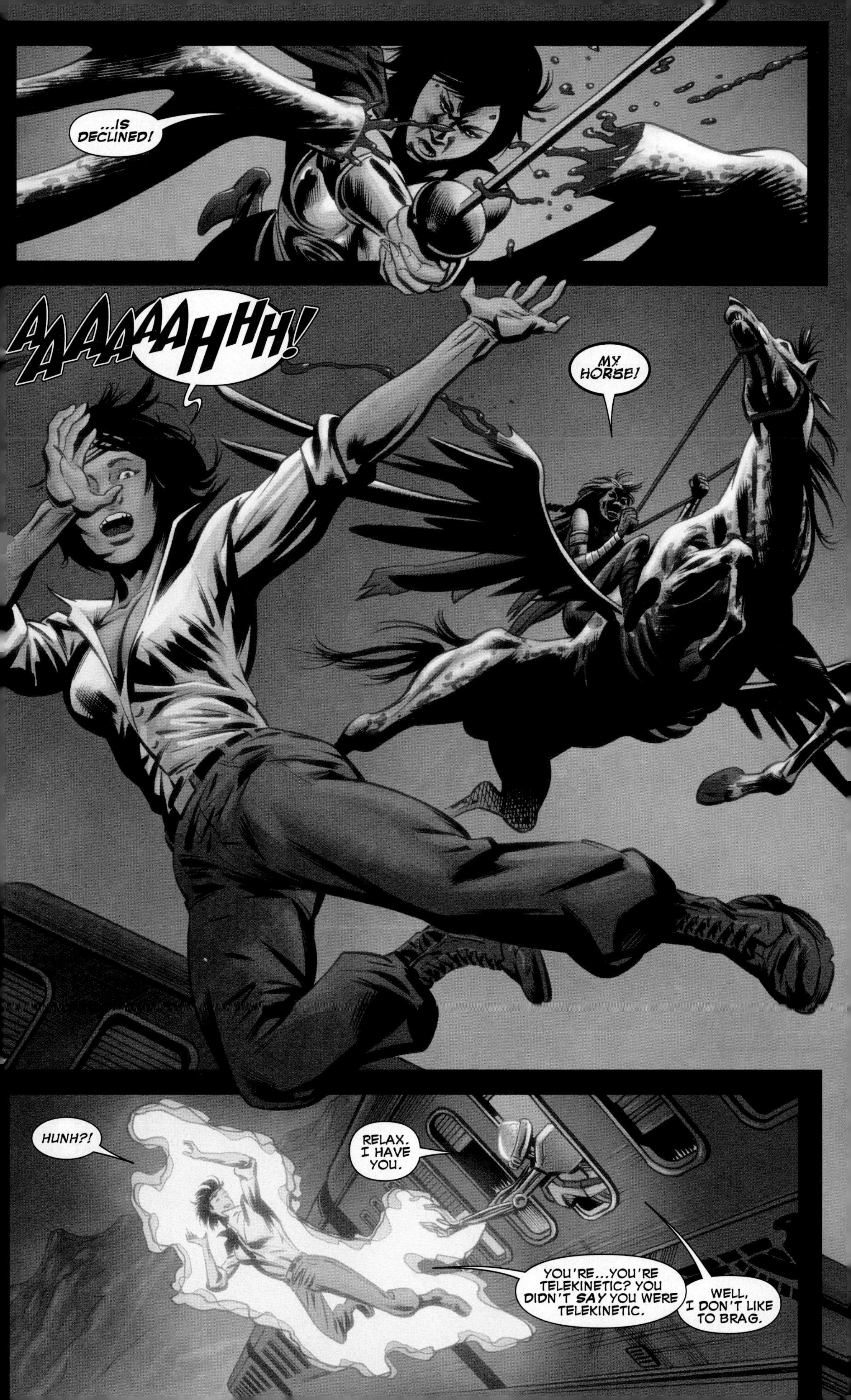
...IS DECLINED!
AAAAAAHHH!
MY HORSE!
HUNH?!
RELAX. I HAVE YOU.
YOU'RE...YOU'RE TELEKINETIC? YOU DIDN'T SAY YOU WERE TELEKINETIC.
WELL, I DON'T LIKE TO BRAG.

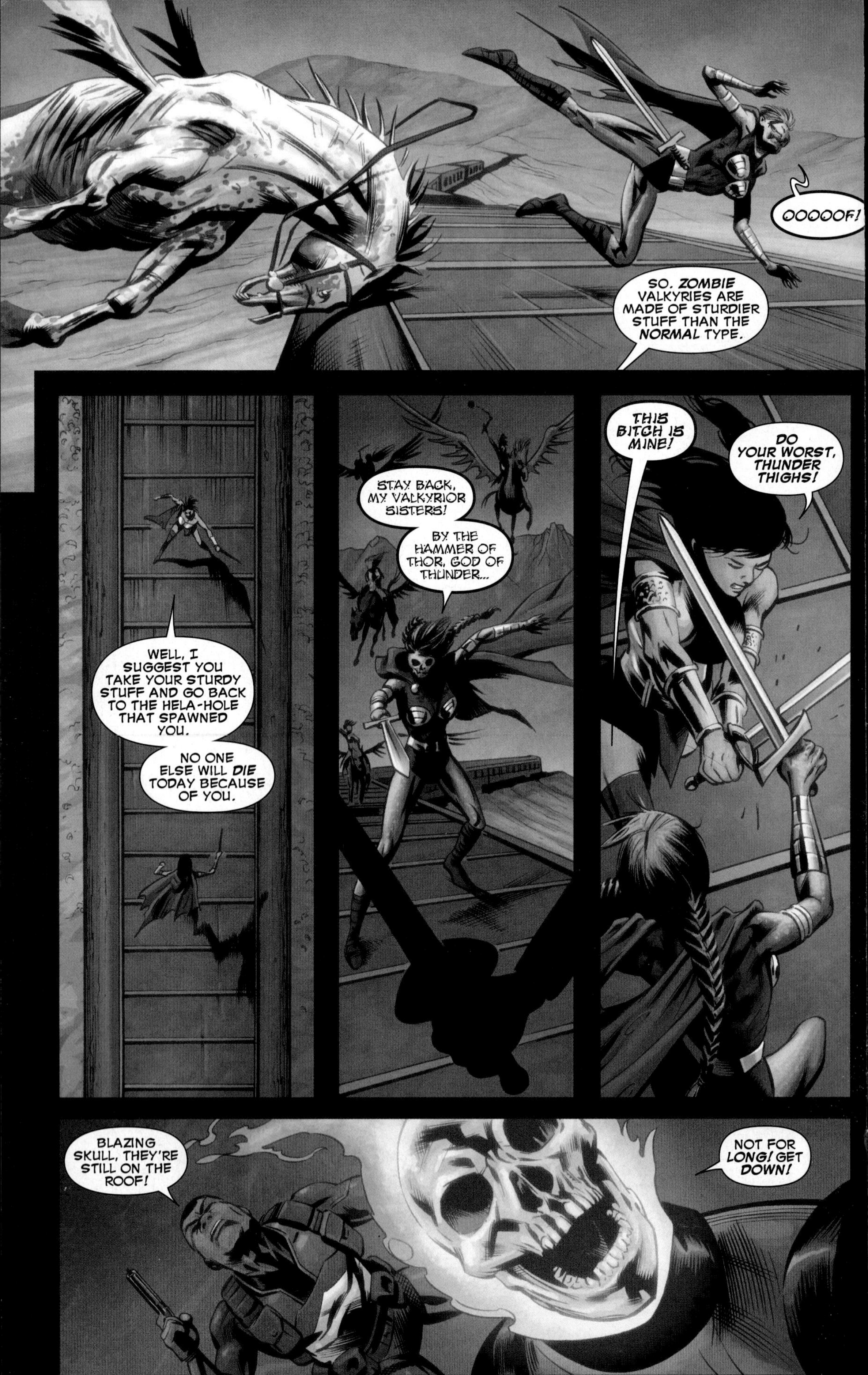

OOOOOF!
SO. ZOMBIE VALKYRIES ARE MADE OF STURDIER STUFF THAN THE NORMAL TYPE.
WELL, I SUGGEST YOU TAKE YOUR STURDY STUFF AND GO BACK TO THE HELA-HOLE THAT SPAWNED YOU.
NO ONE ELSE WILL DIE TODAY BECAUSE OF YOU.
STAY BACK, MY VALKYRIOR SISTERS!
BY THE HAMMER OF THOR, GOD OF THUNDER...
THIS BITCH IS MINE!
DO YOUR WORST, THUNDER THIGHS!
BLAZING SKULL, THEY'RE STILL ON THE ROOF!
NOT FOR LONG! GET DOWN!

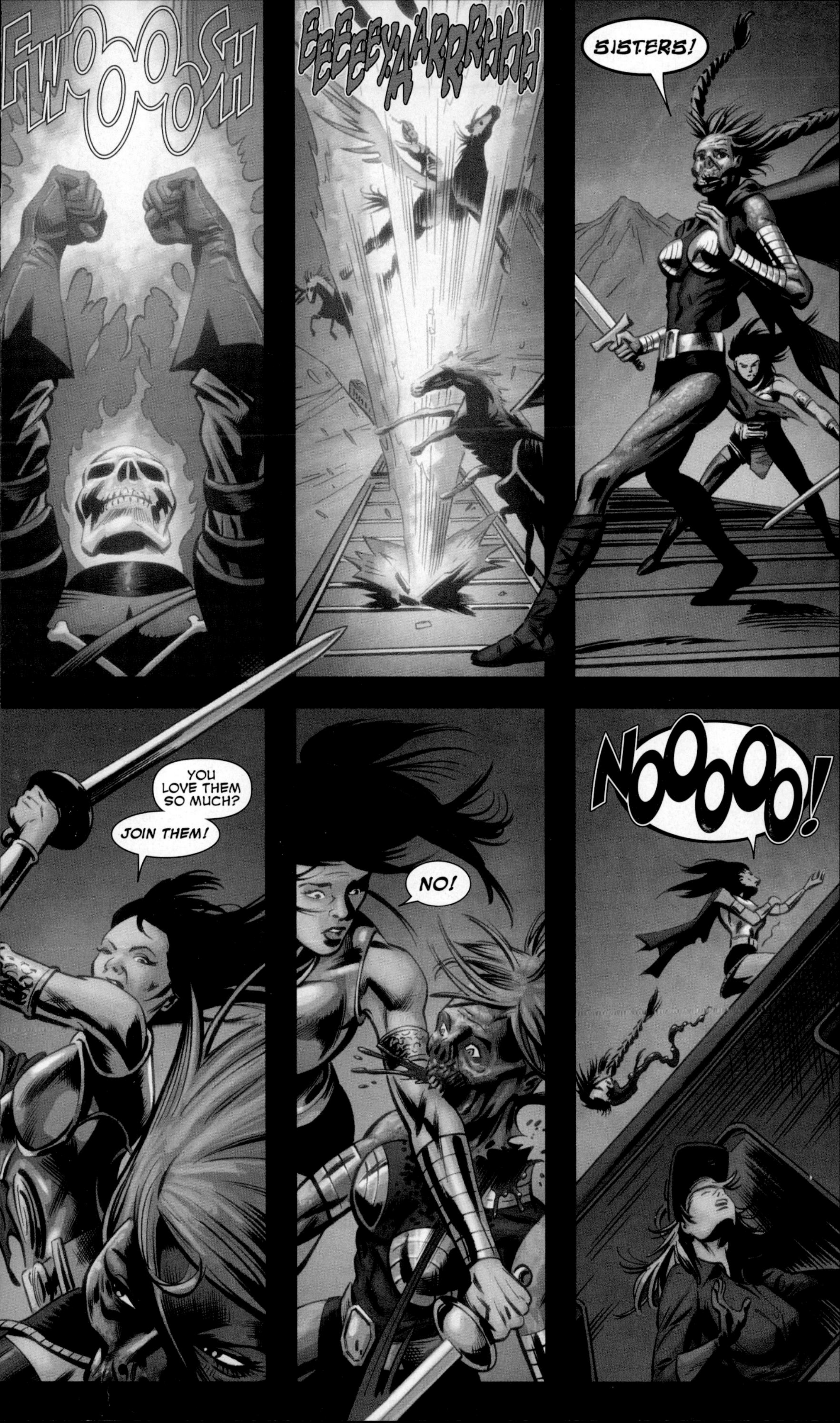
FWOOOOOSH
EEEEEYAARRRHHH
SISTERS!
YOU LOVE THEM SO MUCH?
JOIN THEM!
NO!
NOOOOOO!

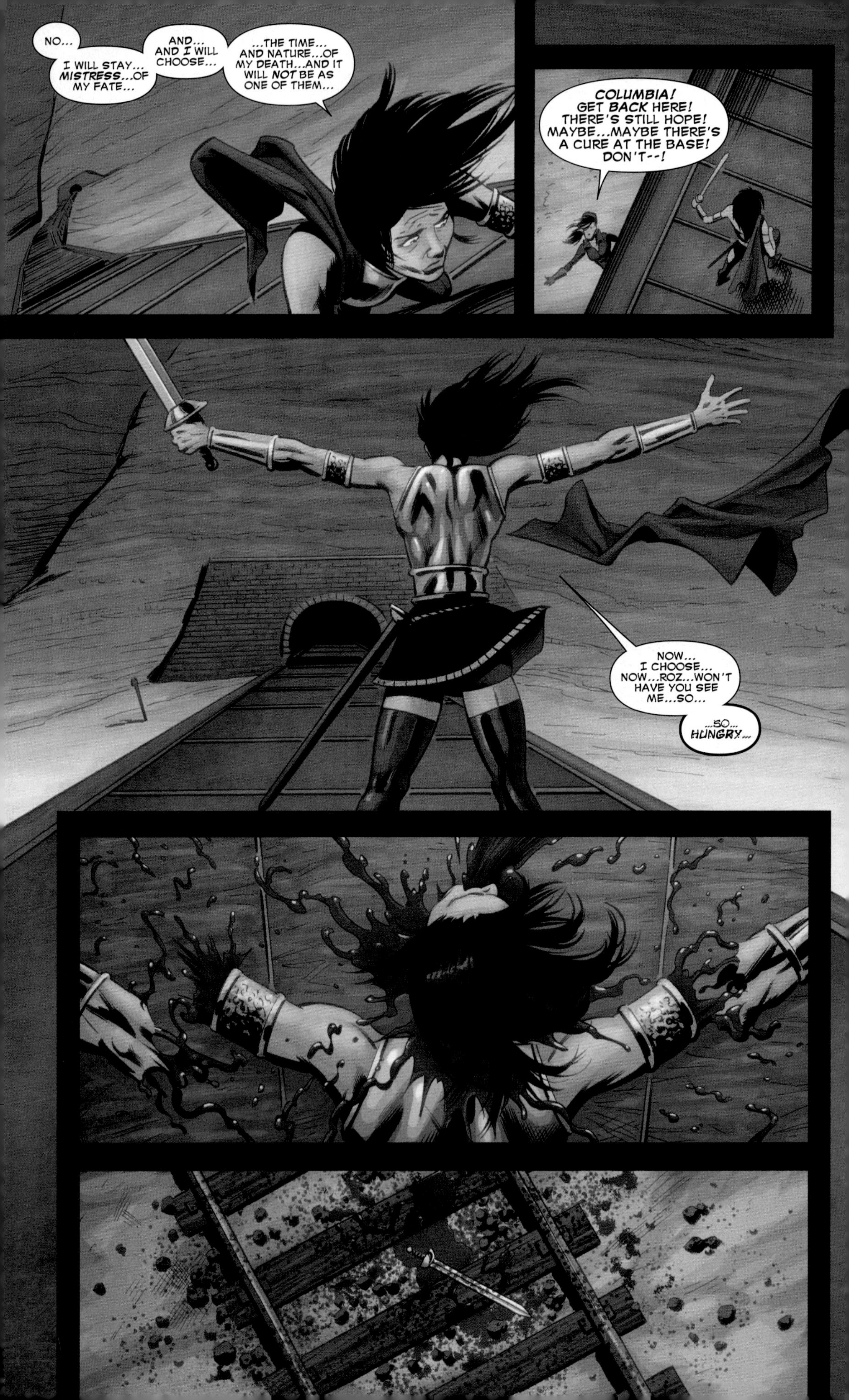
NO...
I WILL STAY... MISTRESS...OF MY FATE...
AND... AND I WILL CHOOSE...
...THE TIME... AND NATURE...OF MY DEATH...AND IT WILL NOT BE AS ONE OF THEM...
COLUMBIA! GET BACK HERE! THERE'S STILL HOPE! MAYBE...MAYBE THERE'S A CURE AT THE BASE! DON'T--!
NOW... I CHOOSE... NOW...ROZ...WON'T HAVE YOU SEE ME...SO...
...SO... HUNGRY...

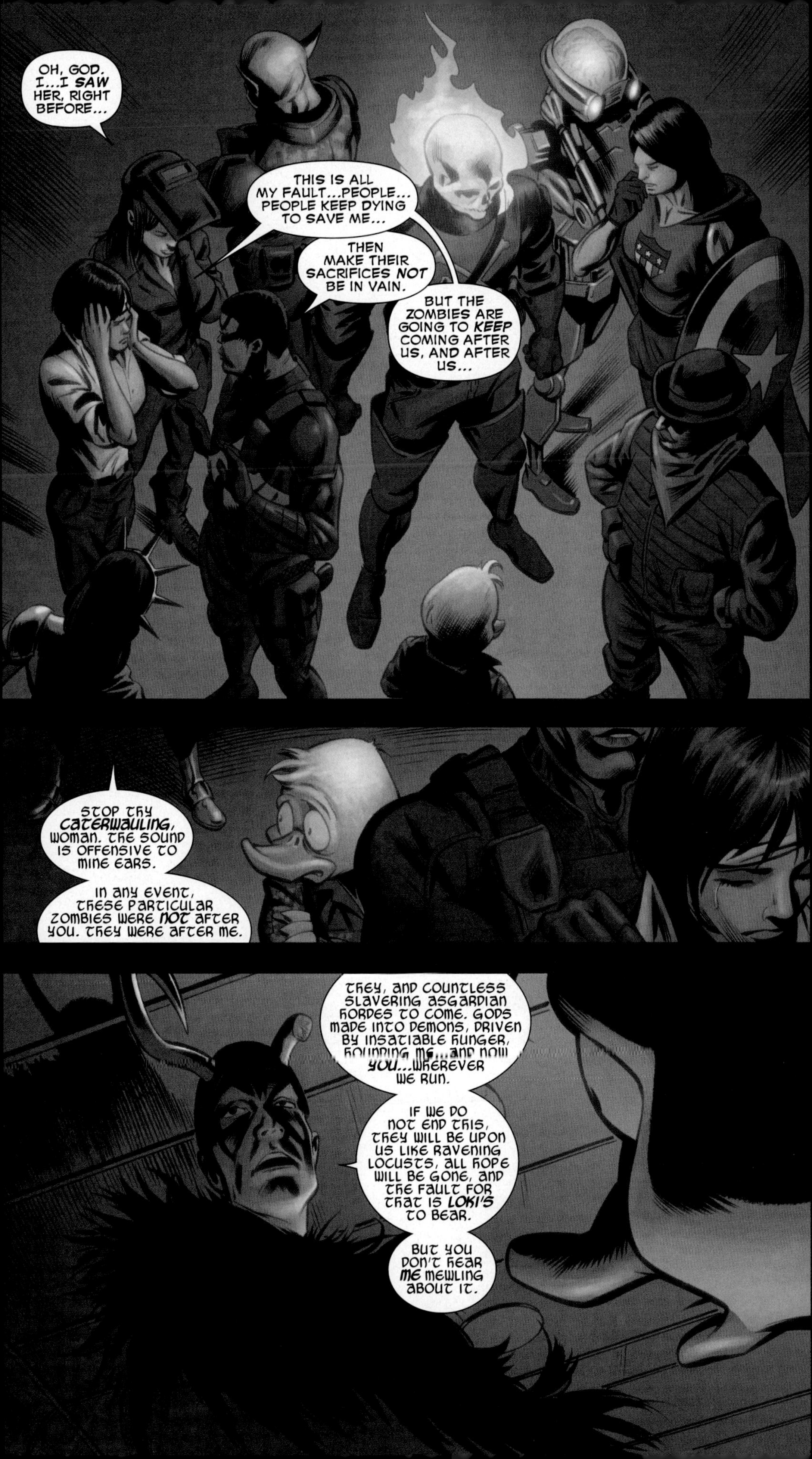
OH, GOD. I...I SAW HER, RIGHT BEFORE...
THIS IS ALL MY FAULT...PEOPLE... PEOPLE KEEP DYING TO SAVE ME...
THEN MAKE THEIR SACRIFICES NOT BE IN VAIN.
BUT THE ZOMBIES ARE GOING TO KEEP COMING AFTER US, AND AFTER US...
STOP THY CATERWAULING, WOMAN. THE SOUND IS OFFENSIVE TO MINE EARS.
IN ANY EVENT, THESE PARTICULAR ZOMBIES WERE NOT AFTER YOU. THEY WERE AFTER ME.
THEY, AND COUNTLESS SLAVERING ASGARDIAN HORDES TO COME. GODS MADE INTO DEMONS, DRIVEN BY INSATIABLE HUNGER, HOUNDING ME... AND NOW YOU... WHEREVER WE RUN.
IF WE DO NOT END THIS, THEY WILL BE UPON US LIKE RAVENING LOCUSTS, ALL HOPE WILL BE GONE, AND THE FAULT FOR THAT IS LOKI'S TO BEAR.
BUT YOU DON'T HEAR ME MEWLING ABOUT IT.

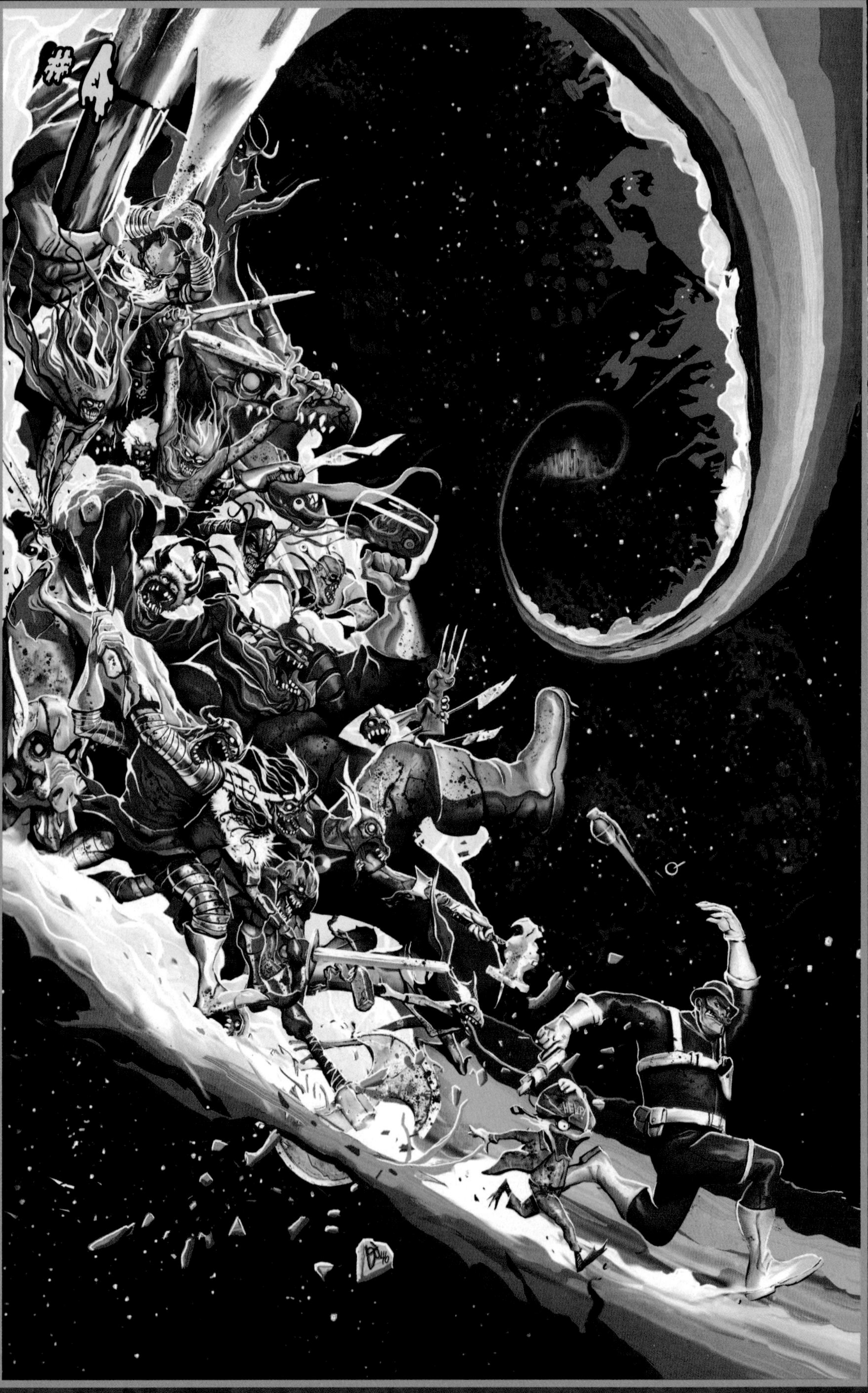
#4
HELP

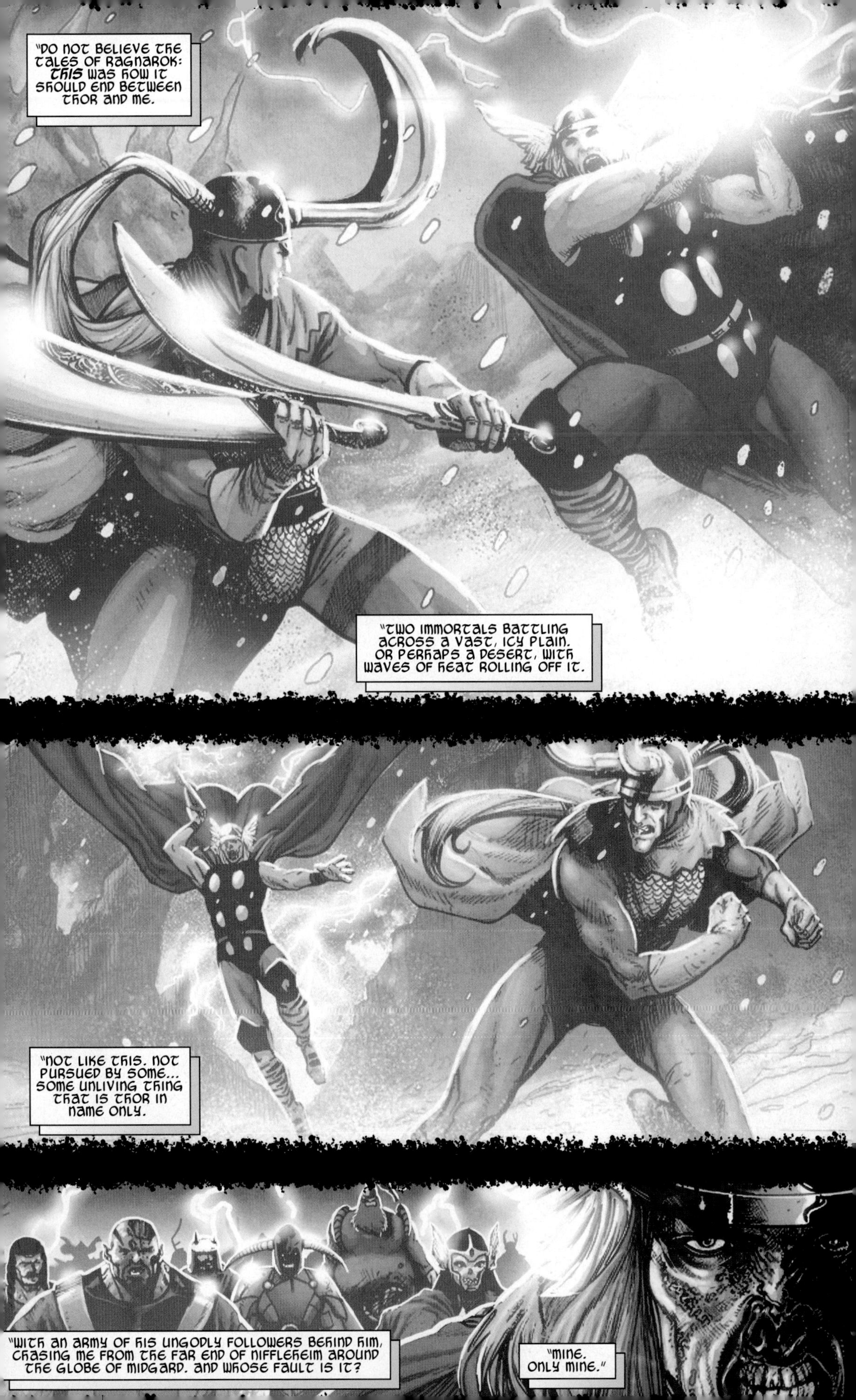
"DO NOT BELIEVE THE TALES OF RAGNAROK: THIS WAS HOW IT SHOULD END BETWEEN THOR AND ME.
"TWO IMMORTALS BATTLING ACROSS A VAST, ICY PLAIN. OR PERHAPS A DESERT, WITH WAVES OF HEAT ROLLING OFF IT.
"NOT LIKE THIS. NOT PURSUED BY SOME... SOME UNLIVING THING THAT IS THOR IN NAME ONLY.
"WITH AN ARMY OF HIS UNGODLY FOLLOWERS BEHIND HIM, CHASING ME FROM THE FAR END OF NIFFLEHEIM AROUND THE GLOBE OF MIDGARD. AND WHOSE FAULT IS IT?
"MINE. ONLY MINE."

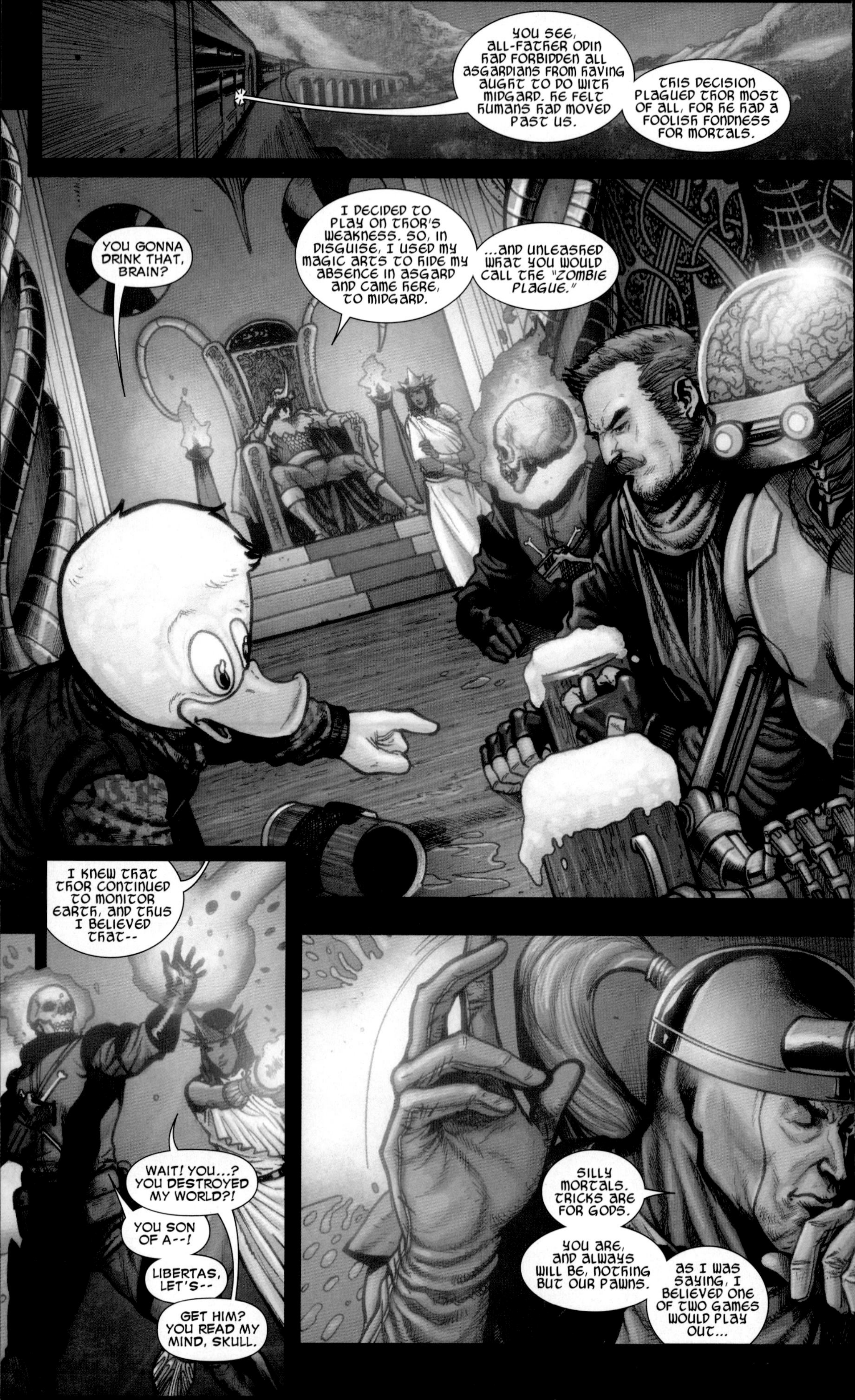
YOU SEE, ALL-FATHER ODIN HAD FORBIDDEN ALL ASGARDIANS FROM HAVING AUGHT TO DO WITH MIDGARD. HE FELT HUMANS HAD MOVED PAST US.
THIS DECISION PLAGUED THOR MOST OF ALL, FOR HE HAD A FOOLISH FONDNESS FOR MORTALS.
YOU GONNA DRINK THAT, BRAIN?
I DECIDED TO PLAY ON THOR'S WEAKNESS. SO, IN DISGUISE, I USED MY MAGIC ARTS TO HIDE MY ABSENCE IN ASGARD AND CAME HERE, TO MIDGARD.
...AND UNLEASHED WHAT YOU WOULD CALL THE "ZOMBIE PLAGUE."
I KNEW THAT THOR CONTINUED TO MONITOR EARTH, AND THUS I BELIEVED THAT--
WAIT! YOU...? YOU DESTROYED MY WORLD?!
YOU SON OF A--!
LIBERTAS, LET'S--
GET HIM? YOU READ MY MIND, SKULL.
SILLY MORTALS. TRICKS ARE FOR GODS.
YOU ARE, AND ALWAYS WILL BE, NOTHING BUT OUR PAWNS.
AS I WAS SAYING, I BELIEVED ONE OF TWO GAMES WOULD PLAY OUT...

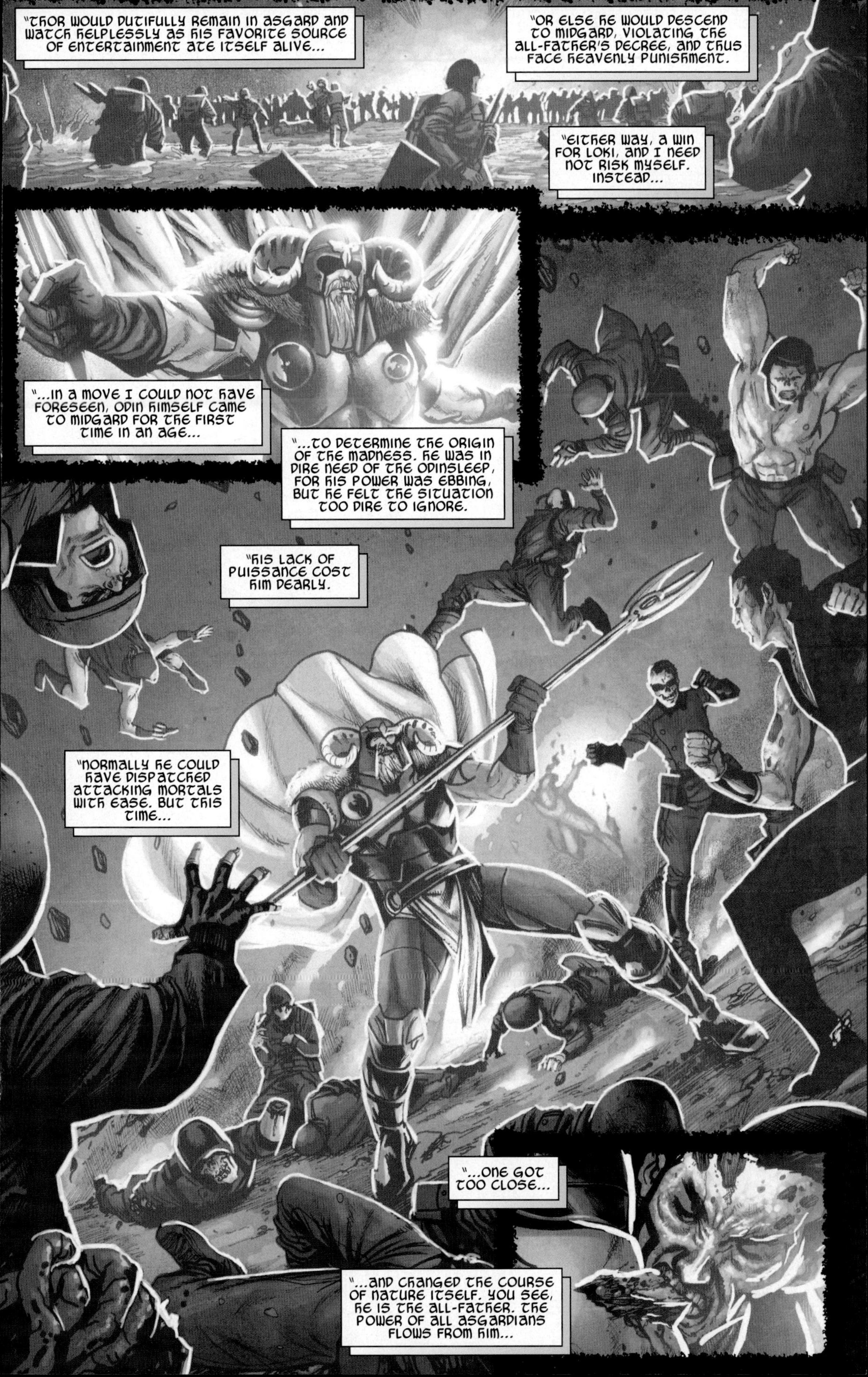
"THOR WOULD DUTIFULLY REMAIN IN ASGARD AND WATCH HELPLESSLY AS HIS FAVORITE SOURCE OF ENTERTAINMENT ATE ITSELF ALIVE...
"OR ELSE HE WOULD DESCEND TO MIDGARD, VIOLATING THE ALL-FATHER'S DECREE, AND THUS FACE HEAVENLY PUNISHMENT.
"EITHER WAY, A WIN FOR LOKI, AND I NEED NOT RISK MYSELF. INSTEAD...
"...IN A MOVE I COULD NOT HAVE FORESEEN, ODIN HIMSELF CAME TO MIDGARD FOR THE FIRST TIME IN AN AGE...
"...TO DETERMINE THE ORIGIN OF THE MADNESS. HE WAS IN DIRE NEED OF THE ODINSLEEP, FOR HIS POWER WAS EBBING, BUT HE FELT THE SITUATION TOO DIRE TO IGNORE.
"HIS LACK OF PUISSANCE COST HIM DEARLY.
"NORMALLY HE COULD HAVE DISPATCHED ATTACKING MORTALS WITH EASE. BUT THIS TIME...
"...ONE GOT TOO CLOSE...
"...AND CHANGED THE COURSE OF NATURE ITSELF. YOU SEE, HE IS THE ALL-FATHER. THE POWER OF ALL ASGARDIANS FLOWS FROM HIM...

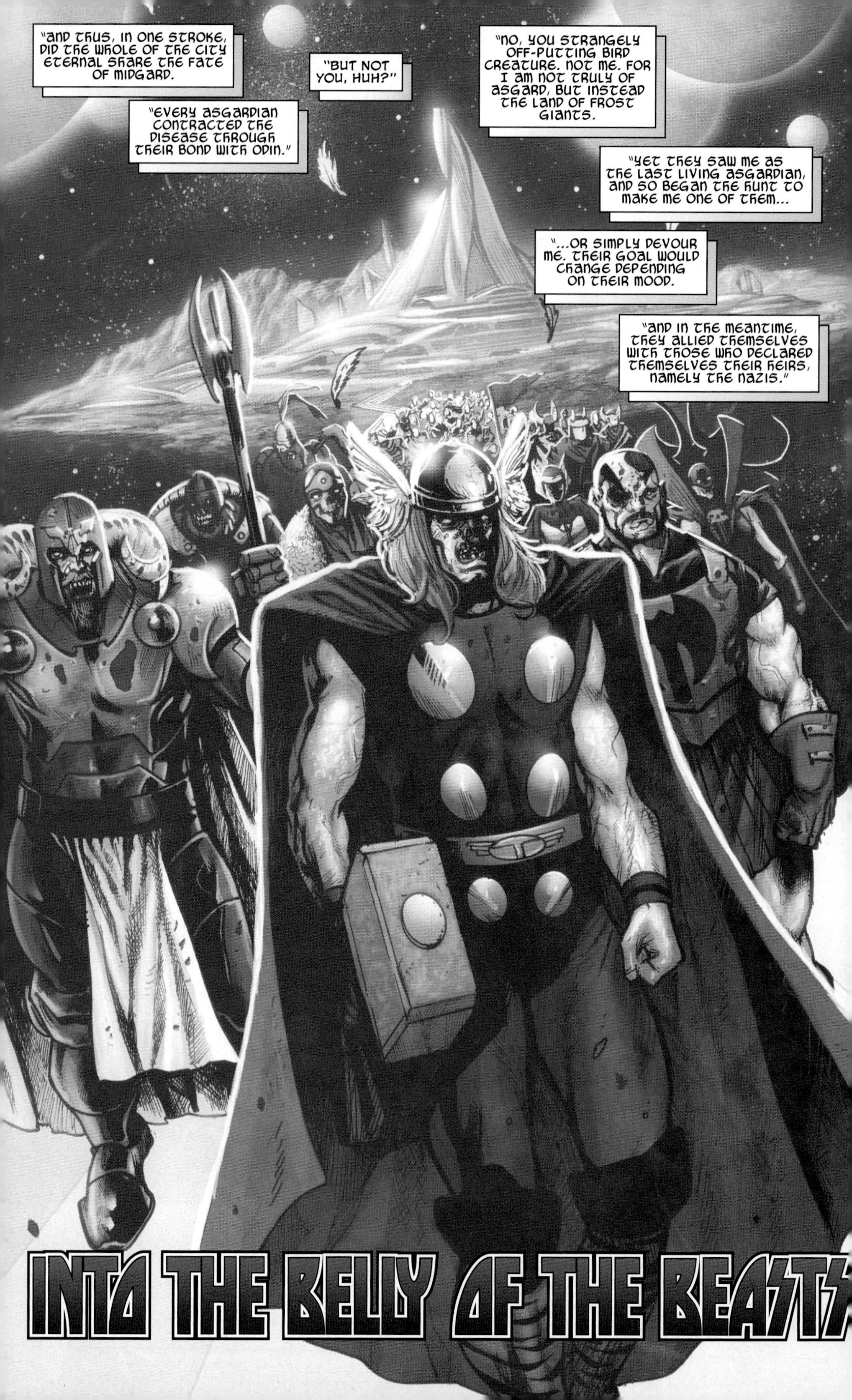
"AND THUS, IN ONE STROKE, DID THE WHOLE OF THE CITY ETERNAL SHARE THE FATE OF MIDGARD.
"EVERY ASGARDIAN CONTRACTED THE DISEASE THROUGH THEIR BOND WITH ODIN."
"BUT NOT YOU, HUH?"
"NO, YOU STRANGELY OFF-PUTTING BIRD CREATURE. NOT ME. FOR I AM NOT TRULY OF ASGARD, BUT INSTEAD THE LAND OF FROST GIANTS.
"YET THEY SAW ME AS THE LAST LIVING ASGARDIAN, AND SO BEGAN THE HUNT TO MAKE ME ONE OF THEM...
"...OR SIMPLY DEVOUR ME. THEIR GOAL WOULD CHANGE DEPENDING ON THEIR MOOD.
"AND IN THE MEANTIME, THEY ALLIED THEMSELVES WITH THOSE WHO DECLARED THEMSELVES THEIR HEIRS, NAMELY THE NAZIS."
INTO THE BELLY OF THE BEASTS

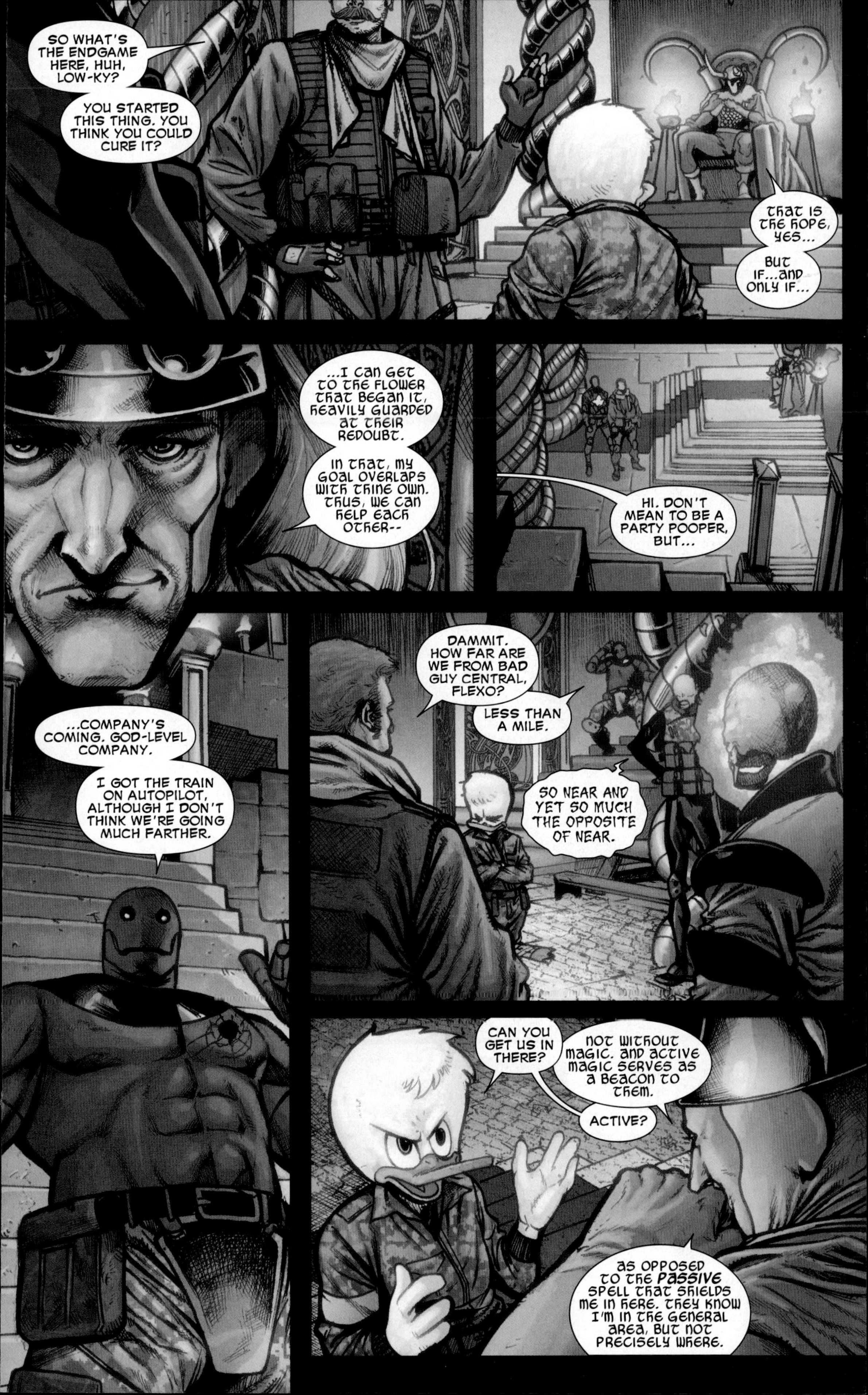
SO WHAT'S THE ENDGAME HERE, HUH, LOW-KY?
YOU STARTED THIS THING. YOU THINK YOU COULD CURE IT?
THAT IS THE HOPE, YES...
BUT IF...AND ONLY IF...
...I CAN GET TO THE FLOWER THAT BEGAN IT, HEAVILY GUARDED AT THEIR REDOUBT.
IN THAT, MY GOAL OVERLAPS WITH THINE OWN. THUS, WE CAN HELP EACH OTHER--
HI. DON'T MEAN TO BE A PARTY POOPER, BUT...
...COMPANY'S COMING. GOD-LEVEL COMPANY.
I GOT THE TRAIN ON AUTOPILOT, ALTHOUGH I DON'T THINK WE'RE GOING MUCH FARTHER.
DAMMIT. HOW FAR ARE WE FROM BAD GUY CENTRAL, FLEXO?
LESS THAN A MILE.
SO NEAR AND YET SO MUCH THE OPPOSITE OF NEAR.
CAN YOU GET US IN THERE?
NOT WITHOUT MAGIC. AND ACTIVE MAGIC SERVES AS A BEACON TO THEM.
ACTIVE?
AS OPPOSED TO THE PASSIVE SPELL THAT SHIELDS ME IN HERE. THEY KNOW I'M IN THE GENERAL AREA, BUT NOT PRECISELY WHERE.

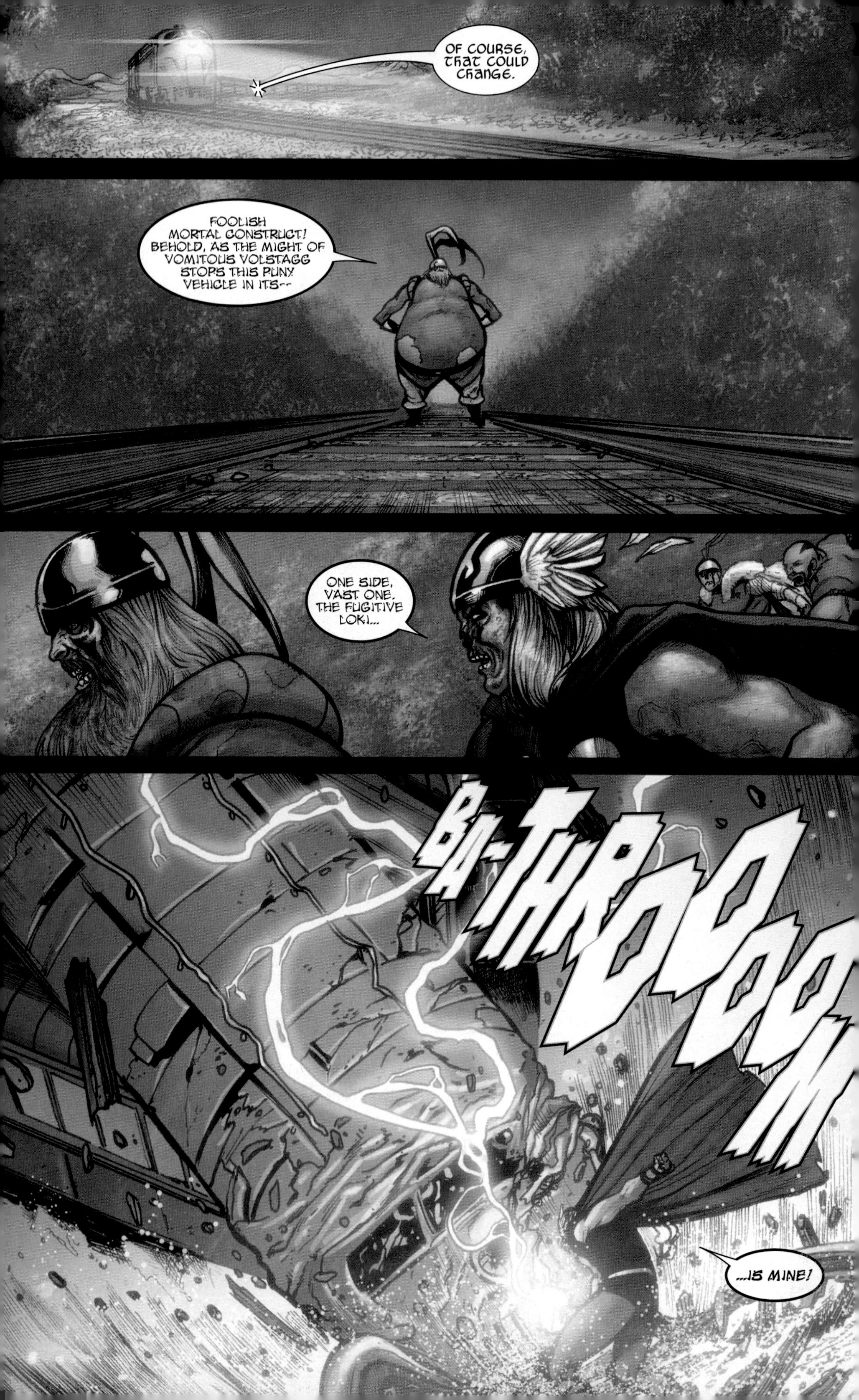
OF COURSE, THAT COULD CHANGE.
FOOLISH MORTAL CONSTRUCT! BEHOLD, AS THE MIGHT OF VOMITOUS VOLSTAGG STOPS THIS PUNY VEHICLE IN ITS--
ONE SIDE, VAST ONE. THE FUGITIVE LOKI...
BA-THROOOOM
...IS MINE!

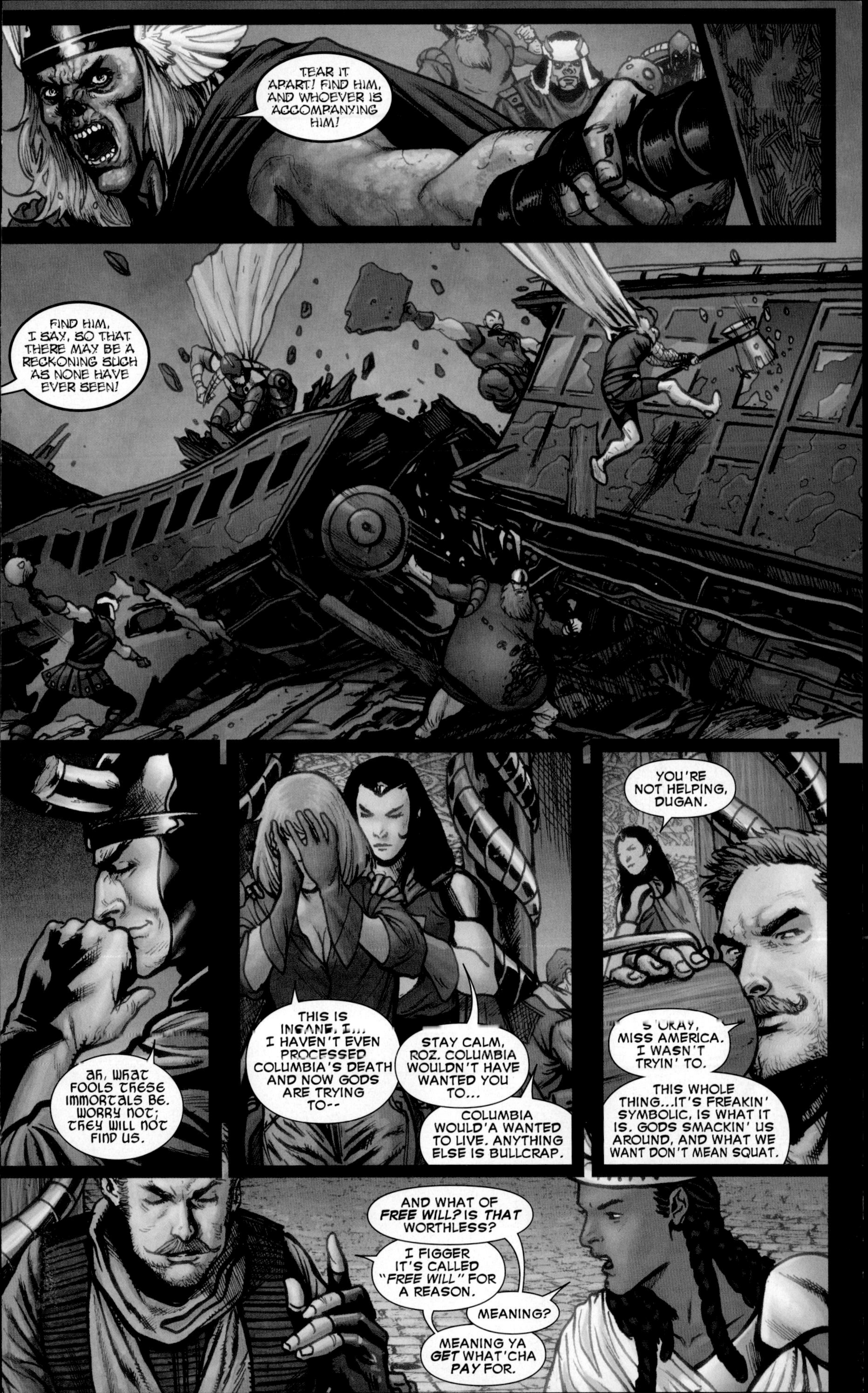
TEAR IT APART! FIND HIM, AND WHOEVER IS ACCOMPANYING HIM!
FIND HIM, I SAY, SO THAT THERE MAY BE A RECKONING SUCH AS NONE HAVE EVER SEEN!
AH, WHAT FOOLS THESE IMMORTALS BE. WORRY NOT; THEY WILL NOT FIND US.
THIS IS INSANE. I... I HAVEN'T EVEN PROCESSED COLUMBIA'S DEATH AND NOW GODS ARE TRYING TO--
STAY CALM, ROZ. COLUMBIA WOULDN'T HAVE WANTED YOU TO...
COLUMBIA WOULD'A WANTED TO LIVE. ANYTHING ELSE IS BULLCRAP.
YOU'RE NOT HELPING, DUGAN.
S'OKAY, MISS AMERICA. I WASN'T TRYIN' TO.
THIS WHOLE THING...IT'S FREAKIN' SYMBOLIC, IS WHAT IT IS. GODS SMACKIN' US AROUND, AND WHAT WE WANT DON'T MEAN SQUAT.
AND WHAT OF FREE WILL? IS THAT WORTHLESS?
I FIGGER IT'S CALLED "FREE WILL" FOR A REASON.
MEANING?
MEANING YA GET WHAT'CHA PAY FOR.

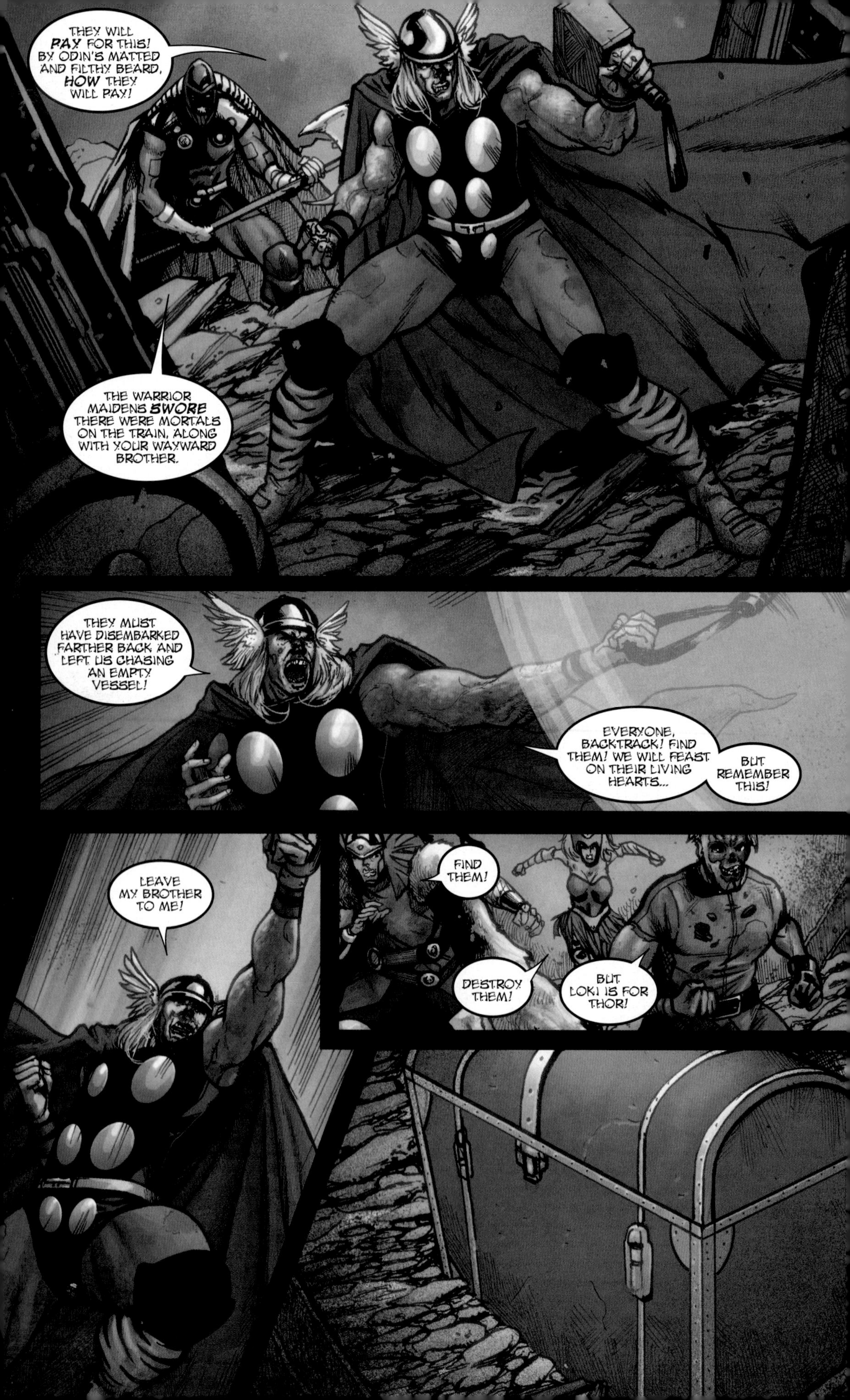
THEY WILL PAY FOR THIS! BY ODIN'S MATTED AND FILTHY BEARD, HOW THEY WILL PAY!
THE WARRIOR MAIDENS SWORE THERE WERE MORTALS ON THE TRAIN, ALONG WITH YOUR WAYWARD BROTHER.
THEY MUST HAVE DISEMBARKED FARTHER BACK AND LEFT US CHASING AN EMPTY VESSEL!
EVERYONE, BACKTRACK! FIND THEM! WE WILL FEAST ON THEIR LIVING HEARTS...
BUT REMEMBER THIS!
LEAVE MY BROTHER TO ME!
FIND THEM!
DESTROY THEM!
BUT LOKI IS FOR THOR!

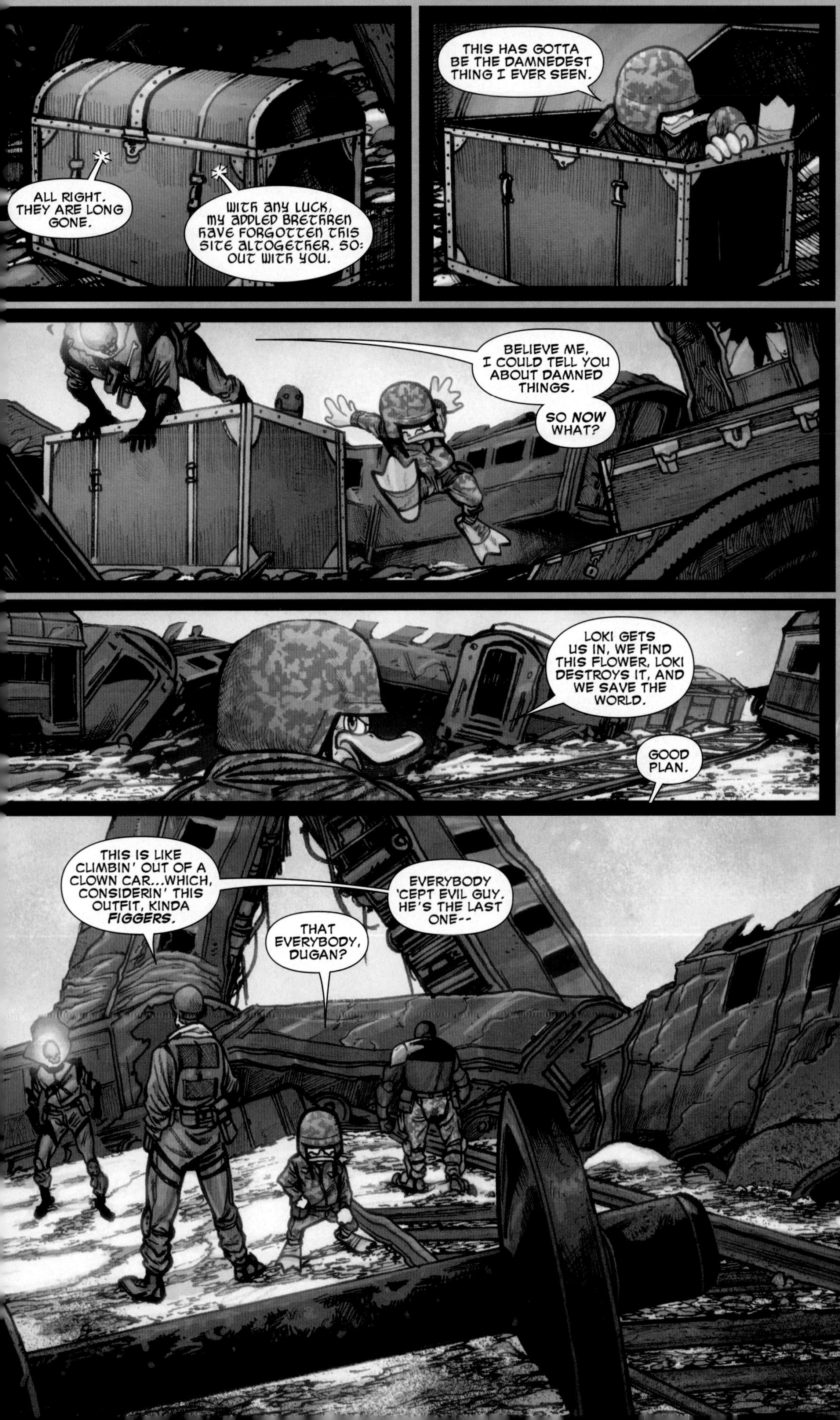
ALL RIGHT. THEY ARE LONG GONE.
WITH ANY LUCK, MY ADDLED BRETHREN HAVE FORGOTTEN THIS SITE ALTOGETHER. SO: OUT WITH YOU.
THIS HAS GOTTA BE THE DAMNEDEST THING I EVER SEEN.
BELIEVE ME, I COULD TELL YOU ABOUT DAMNED THINGS.
SO NOW WHAT?
LOKI GETS US IN, WE FIND THIS FLOWER, LOKI DESTROYS IT, AND WE SAVE THE WORLD.
GOOD PLAN.
THIS IS LIKE CLIMBIN' OUT OF A CLOWN CAR...WHICH, CONSIDERIN' THIS OUTFIT, KINDA FIGGERS.
EVERYBODY 'CEPT EVIL GUY. HE'S THE LAST ONE--
THAT EVERYBODY, DUGAN?

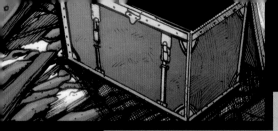

WHAT THE--?

AWWWW! I *LIKED* HIM! FOR AN EVIL GUY, HE WAS KIND OF NICE!

EITHER HE NEVER CAME OUT OR HE HAD ANOTHER EXIT.

I HATE TO KEEP ASKING THIS, BUT... NOW WHAT?

NOW IT'S BACK TO PLAN A.

ME PRETENDIN' TO BE MY OWN ZOMBIE. I HATE THIS.

THERE'S NOTHIN' ABOUT THIS *NOT* TO HATE, BUT IT *IS* WHAT IT IS.

"SO LET'S GET TO IT AND SEE JUST WHAT IT IS THAT THEY'RE HIDING UP THERE."

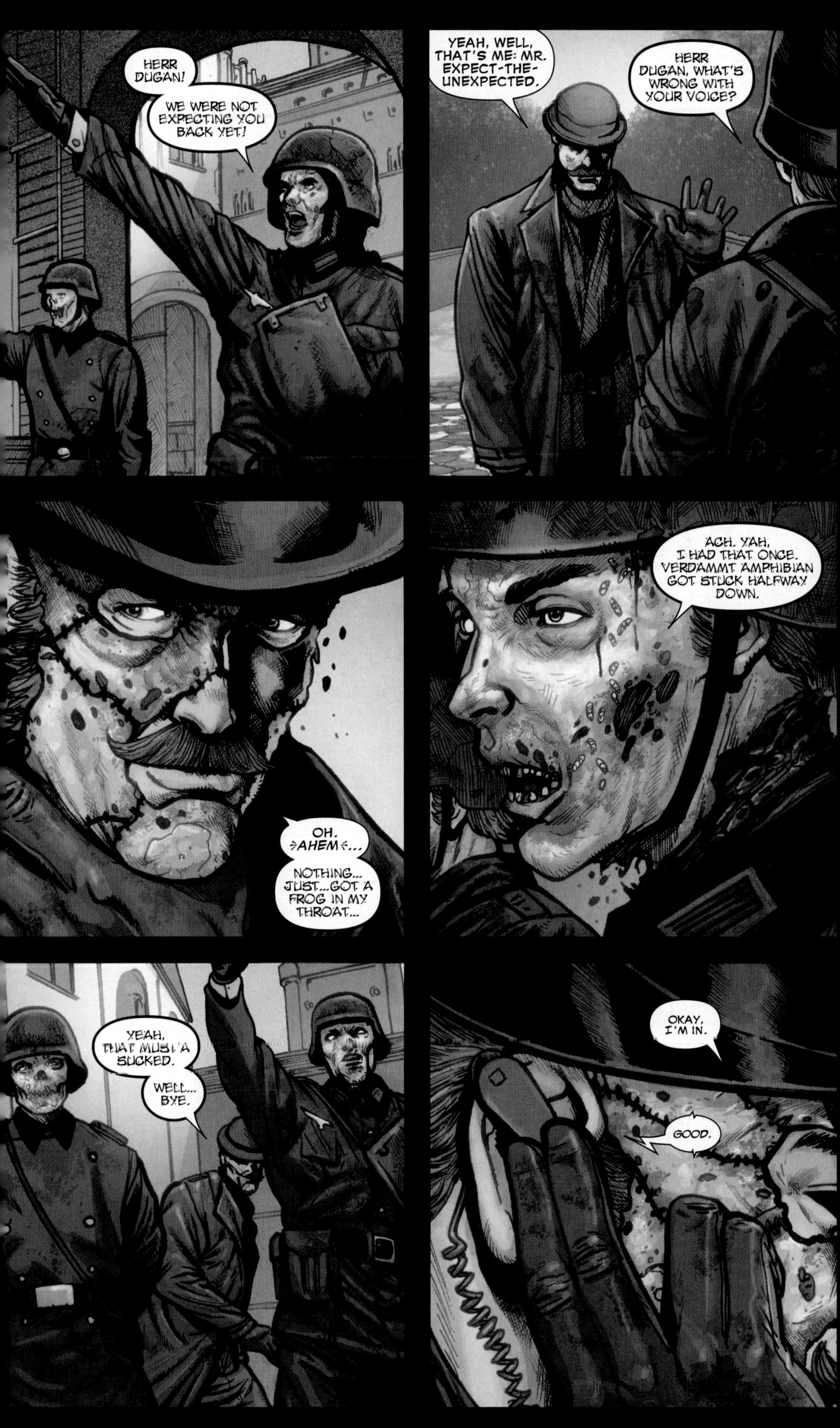
HERR DUGAN!
WE WERE NOT EXPECTING YOU BACK YET!
YEAH, WELL, THAT'S ME: MR. EXPECT-THE-UNEXPECTED.
HERR DUGAN, WHAT'S WRONG WITH YOUR VOICE?
OH. *AHEM*...
NOTHING... JUST...GOT A FROG IN MY THROAT...
ACH. YAH, I HAD THAT ONCE. VERDAMMT AMPHIBIAN GOT STUCK HALFWAY DOWN.
YEAH, THAT MUST'A SUCKED.
WELL... BYE.
OKAY, I'M IN.
GOOD.

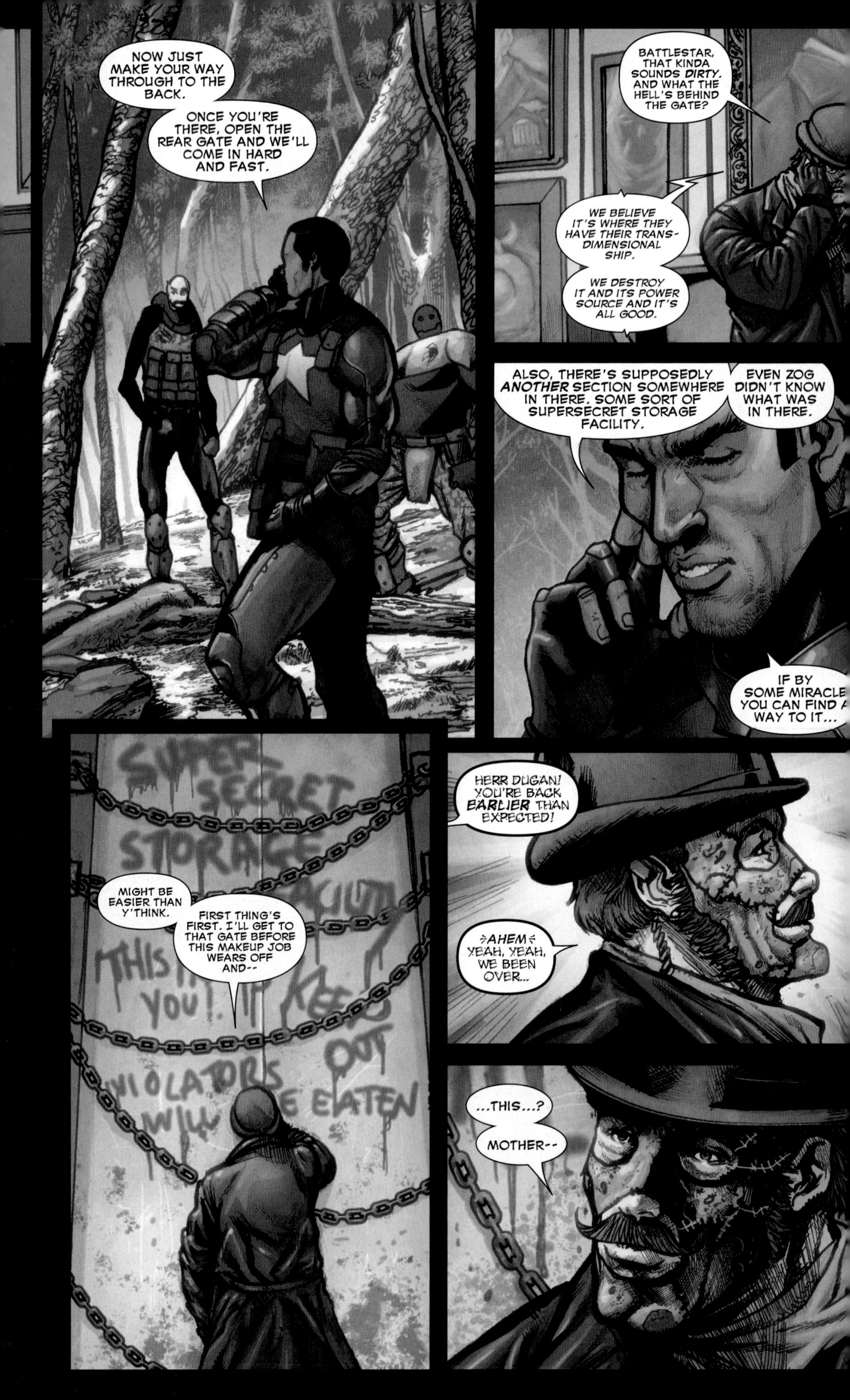
NOW JUST MAKE YOUR WAY THROUGH TO THE BACK.
ONCE YOU'RE THERE, OPEN THE REAR GATE AND WE'LL COME IN HARD AND FAST.
BATTLESTAR, THAT KINDA SOUNDS DIRTY. AND WHAT THE HELL'S BEHIND THE GATE?
WE BELIEVE IT'S WHERE THEY HAVE THEIR TRANS-DIMENSIONAL SHIP.
WE DESTROY IT AND ITS POWER SOURCE AND IT'S ALL GOOD.
ALSO, THERE'S SUPPOSEDLY ANOTHER SECTION SOMEWHERE IN THERE. SOME SORT OF SUPERSECRET STORAGE FACILITY.
EVEN ZOG DIDN'T KNOW WHAT WAS IN THERE.
IF BY SOME MIRACLE YOU CAN FIND A WAY TO IT...
SUPER SECRET
STORAGE
MIGHT BE EASIER THAN Y'THINK.
FIRST THING'S FIRST. I'LL GET TO THAT GATE BEFORE THIS MAKEUP JOB WEARS OFF AND--
HERR DUGAN! YOU'RE BACK EARLIER THAN EXPECTED!
AHEM YEAH, YEAH, WE BEEN OVER...
...THIS...?
MOTHER--

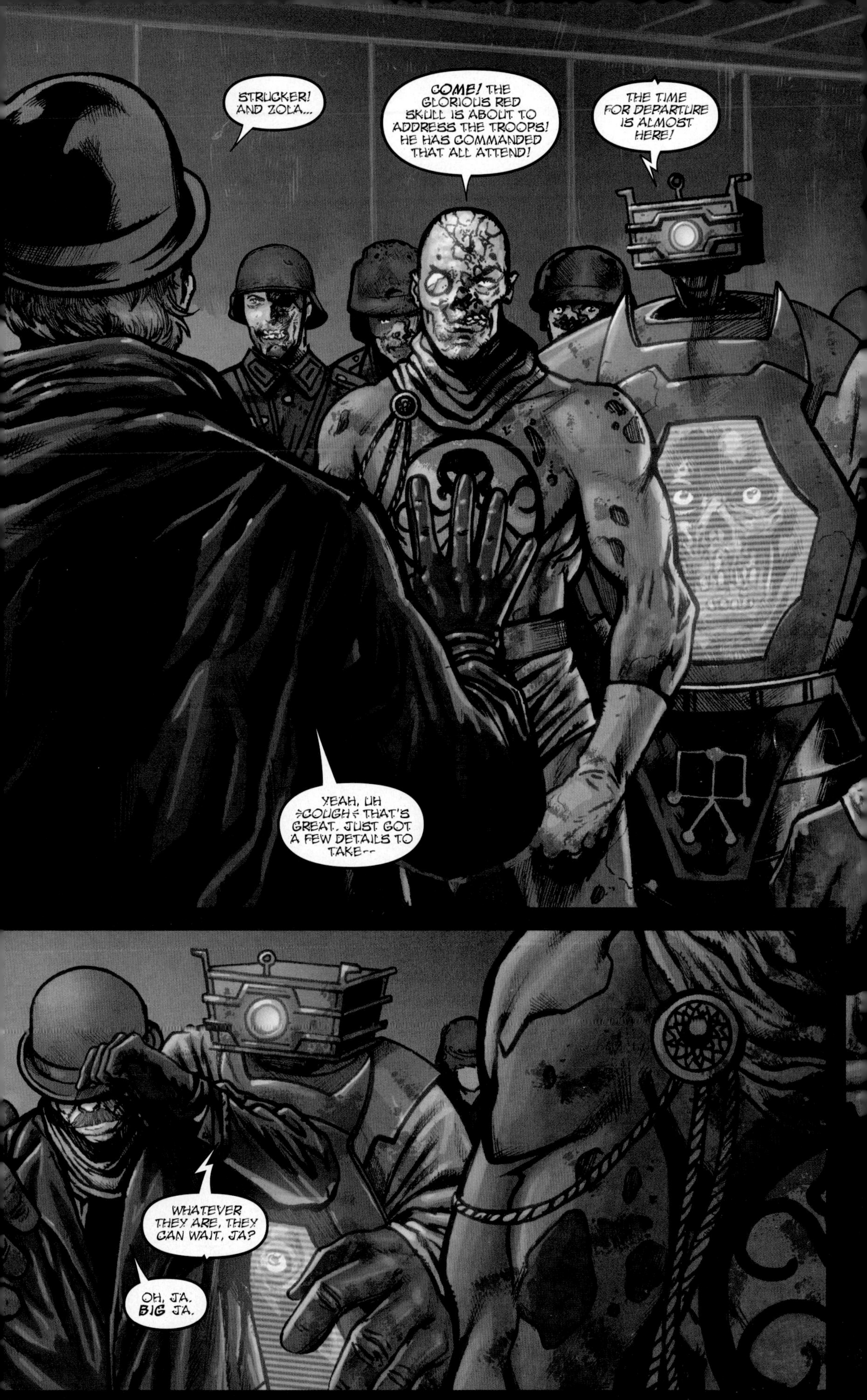
STRUCKER! AND ZOLA...
COME! THE GLORIOUS RED SKULL IS ABOUT TO ADDRESS THE TROOPS! HE HAS COMMANDED THAT ALL ATTEND!
THE TIME FOR DEPARTURE IS ALMOST HERE!
YEAH, UH *COUGH* THAT'S GREAT. JUST GOT A FEW DETAILS TO TAKE--
WHATEVER THEY ARE, THEY CAN WAIT, JA?
OH, JA. BIG JA.

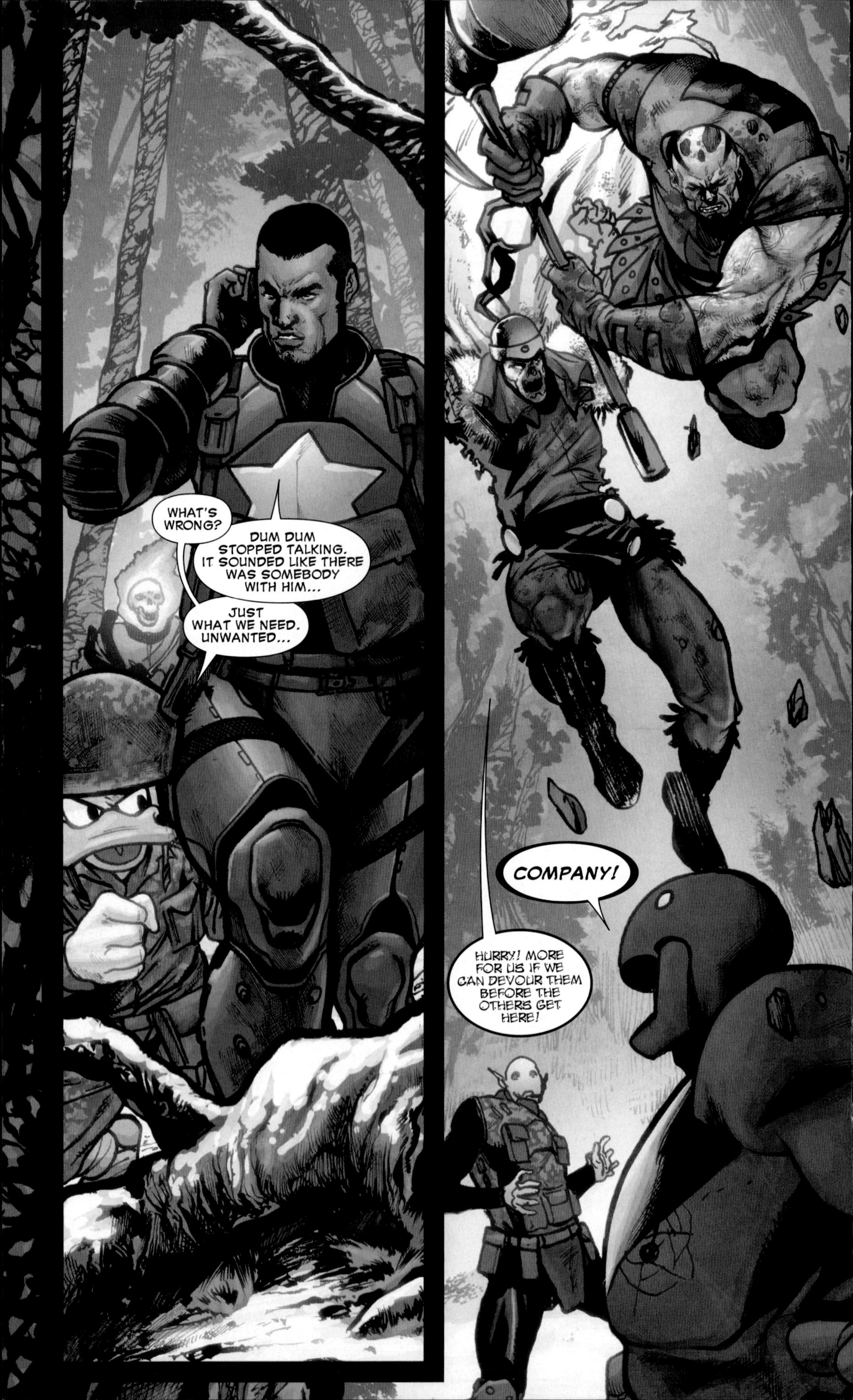
WHAT'S WRONG?
DUM DUM STOPPED TALKING. IT SOUNDED LIKE THERE WAS SOMEBODY WITH HIM...
JUST WHAT WE NEED. UNWANTED...
COMPANY!
HURRY! MORE FOR US IF WE CAN DEVOUR THEM BEFORE THE OTHERS GET HERE!

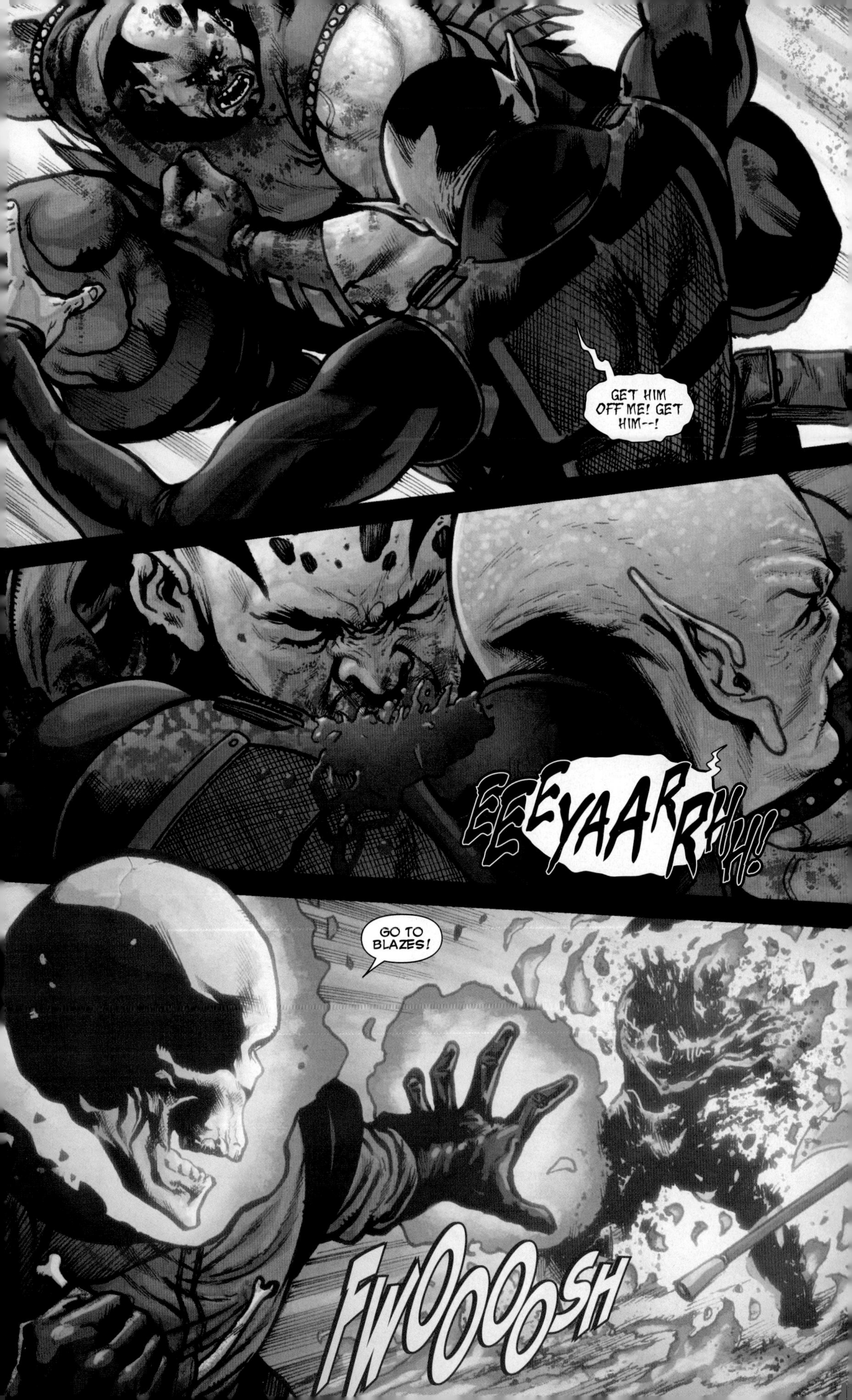
GET HIM OFF ME! GET HIM--!
EEEYAARRHH!
GO TO BLAZES!
FWOOOOOSH

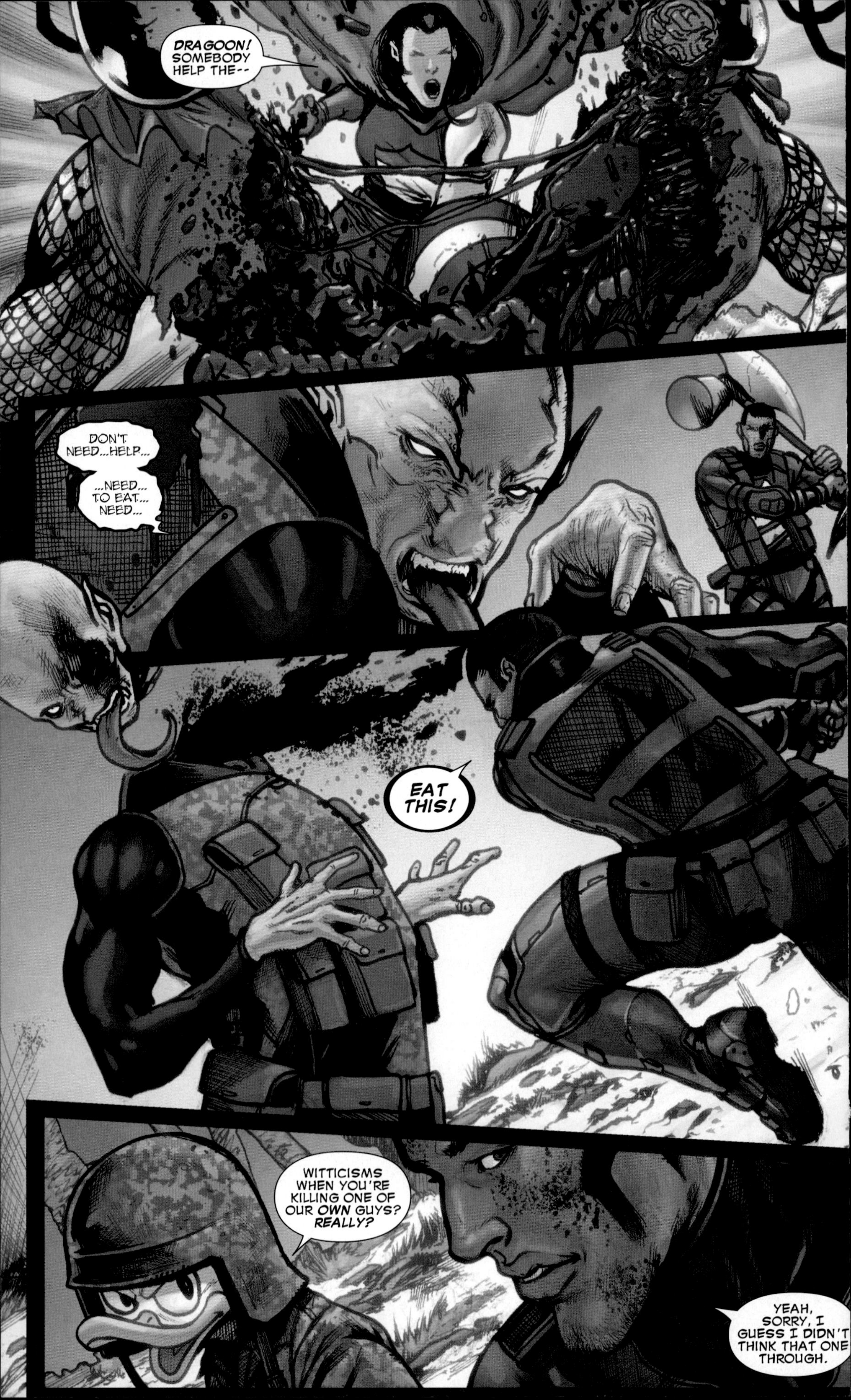
DRAGOON! SOMEBODY HELP THE--
DON'T NEED...HELP...
...NEED... TO EAT... NEED...
EAT THIS!
WITTICISMS WHEN YOU'RE KILLING ONE OF OUR OWN GUYS? REALLY?
YEAH, SORRY, I GUESS I DIDN'T THINK THAT ONE THROUGH.

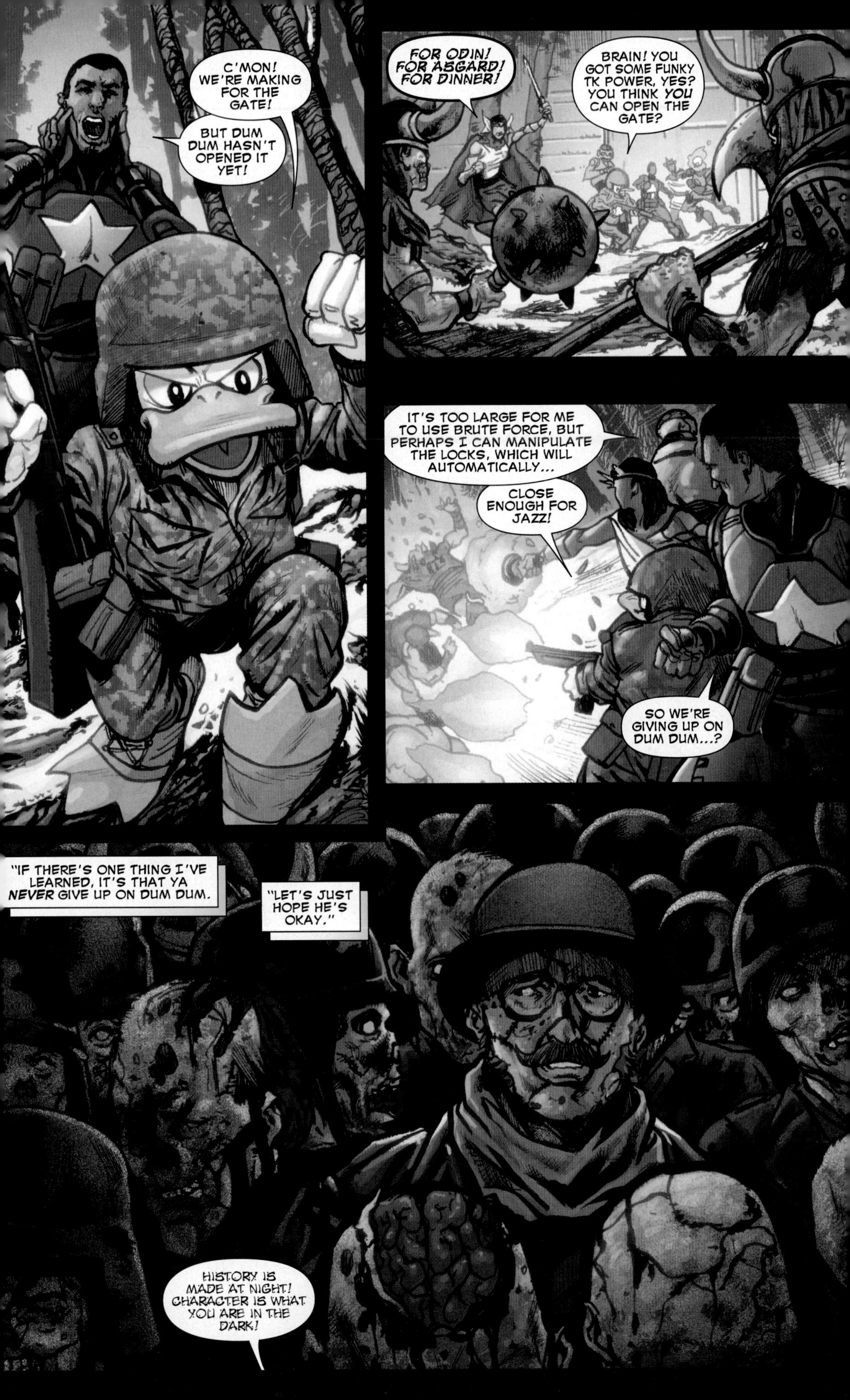

C'MON! WE'RE MAKING FOR THE GATE!
BUT DUM DUM HASN'T OPENED IT YET!
FOR ODIN! FOR ASGARD! FOR DINNER!
BRAIN! YOU GOT SOME FUNKY TK POWER, YES? YOU THINK YOU CAN OPEN THE GATE?
IT'S TOO LARGE FOR ME TO USE BRUTE FORCE, BUT PERHAPS I CAN MANIPULATE THE LOCKS, WHICH WILL AUTOMATICALLY...
CLOSE ENOUGH FOR JAZZ!
SO WE'RE GIVING UP ON DUM DUM...?
"IF THERE'S ONE THING I'VE LEARNED, IT'S THAT YA NEVER GIVE UP ON DUM DUM.
"LET'S JUST HOPE HE'S OKAY."
HISTORY IS MADE AT NIGHT! CHARACTER IS WHAT YOU ARE IN THE DARK!

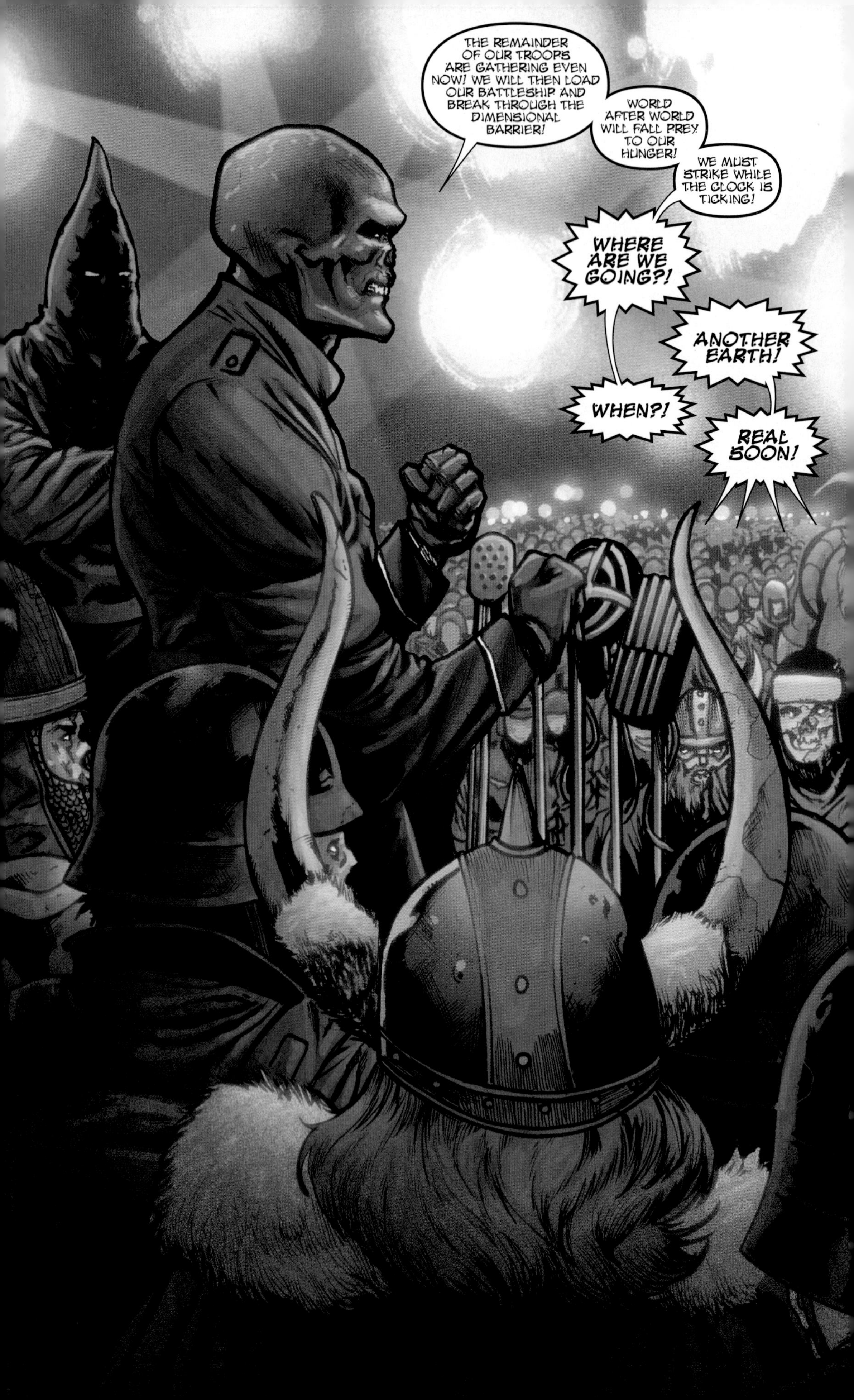
THE REMAINDER OF OUR TROOPS ARE GATHERING EVEN NOW! WE WILL THEN LOAD OUR BATTLESHIP AND BREAK THROUGH THE DIMENSIONAL BARRIER!
WORLD AFTER WORLD WILL FALL PREY TO OUR HUNGER!
WE MUST STRIKE WHILE THE CLOCK IS TICKING!
WHERE ARE WE GOING?!
WHEN?!
ANOTHER EARTH!
REAL SOON!

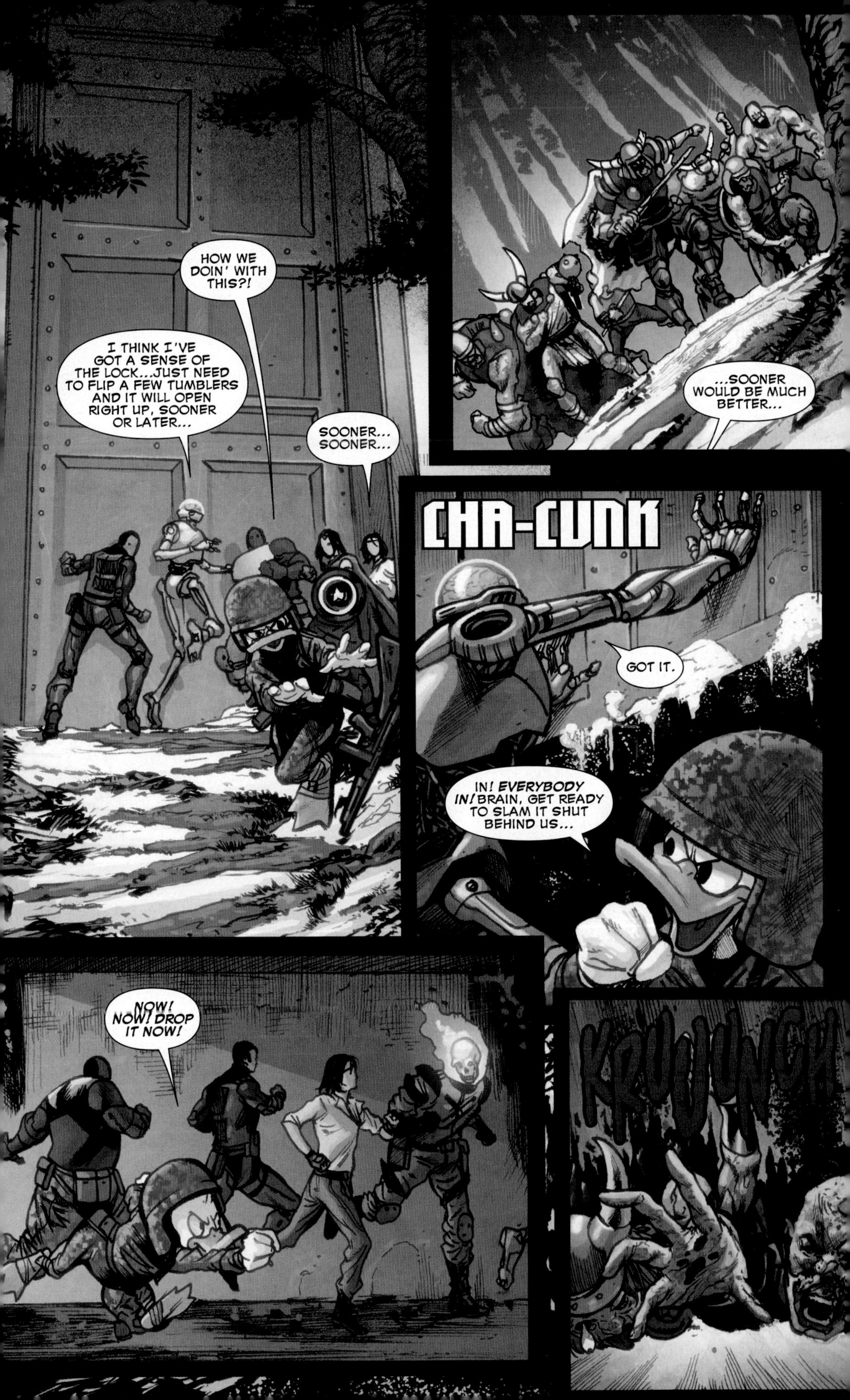

HOW WE DOIN' WITH THIS?!
I THINK I'VE GOT A SENSE OF THE LOCK...JUST NEED TO FLIP A FEW TUMBLERS AND IT WILL OPEN RIGHT UP, SOONER OR LATER...
SOONER... SOONER...
...SOONER WOULD BE MUCH BETTER...
CHA-CUNK
GOT IT.
IN! EVERYBODY IN! BRAIN, GET READY TO SLAM IT SHUT BEHIND US...
NOW! NOW! DROP IT NOW!
KRUUUNCH

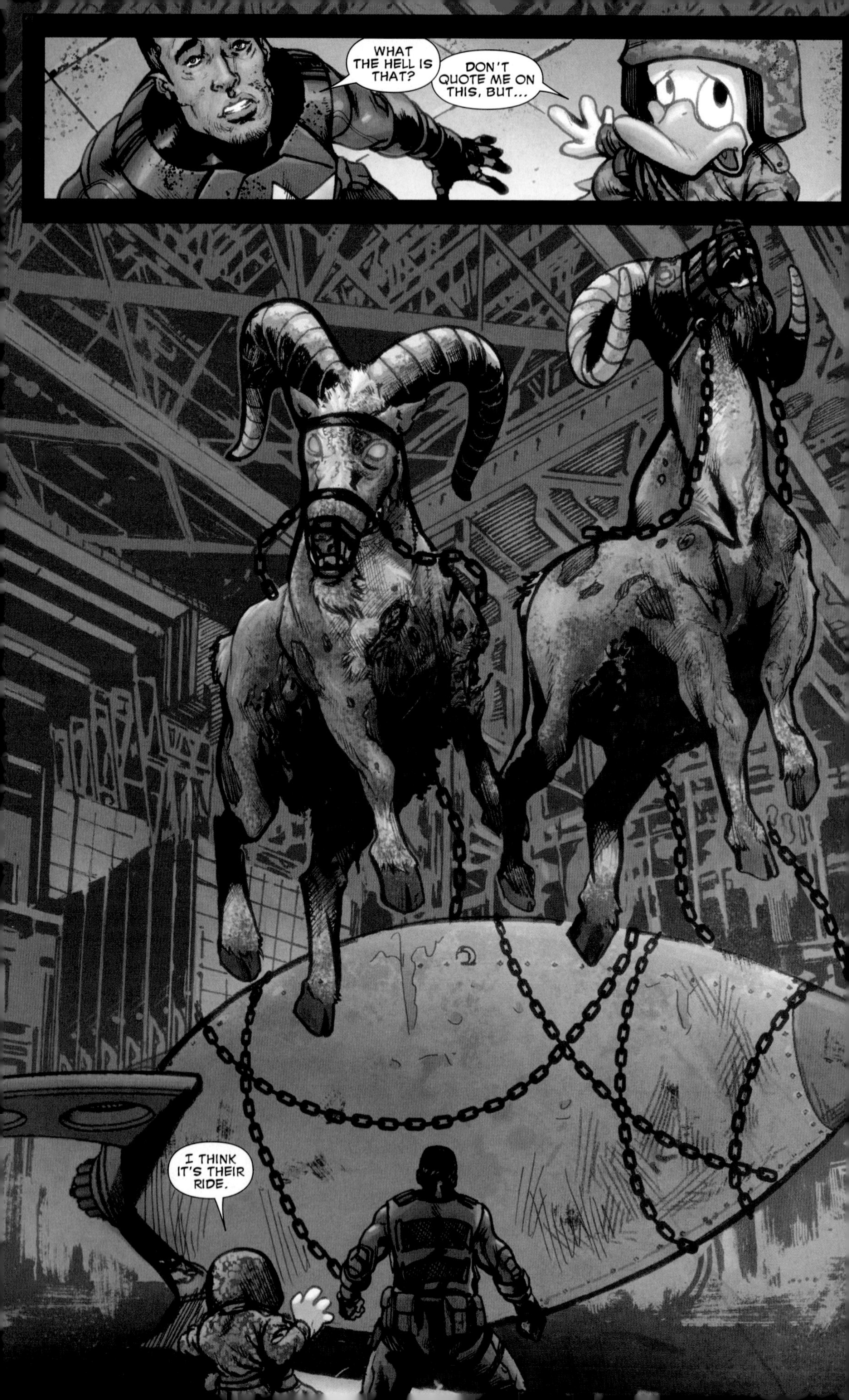
WHAT THE HELL IS THAT?
DON'T QUOTE ME ON THIS, BUT...
I THINK IT'S THEIR RIDE.

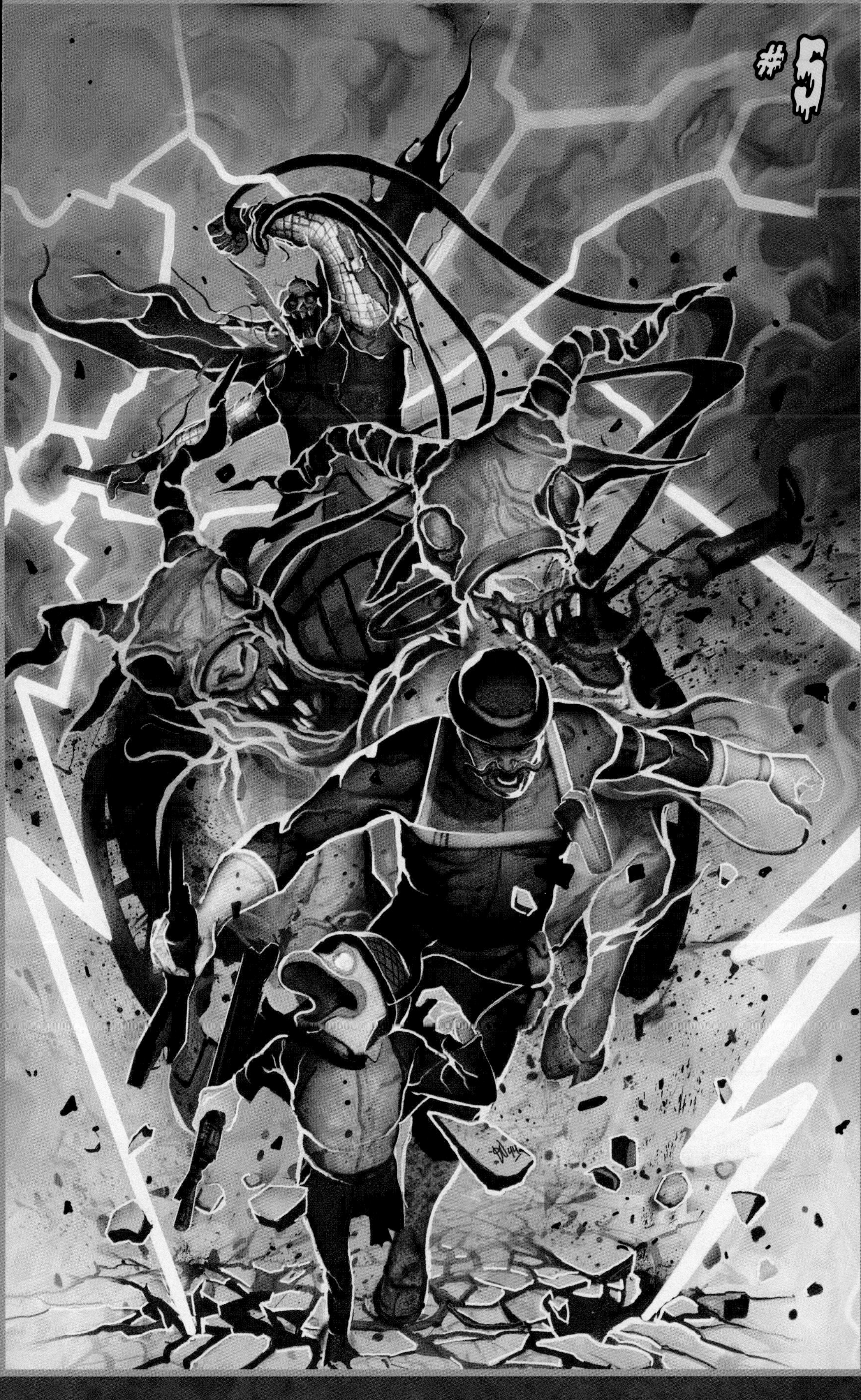
#5

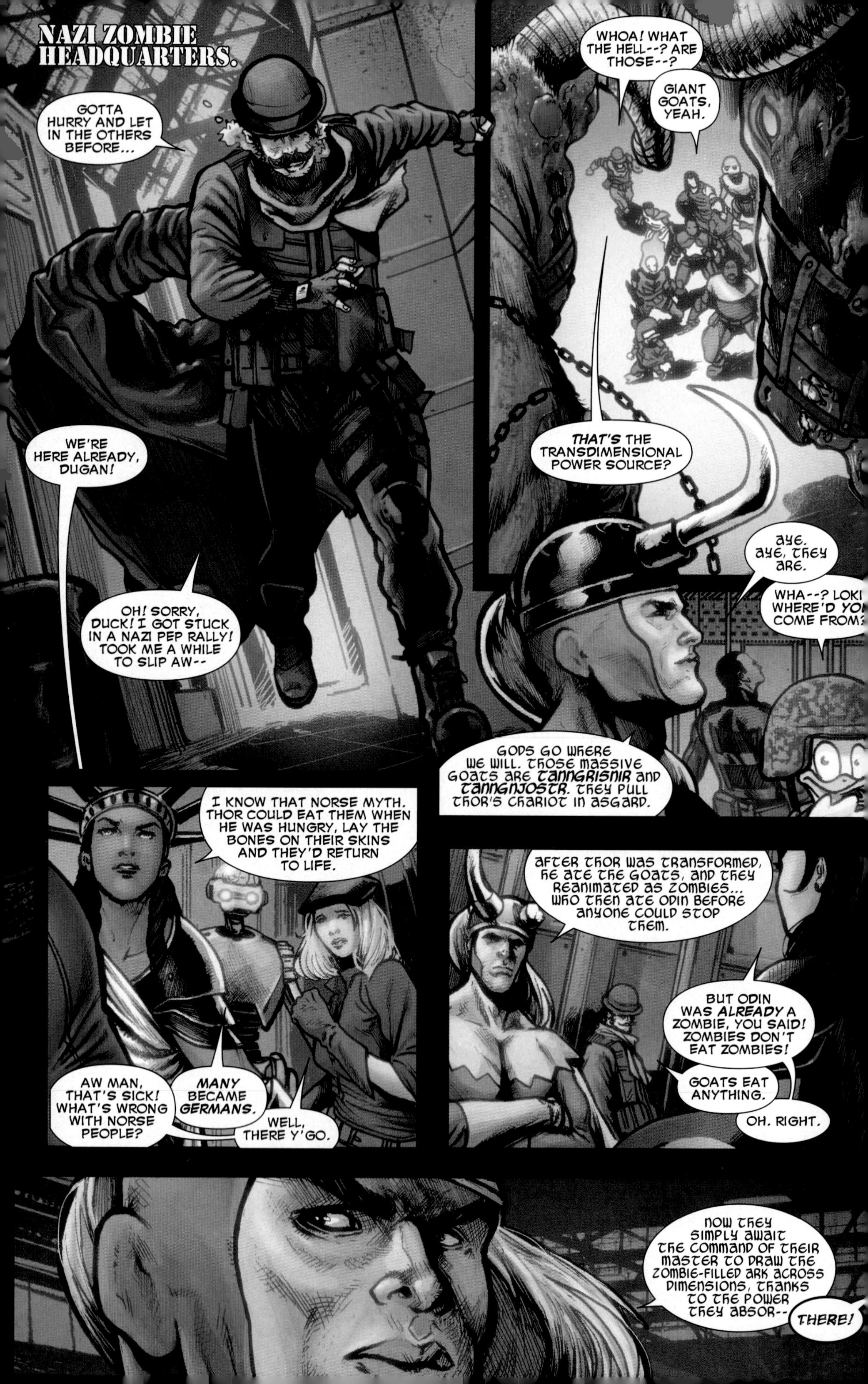
NAZI ZOMBIE HEADQUARTERS.
GOTTA HURRY AND LET IN THE OTHERS BEFORE...
WE'RE HERE ALREADY, DUGAN!
OH! SORRY, DUCK! I GOT STUCK IN A NAZI PEP RALLY! TOOK ME A WHILE TO SLIP AW--
WHOA! WHAT THE HELL--? ARE THOSE--?
GIANT GOATS, YEAH.
THAT'S THE TRANSDIMENSIONAL POWER SOURCE?
AYE. AYE, THEY ARE.
WHA--? LOKI WHERE'D YO COME FROM?
GODS GO WHERE WE WILL. THOSE MASSIVE GOATS ARE TANNGRISNIR AND TANNGNJOSTR. THEY PULL THOR'S CHARIOT IN ASGARD.
I KNOW THAT NORSE MYTH. THOR COULD EAT THEM WHEN HE WAS HUNGRY, LAY THE BONES ON THEIR SKINS AND THEY'D RETURN TO LIFE.
AW MAN, THAT'S SICK! WHAT'S WRONG WITH NORSE PEOPLE?
MANY BECAME GERMANS.
WELL, THERE Y'GO.
AFTER THOR WAS TRANSFORMED, HE ATE THE GOATS, AND THEY REANIMATED AS ZOMBIES... WHO THEN ATE ODIN BEFORE ANYONE COULD STOP THEM.
BUT ODIN WAS ALREADY A ZOMBIE, YOU SAID! ZOMBIES DON'T EAT ZOMBIES!
GOATS EAT ANYTHING.
OH. RIGHT.
NOW THEY SIMPLY AWAIT THE COMMAND OF THEIR MASTER TO DRAW THE ZOMBIE-FILLED ARK ACROSS DIMENSIONS, THANKS TO THE POWER THEY ABSOR--
THERE!

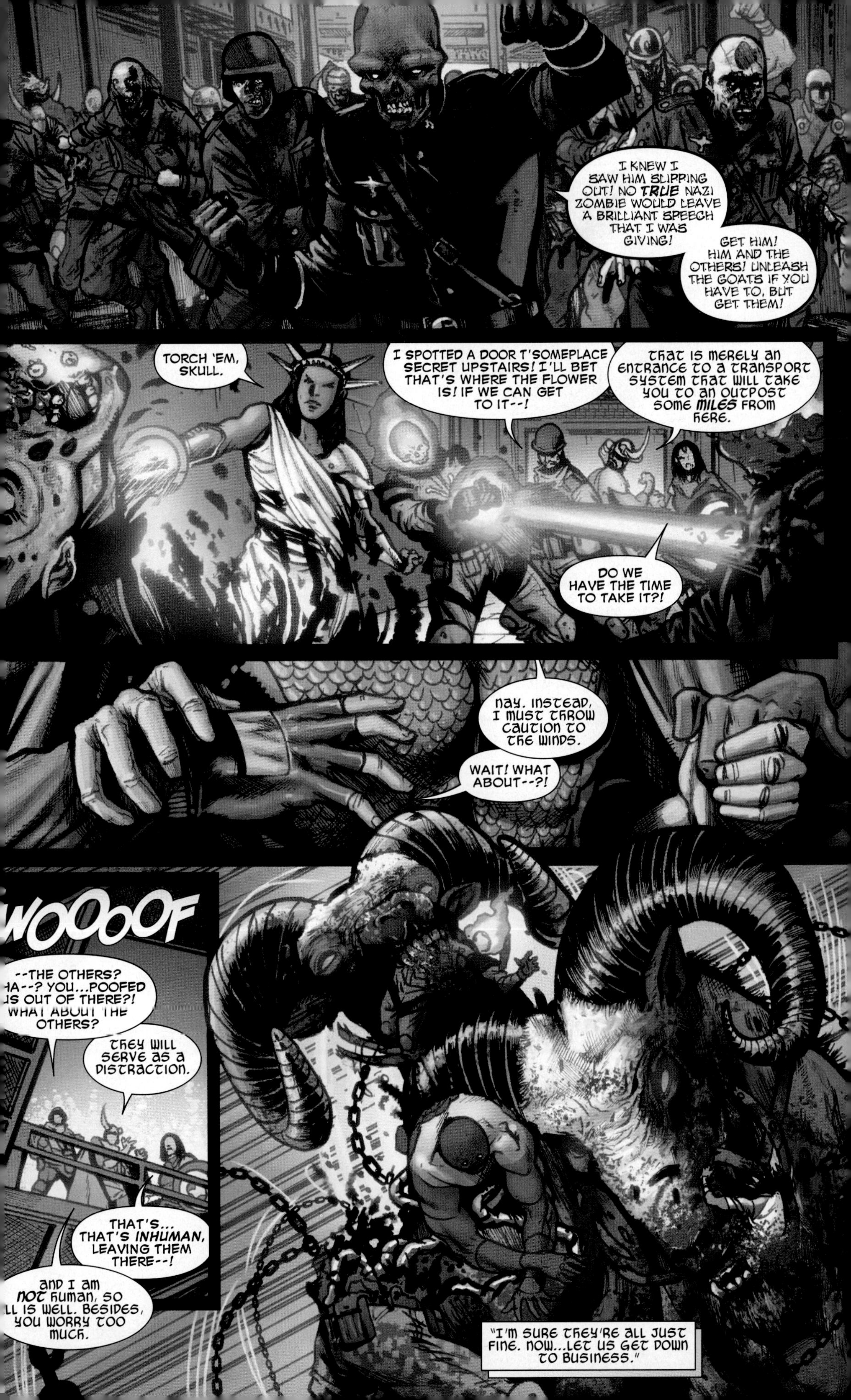
I KNEW I SAW HIM SLIPPING OUT! NO TRUE NAZI ZOMBIE WOULD LEAVE A BRILLIANT SPEECH THAT I WAS GIVING!
GET HIM! HIM AND THE OTHERS! UNLEASH THE GOATS IF YOU HAVE TO, BUT GET THEM!
TORCH 'EM, SKULL.
I SPOTTED A DOOR T'SOMEPLACE SECRET UPSTAIRS! I'LL BET THAT'S WHERE THE FLOWER IS! IF WE CAN GET TO IT--!
THAT IS MERELY AN ENTRANCE TO A TRANSPORT SYSTEM THAT WILL TAKE YOU TO AN OUTPOST SOME MILES FROM HERE.
DO WE HAVE THE TIME TO TAKE IT?!
NAY. INSTEAD, I MUST THROW CAUTION TO THE WINDS.
WAIT! WHAT ABOUT--?!
WOOOOF
--THE OTHERS? HA--? YOU...POOFED US OUT OF THERE?! WHAT ABOUT THE OTHERS?
THEY WILL SERVE AS A DISTRACTION.
THAT'S... THAT'S INHUMAN, LEAVING THEM THERE--!
AND I AM NOT HUMAN, SO LL IS WELL. BESIDES, YOU WORRY TOO MUCH.
"I'M SURE THEY'RE ALL JUST FINE. NOW...LET US GET DOWN TO BUSINESS."

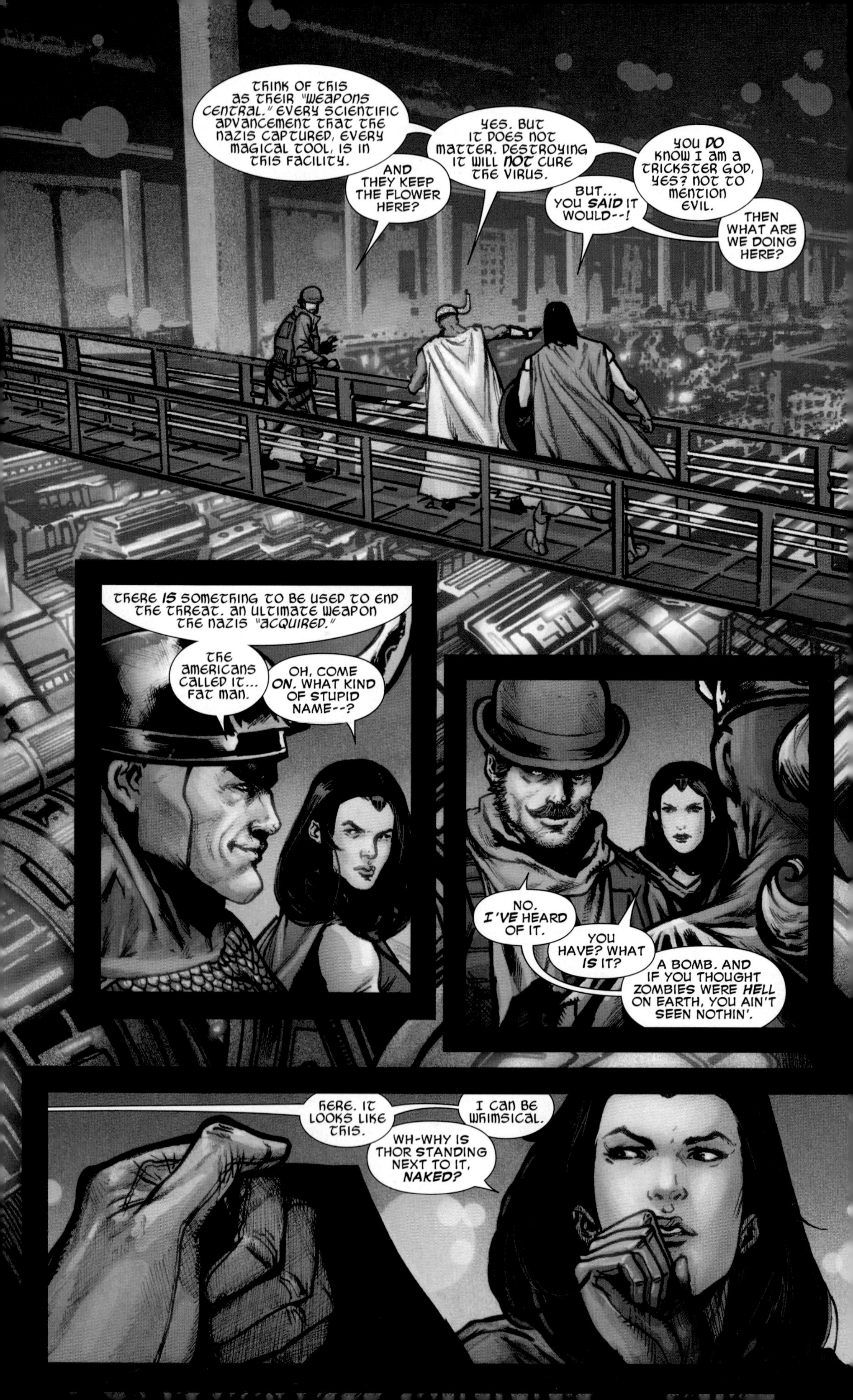
THINK OF THIS AS THEIR "WEAPONS CENTRAL." EVERY SCIENTIFIC ADVANCEMENT THAT THE NAZIS CAPTURED, EVERY MAGICAL TOOL, IS IN THIS FACILITY.
AND THEY KEEP THE FLOWER HERE?
YES. BUT IT DOES NOT MATTER. DESTROYING IT WILL NOT CURE THE VIRUS.
BUT... YOU SAID IT WOULD--!
YOU DO KNOW I AM A TRICKSTER GOD, YES? NOT TO MENTION EVIL.
THEN WHAT ARE WE DOING HERE?
THERE IS SOMETHING TO BE USED TO END THE THREAT. AN ULTIMATE WEAPON THE NAZIS "ACQUIRED."
THE AMERICANS CALLED IT... FAT MAN.
OH, COME ON. WHAT KIND OF STUPID NAME--?
NO. I'VE HEARD OF IT.
YOU HAVE? WHAT IS IT?
A BOMB. AND IF YOU THOUGHT ZOMBIES WERE HELL ON EARTH, YOU AIN'T SEEN NOTHIN'.
HERE. IT LOOKS LIKE THIS.
I CAN BE WHIMSICAL.
WH-WHY IS THOR STANDING NEXT TO IT, NAKED?

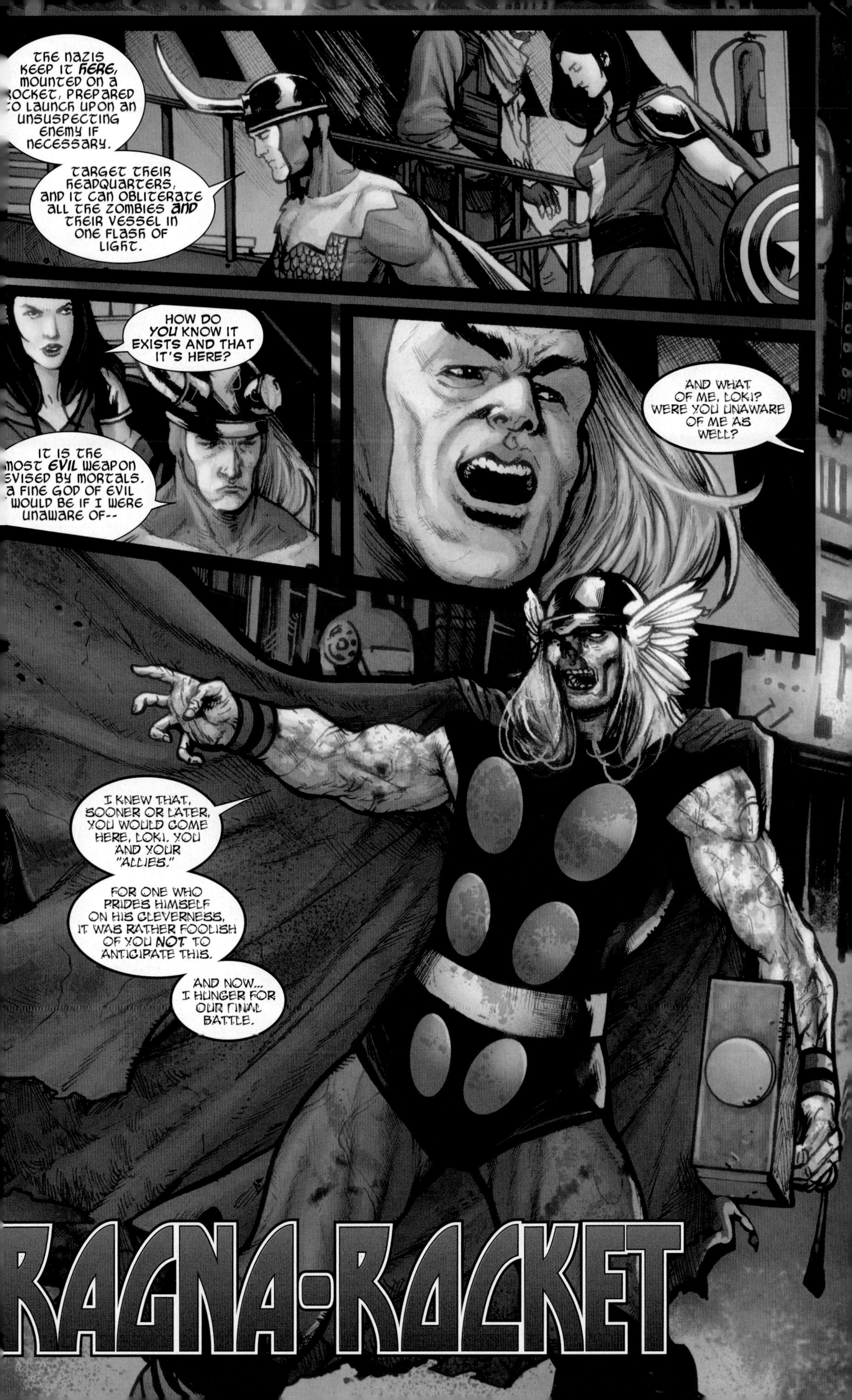
THE NAZIS KEEP IT HERE, MOUNTED ON A ROCKET, PREPARED TO LAUNCH UPON AN UNSUSPECTING ENEMY IF NECESSARY.
TARGET THEIR HEADQUARTERS, AND IT CAN OBLITERATE ALL THE ZOMBIES AND THEIR VESSEL IN ONE FLASH OF LIGHT.
HOW DO YOU KNOW IT EXISTS AND THAT IT'S HERE?
IT IS THE MOST EVIL WEAPON EVISED BY MORTALS. A FINE GOD OF EVIL WOULD BE IF I WERE UNAWARE OF--
AND WHAT OF ME, LOKI? WERE YOU UNAWARE OF ME AS WELL?
I KNEW THAT, SOONER OR LATER, YOU WOULD COME HERE, LOKI. YOU AND YOUR "ALLIES."
FOR ONE WHO PRIDES HIMSELF ON HIS CLEVERNESS, IT WAS RATHER FOOLISH OF YOU NOT TO ANTICIPATE THIS.
AND NOW... I HUNGER FOR OUR FINAL BATTLE.
RAGNA-ROCKET

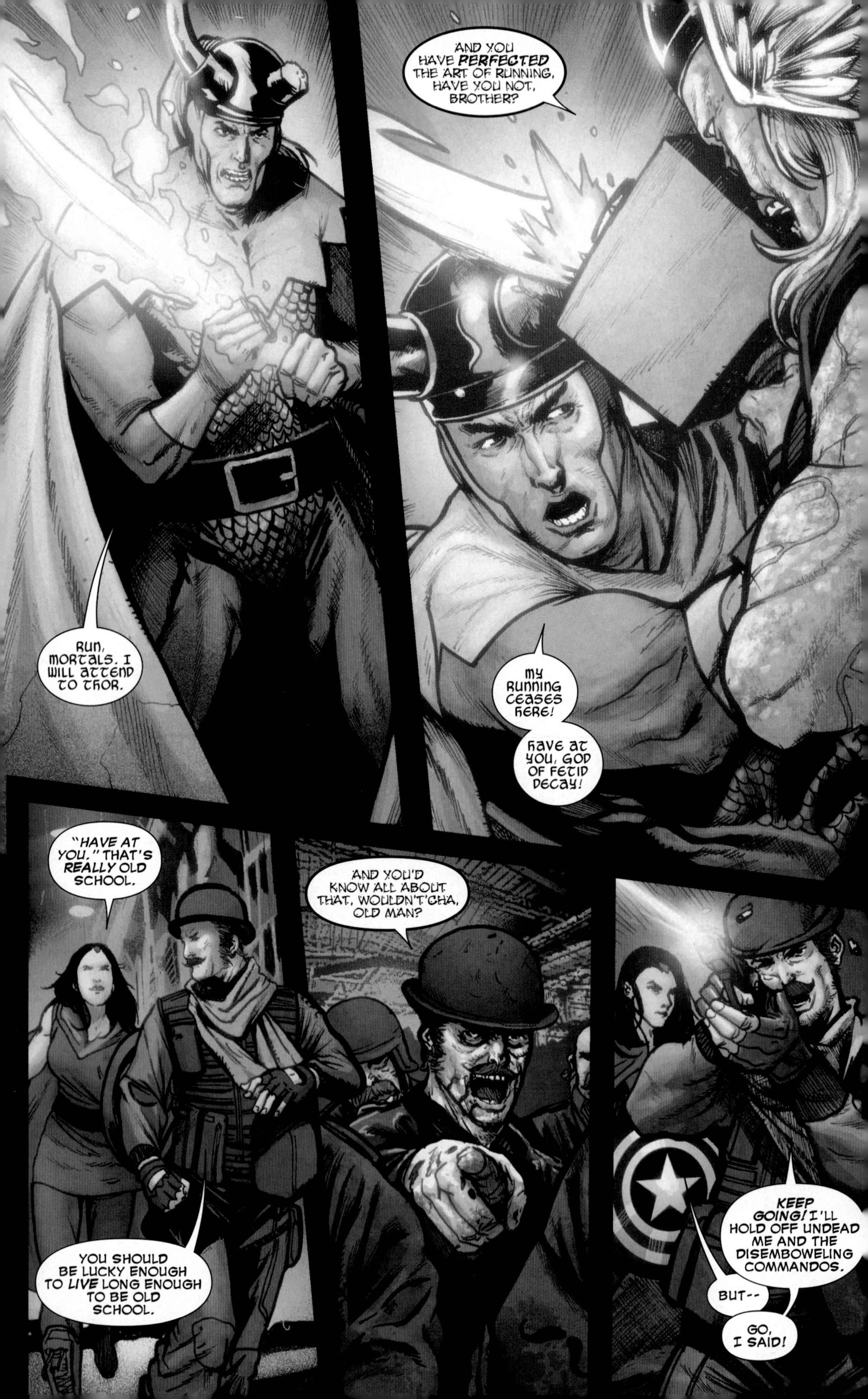
AND YOU HAVE PERFECTED THE ART OF RUNNING, HAVE YOU NOT, BROTHER?
RUN, MORTALS. I WILL ATTEND TO THOR.
MY RUNNING CEASES HERE!
HAVE AT YOU, GOD OF FETID DECAY!
"HAVE AT YOU." THAT'S REALLY OLD SCHOOL.
AND YOU'D KNOW ALL ABOUT THAT, WOULDN'T'CHA, OLD MAN?
YOU SHOULD BE LUCKY ENOUGH TO LIVE LONG ENOUGH TO BE OLD SCHOOL.
KEEP GOING! I'LL HOLD OFF UNDEAD ME AND THE DISEMBOWELING COMMANDOS.
BUT--
GO, I SAID!

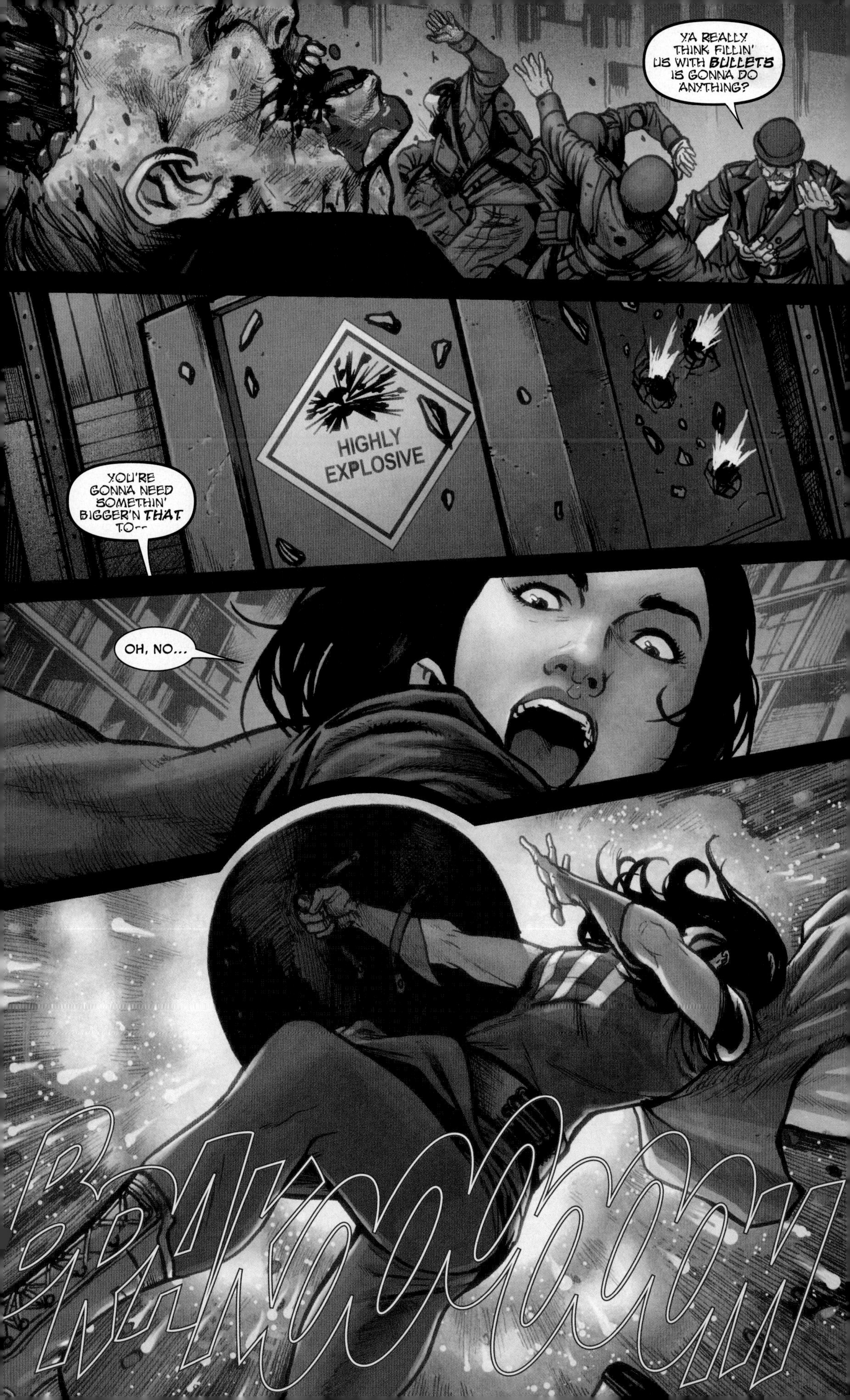

YA REALLY THINK FILLIN' US WITH BULLETS IS GONNA DO ANYTHING?
HIGHLY EXPLOSIVE
YOU'RE GONNA NEED SOMETHIN' BIGGER'N THAT TO--
OH, NO...

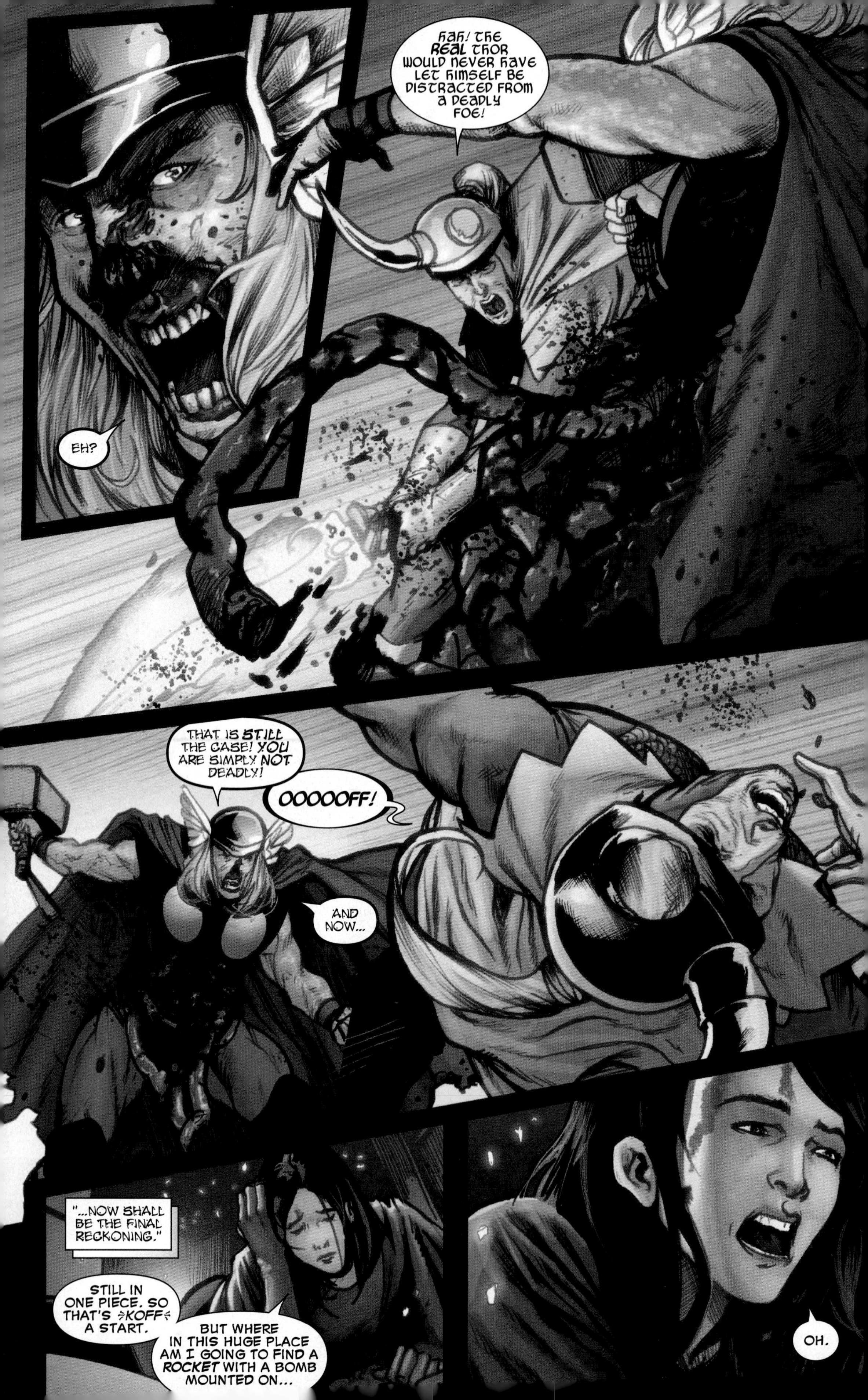
HAH! THE REAL THOR WOULD NEVER HAVE LET HIMSELF BE DISTRACTED FROM A DEADLY FOE!
EH?
THAT IS STILL THE CASE! YOU ARE SIMPLY NOT DEADLY!
OOOOOFF!
AND NOW...
"...NOW SHALL BE THE FINAL RECKONING."
STILL IN ONE PIECE. SO THAT'S ≯KOFF≮ A START.
BUT WHERE IN THIS HUGE PLACE AM I GOING TO FIND A ROCKET WITH A BOMB MOUNTED ON...
OH.

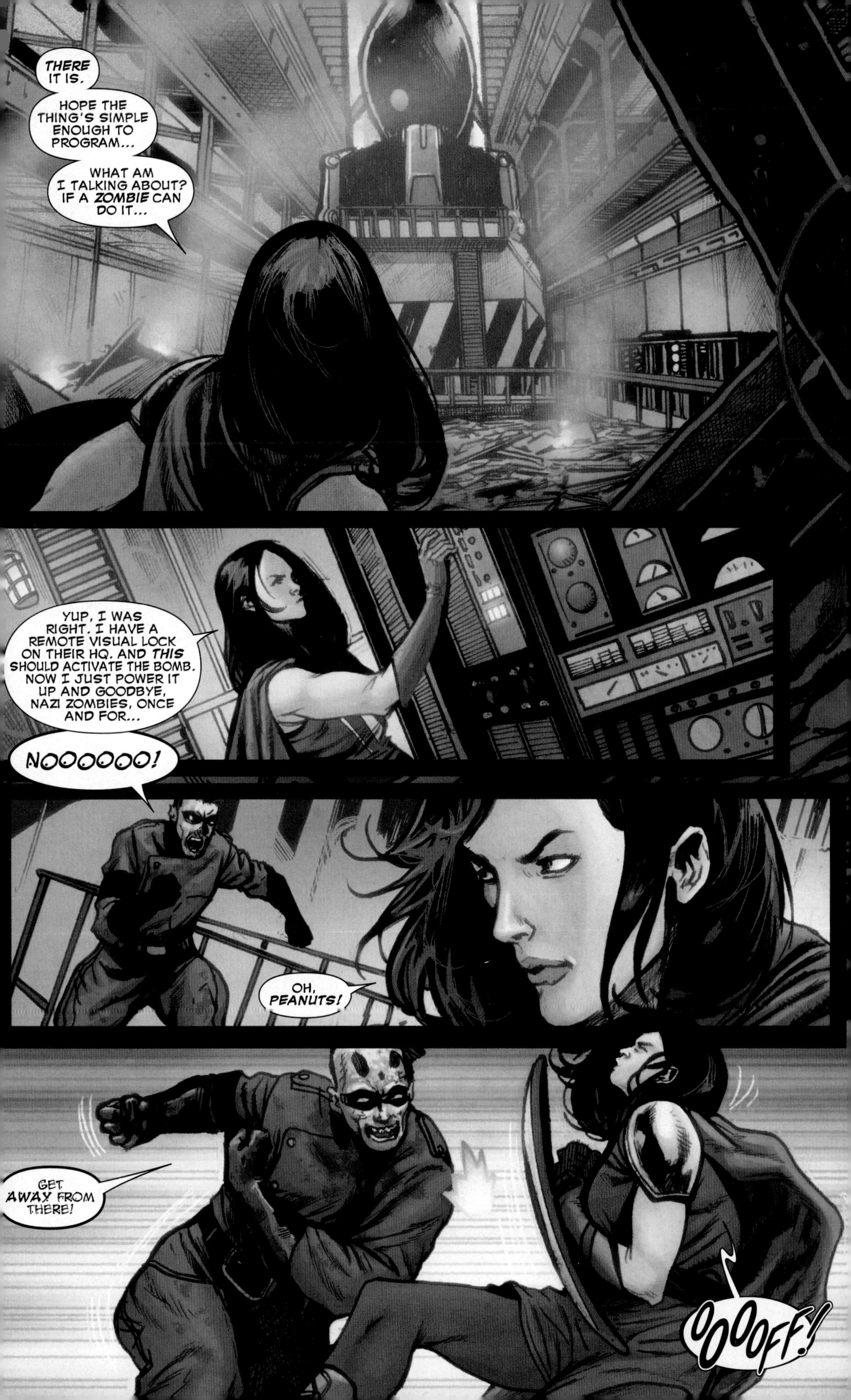
THERE IT IS.
HOPE THE THING'S SIMPLE ENOUGH TO PROGRAM...
WHAT AM I TALKING ABOUT? IF A ZOMBIE CAN DO IT...
YUP, I WAS RIGHT. I HAVE A REMOTE VISUAL LOCK ON THEIR HQ. AND THIS SHOULD ACTIVATE THE BOMB. NOW I JUST POWER IT UP AND GOODBYE, NAZI ZOMBIES, ONCE AND FOR...
NOOOOOO!
OH, PEANUTS!
GET AWAY FROM THERE!
OOOOFF!

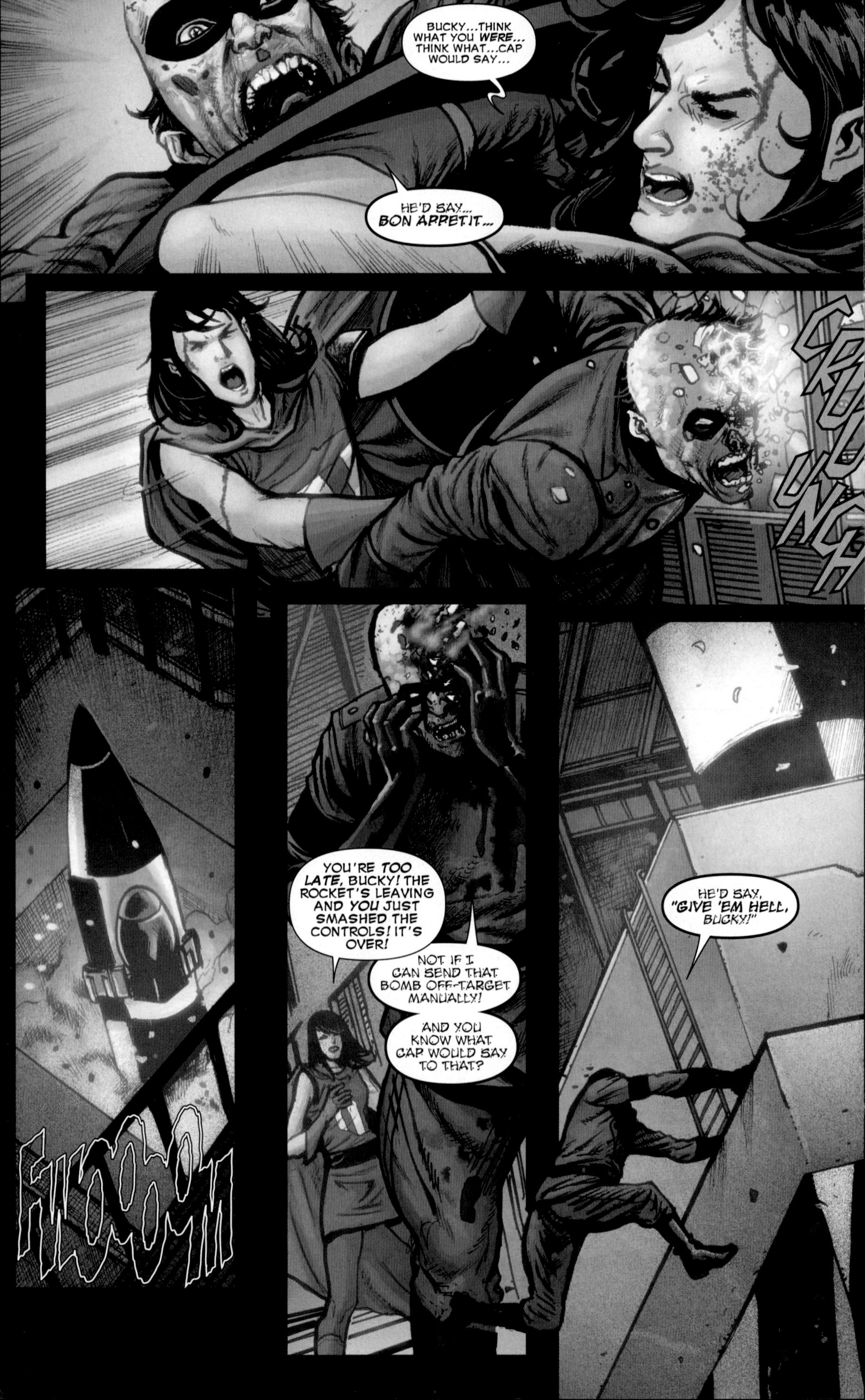

BUCKY...THINK WHAT YOU WERE... THINK WHAT...CAP WOULD SAY...
HE'D SAY... BON APPETIT...
CRUNCH
FWOOOOM
YOU'RE TOO LATE, BUCKY! THE ROCKET'S LEAVING AND YOU JUST SMASHED THE CONTROLS! IT'S OVER!
NOT IF I CAN SEND THAT BOMB OFF-TARGET MANUALLY!
AND YOU KNOW WHAT CAP WOULD SAY TO THAT?
HE'D SAY, "GIVE 'EM HELL, BUCKY!"

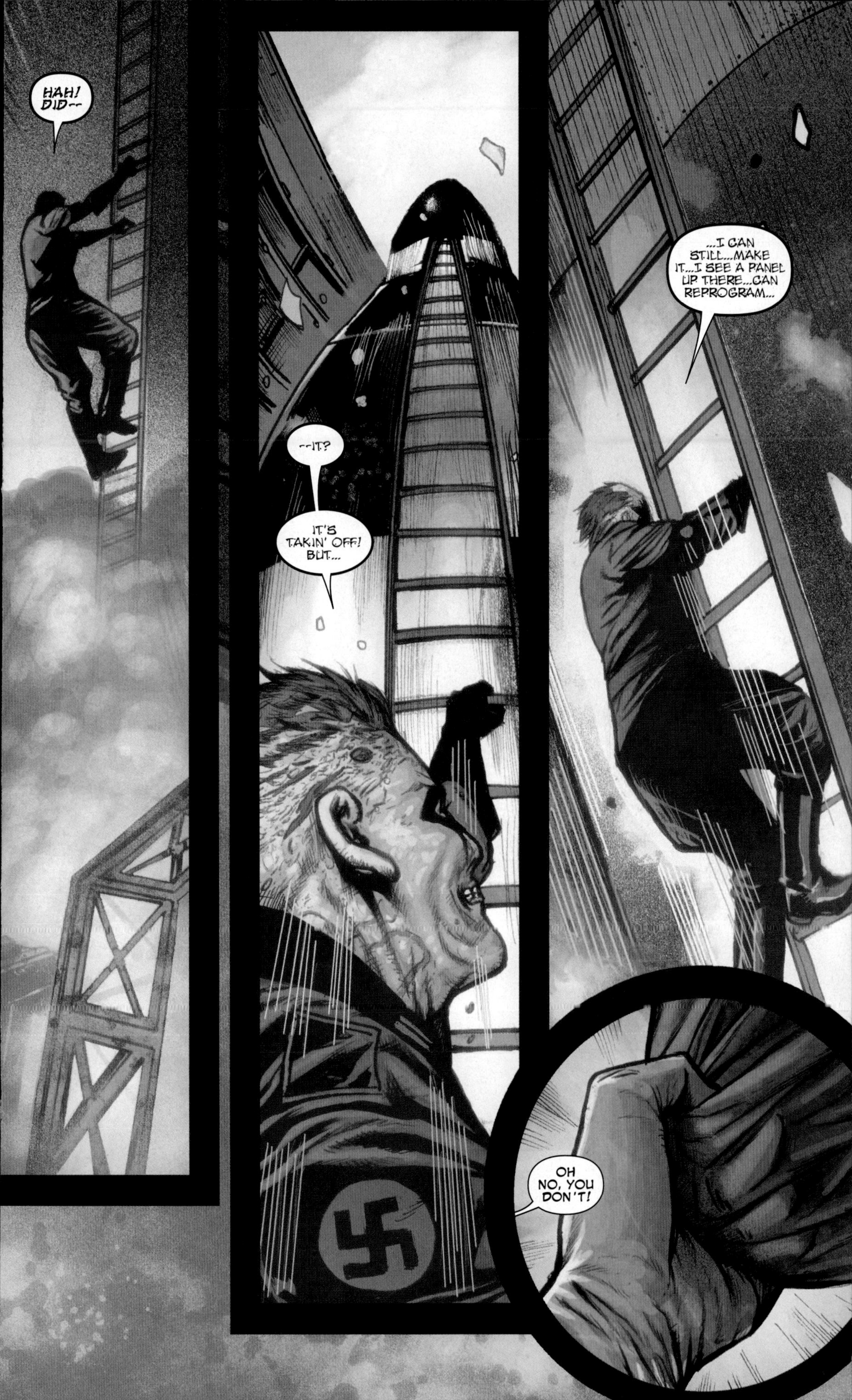
HAH! DID--
--IT?
IT'S TAKIN' OFF! BUT...
...I CAN STILL...MAKE IT...I SEE A PANEL UP THERE...CAN REPROGRAM...
OH NO, YOU DON'T!

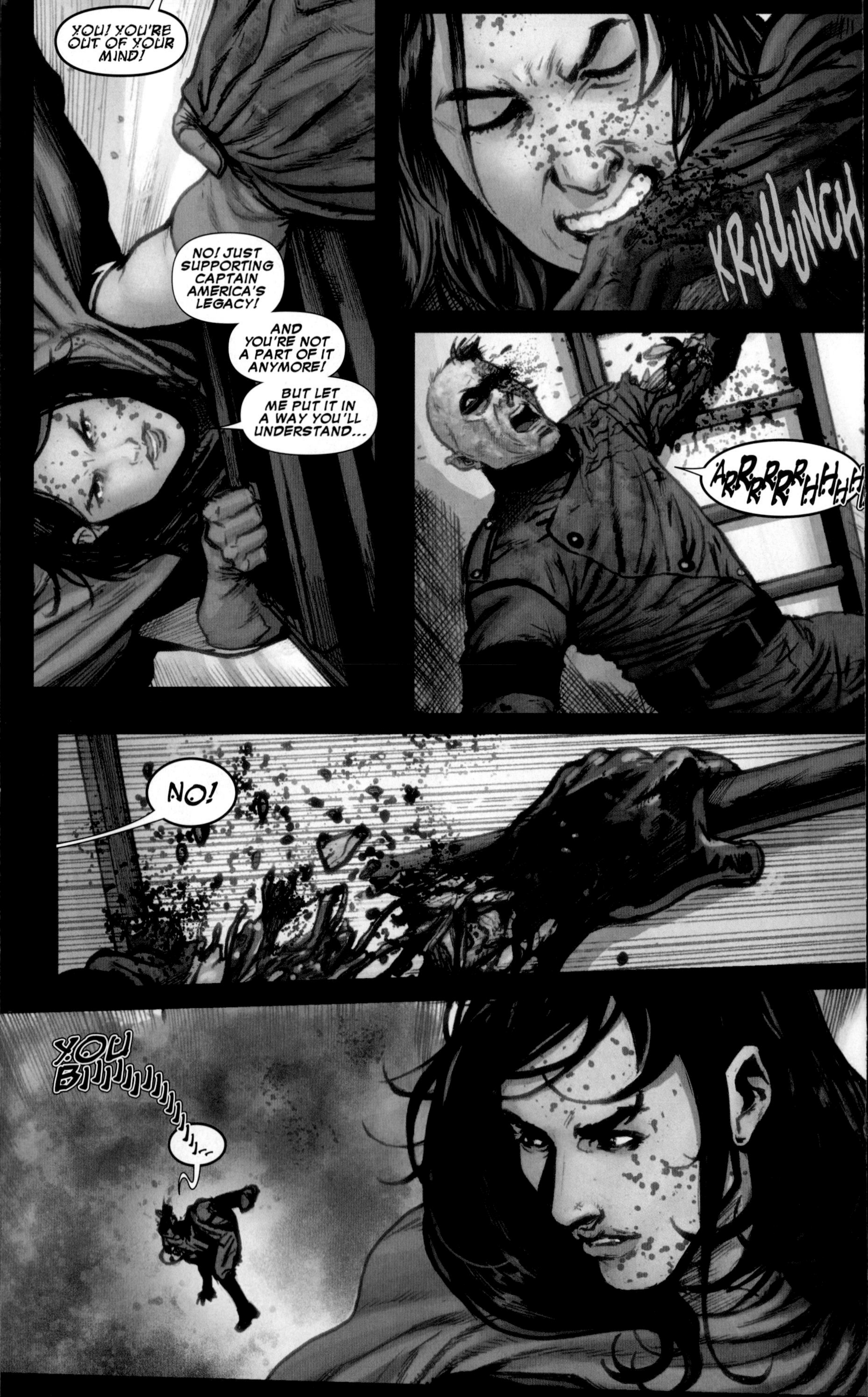

YOU! YOU'RE OUT OF YOUR MIND!
NO! JUST SUPPORTING CAPTAIN AMERICA'S LEGACY!
AND YOU'RE NOT A PART OF IT ANYMORE!
BUT LET ME PUT IT IN A WAY YOU'LL UNDERSTAND...
KRUUUNCH
ARRRRRRHHHH
NO!
YOU BIIIIIIIIIIII---

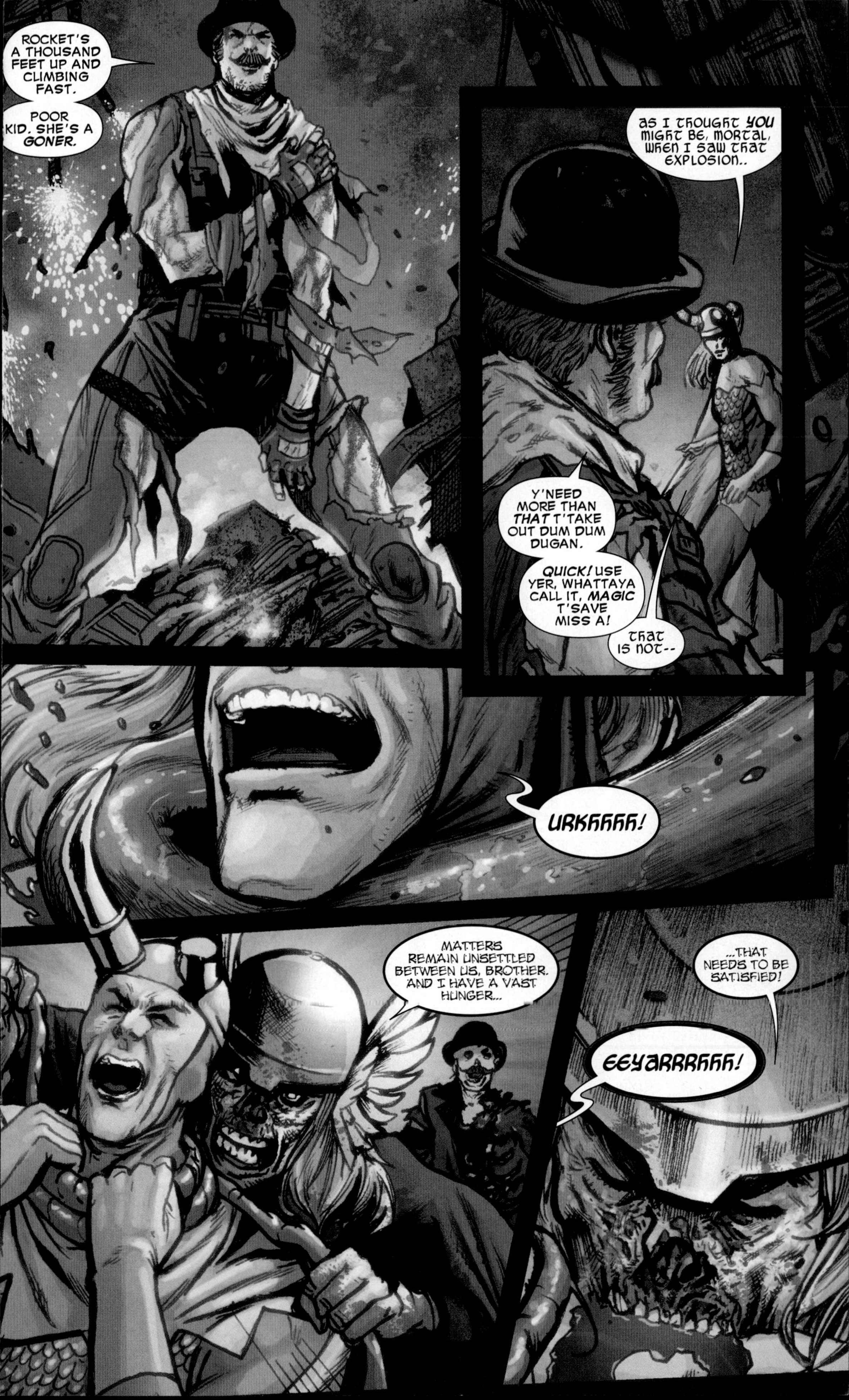
ROCKET'S A THOUSAND FEET UP AND CLIMBING FAST.
POOR KID. SHE'S A GONER.
AS I THOUGHT YOU MIGHT BE, MORTAL, WHEN I SAW THAT EXPLOSION..
Y'NEED MORE THAN THAT T'TAKE OUT DUM DUM DUGAN.
QUICK! USE YER, WHATTAYA CALL IT, MAGIC T'SAVE MISS A!
THAT IS NOT--
URKHHHH!
MATTERS REMAIN UNSETTLED BETWEEN US, BROTHER. AND I HAVE A VAST HUNGER...
...THAT NEEDS TO BE SATISFIED!
EEYARRRHHH!

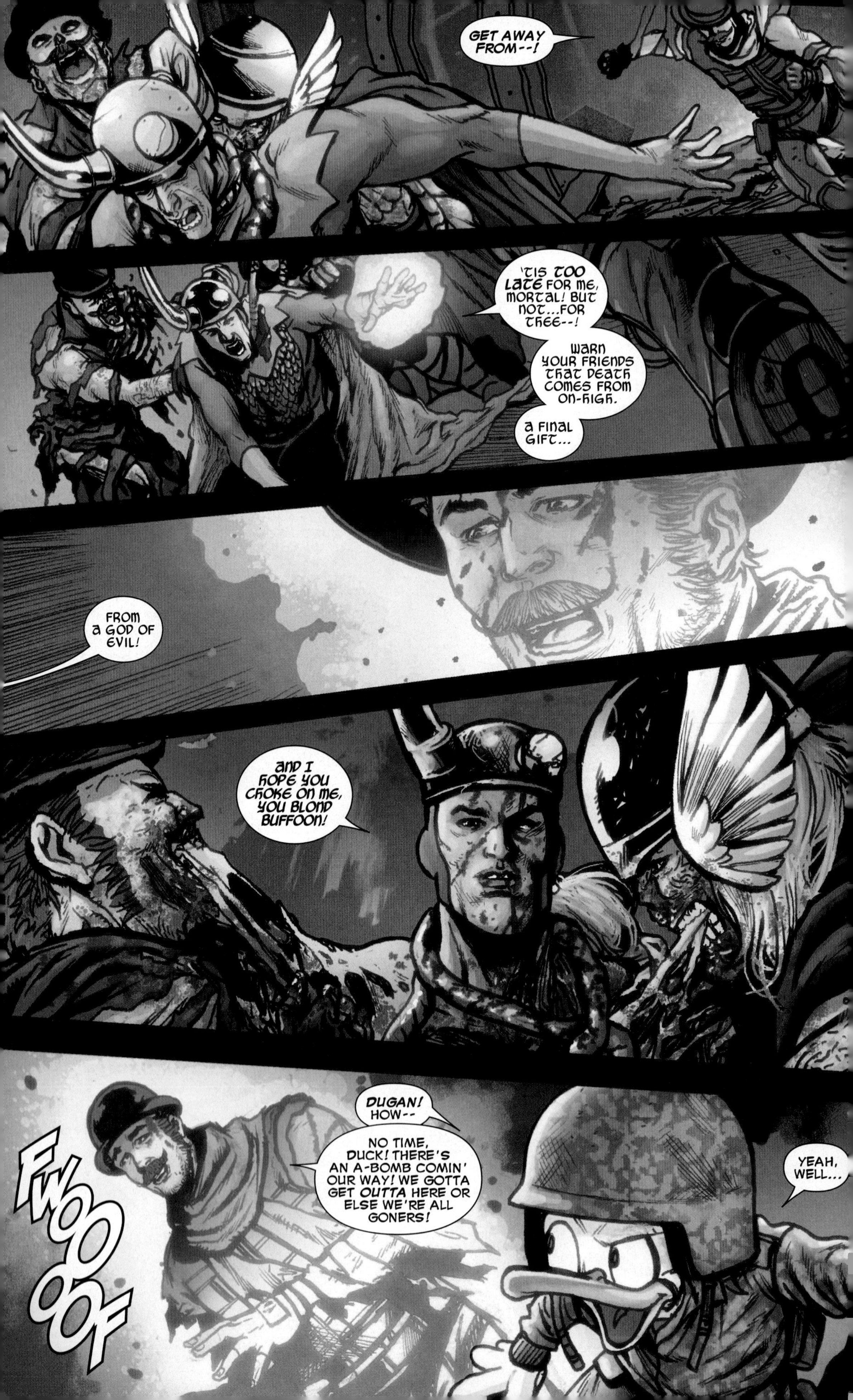
GET AWAY FROM--!
'TIS TOO LATE FOR ME, MORTAL! BUT NOT...FOR THEE--!
WARN YOUR FRIENDS THAT DEATH COMES FROM ON-HIGH.
A FINAL GIFT...
FROM A GOD OF EVIL!
AND I HOPE YOU CHOKE ON ME, YOU BLOND BUFFOON!
FWOOOOF
DUGAN! HOW--
NO TIME, DUCK! THERE'S AN A-BOMB COMIN' OUR WAY! WE GOTTA GET OUTTA HERE OR ELSE WE'RE ALL GONERS!
YEAH, WELL...

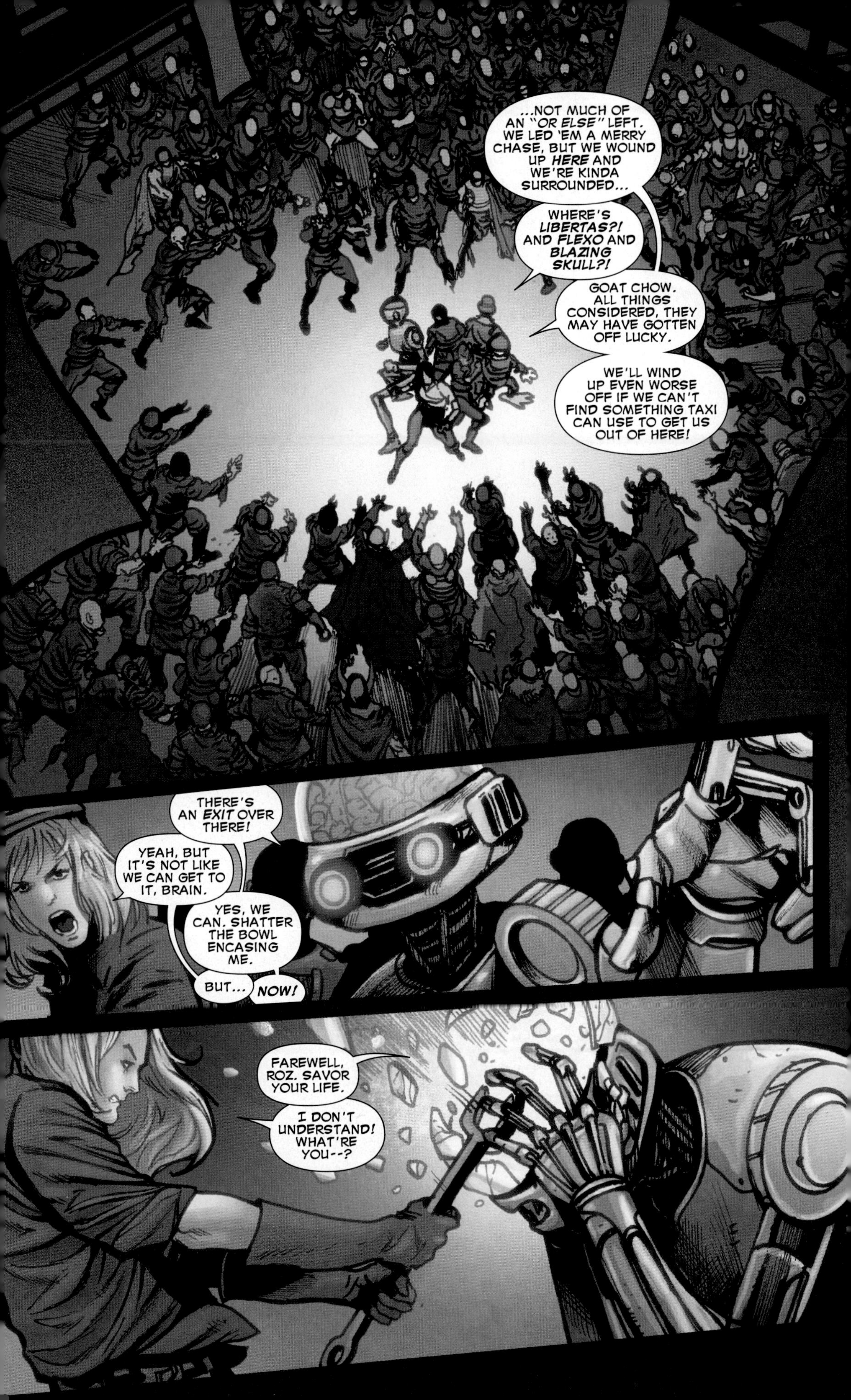
...NOT MUCH OF AN "OR ELSE" LEFT. WE LED 'EM A MERRY CHASE, BUT WE WOUND UP HERE AND WE'RE KINDA SURROUNDED...
WHERE'S LIBERTAS?! AND FLEXO AND BLAZING SKULL?!
GOAT CHOW. ALL THINGS CONSIDERED, THEY MAY HAVE GOTTEN OFF LUCKY.
WE'LL WIND UP EVEN WORSE OFF IF WE CAN'T FIND SOMETHING TAXI CAN USE TO GET US OUT OF HERE!
THERE'S AN EXIT OVER THERE!
YEAH, BUT IT'S NOT LIKE WE CAN GET TO IT, BRAIN.
YES, WE CAN. SHATTER THE BOWL ENCASING ME.
BUT...
NOW!
FAREWELL, ROZ. SAVOR YOUR LIFE.
I DON'T UNDERSTAND! WHAT'RE YOU--?

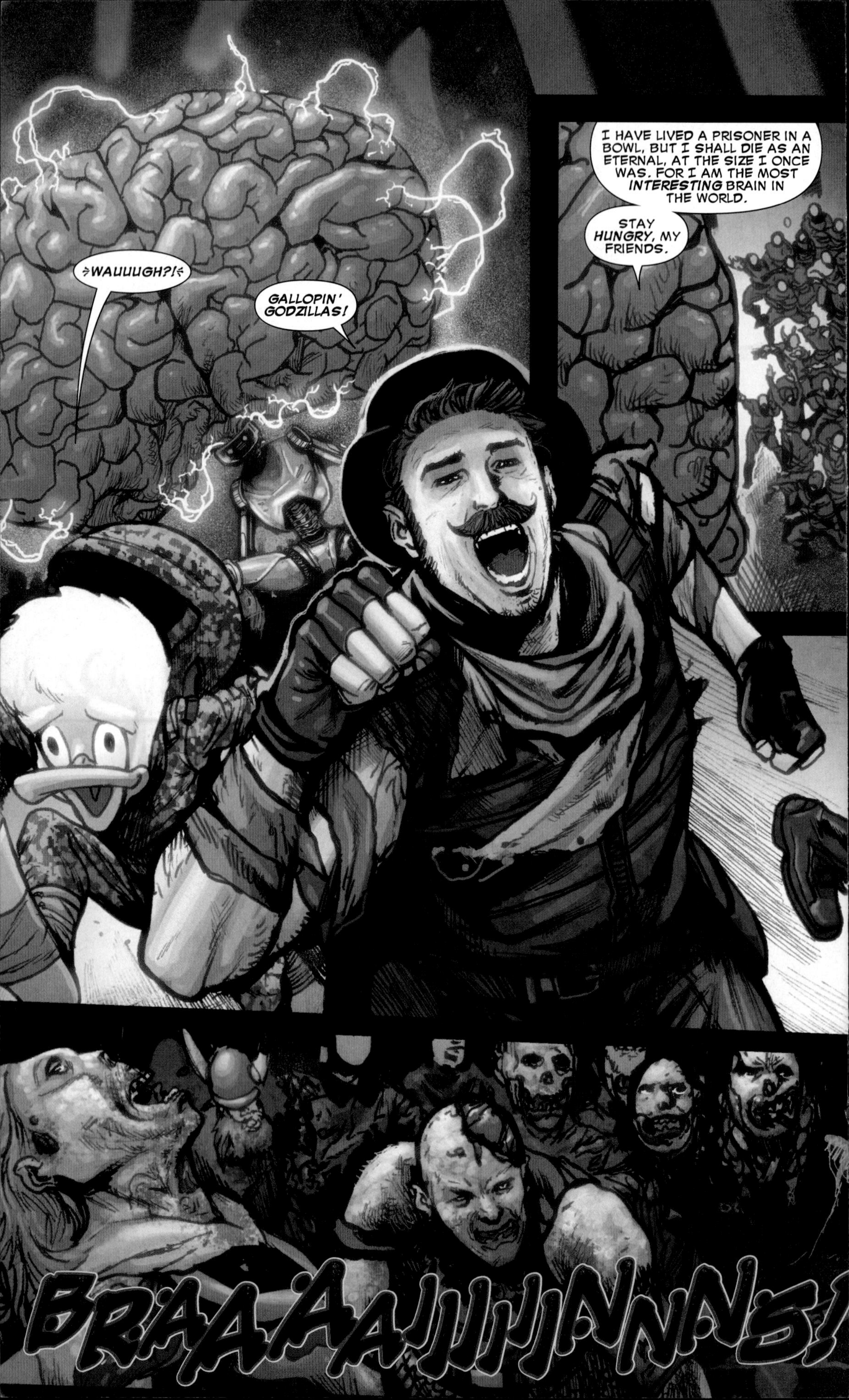

⋟WAUUUGH?!⋞
GALLOPIN' GODZILLAS!
I HAVE LIVED A PRISONER IN A BOWL, BUT I SHALL DIE AS AN ETERNAL, AT THE SIZE I ONCE WAS. FOR I AM THE MOST INTERESTING BRAIN IN THE WORLD.
STAY HUNGRY, MY FRIENDS.
BRAAAAIIIINNNS!

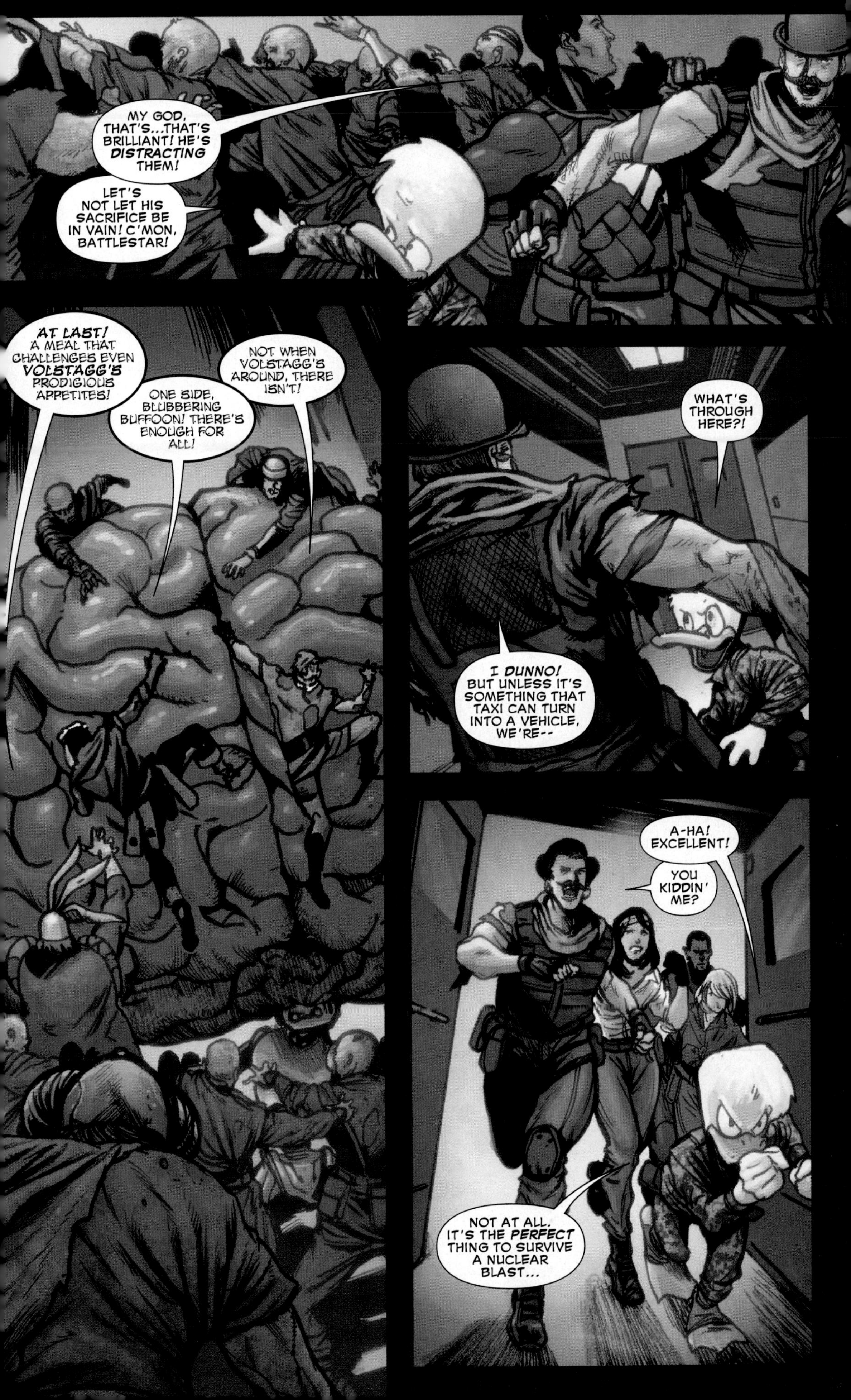
MY GOD, THAT'S...THAT'S BRILLIANT! HE'S DISTRACTING THEM!
LET'S NOT LET HIS SACRIFICE BE IN VAIN! C'MON, BATTLESTAR!
AT LAST! A MEAL THAT CHALLENGES EVEN VOLSTAGG'S PRODIGIOUS APPETITES!
ONE SIDE, BLUBBERING BUFFOON! THERE'S ENOUGH FOR ALL!
NOT WHEN VOLSTAGG'S AROUND, THERE ISN'T!
WHAT'S THROUGH HERE?!
I DUNNO! BUT UNLESS IT'S SOMETHING THAT TAXI CAN TURN INTO A VEHICLE, WE'RE--
A-HA! EXCELLENT!
YOU KIDDIN' ME?
NOT AT ALL. IT'S THE PERFECT THING TO SURVIVE A NUCLEAR BLAST...

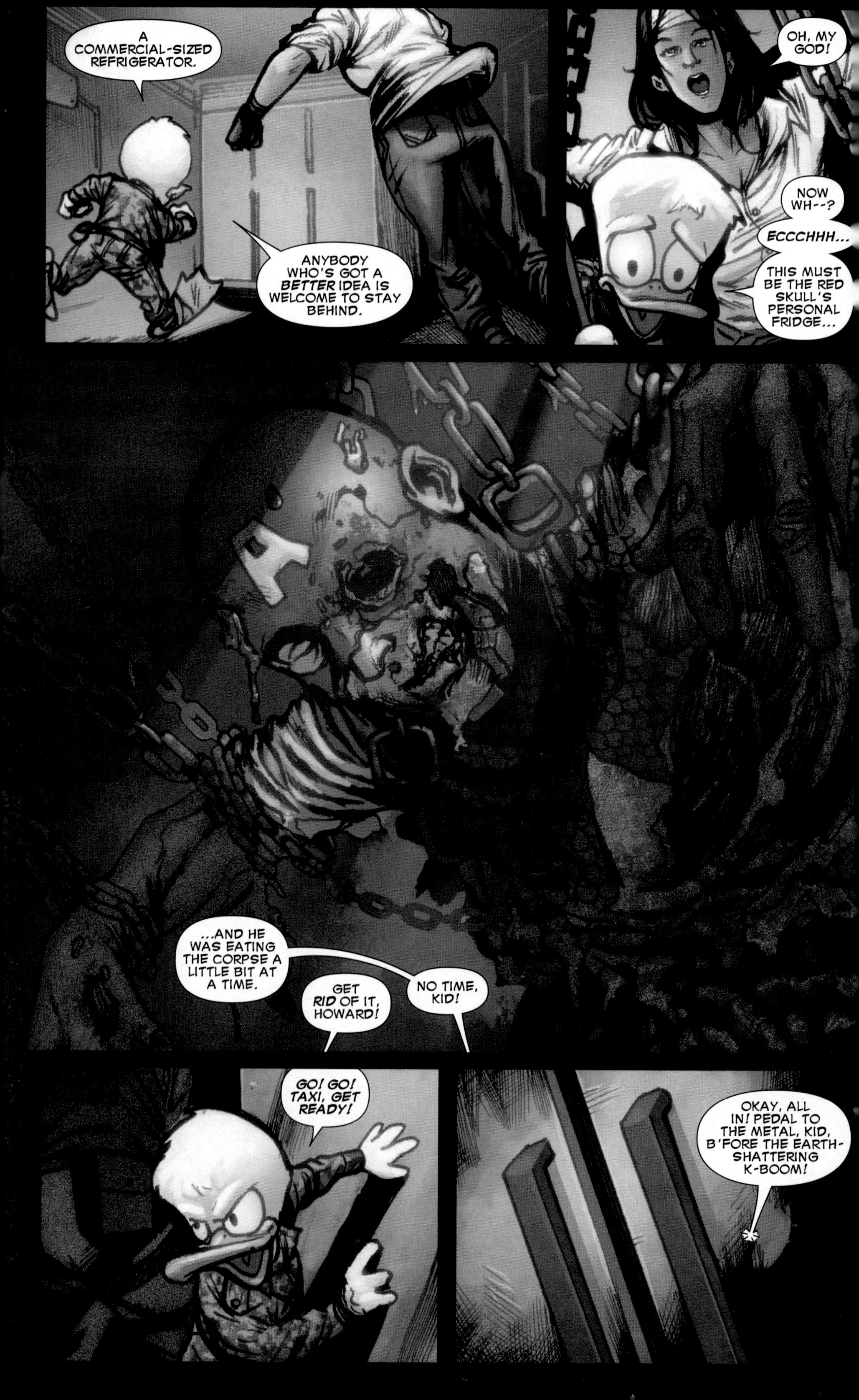
A COMMERCIAL-SIZED REFRIGERATOR.
ANYBODY WHO'S GOT A BETTER IDEA IS WELCOME TO STAY BEHIND.
OH, MY GOD!
NOW WH--?
ECCCHHH...
THIS MUST BE THE RED SKULL'S PERSONAL FRIDGE...
...AND HE WAS EATING THE CORPSE A LITTLE BIT AT A TIME.
GET RID OF IT, HOWARD!
NO TIME, KID!
GO! GO! TAXI, GET READY!
OKAY, ALL IN! PEDAL TO THE METAL, KID, B'FORE THE EARTH-SHATTERING K-BOOM!

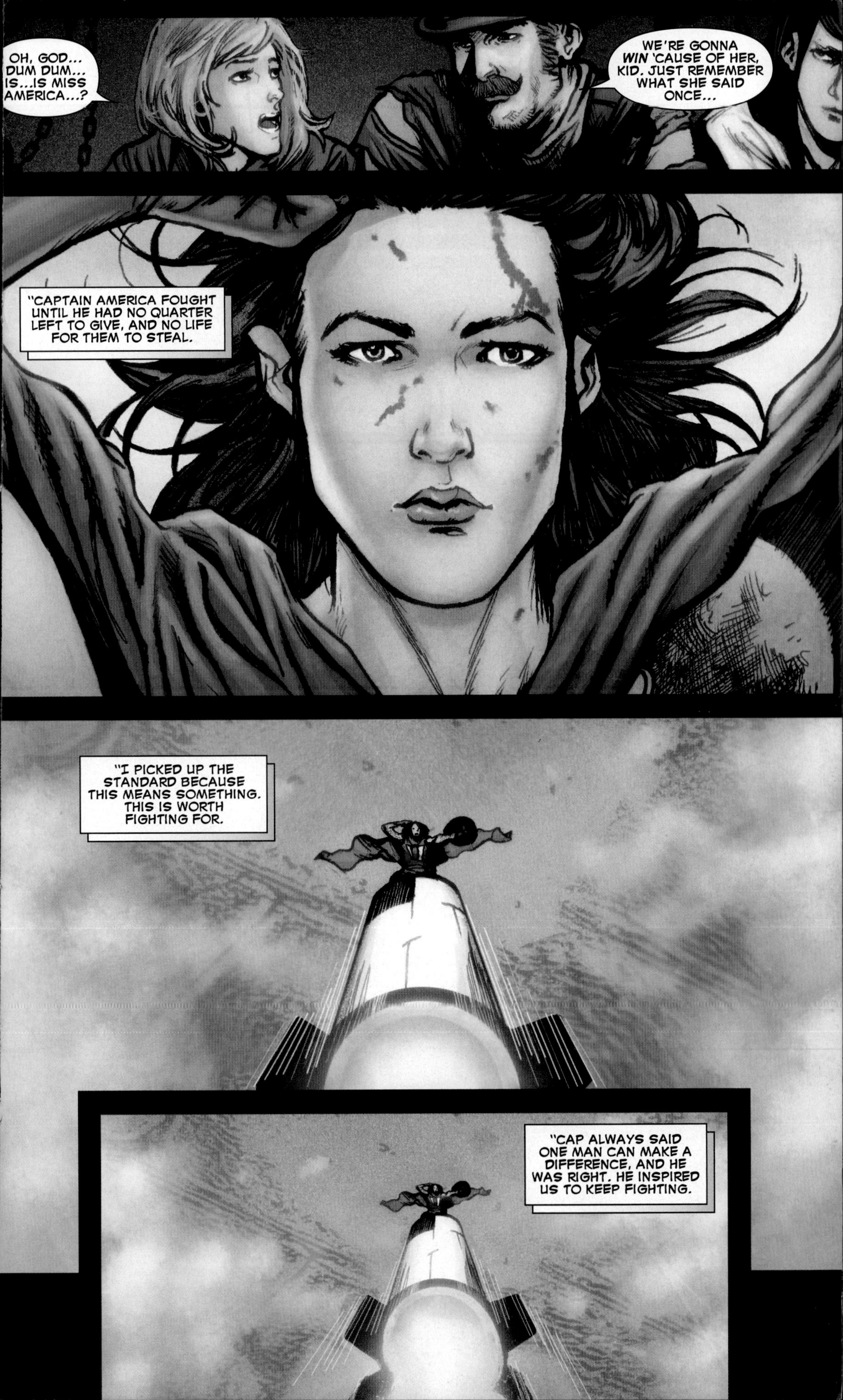
OH, GOD... DUM DUM... IS...IS MISS AMERICA...?
WE'RE GONNA WIN 'CAUSE OF HER, KID. JUST REMEMBER WHAT SHE SAID ONCE...
"CAPTAIN AMERICA FOUGHT UNTIL HE HAD NO QUARTER LEFT TO GIVE, AND NO LIFE FOR THEM TO STEAL.
"I PICKED UP THE STANDARD BECAUSE THIS MEANS SOMETHING. THIS IS WORTH FIGHTING FOR.
"CAP ALWAYS SAID ONE MAN CAN MAKE A DIFFERENCE, AND HE WAS RIGHT. HE INSPIRED US TO KEEP FIGHTING.

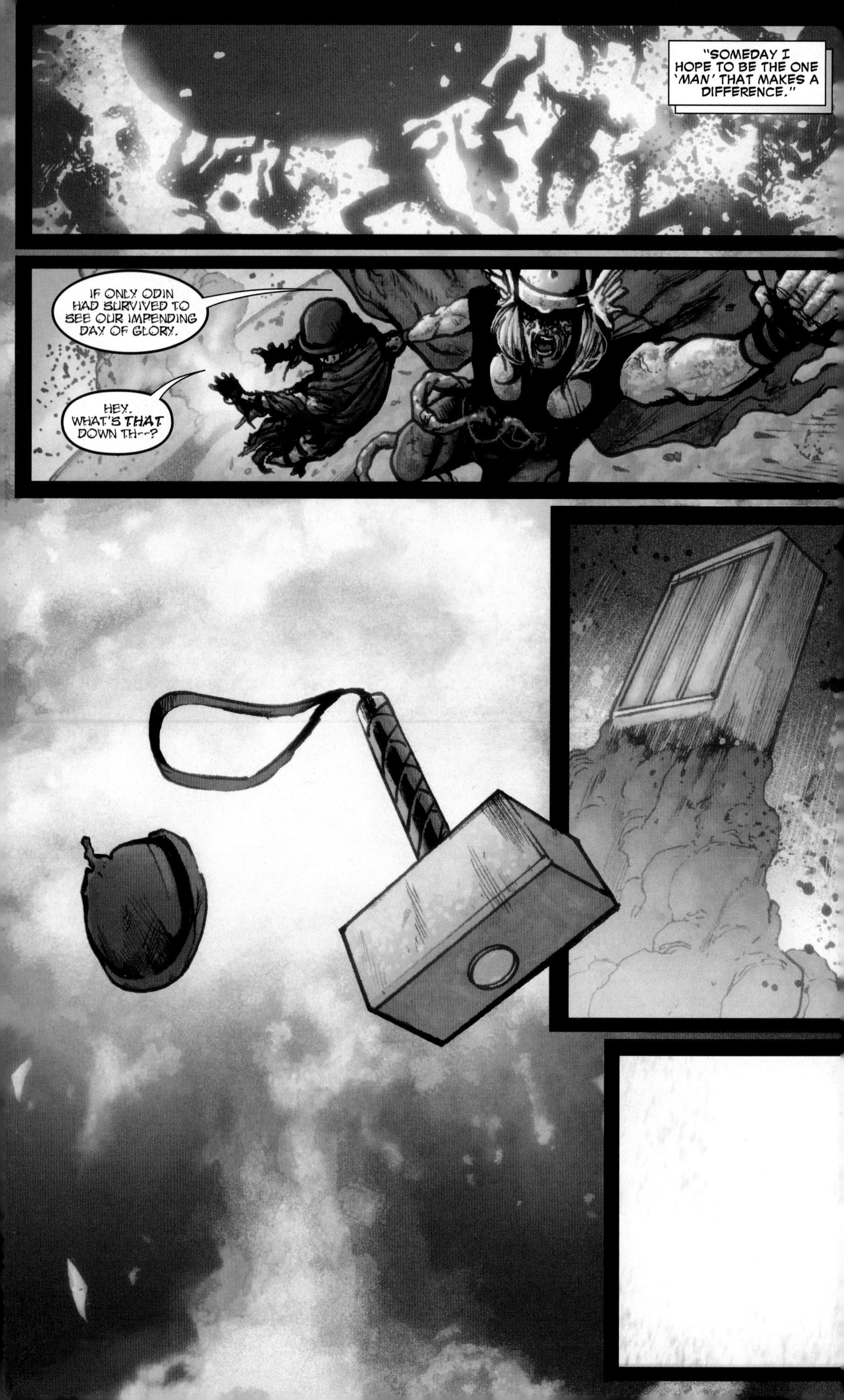
"SOMEDAY I HOPE TO BE THE ONE 'MAN' THAT MAKES A DIFFERENCE."
IF ONLY ODIN HAD SURVIVED TO SEE OUR IMPENDING DAY OF GLORY.
HEY. WHAT'S THAT DOWN TH--?

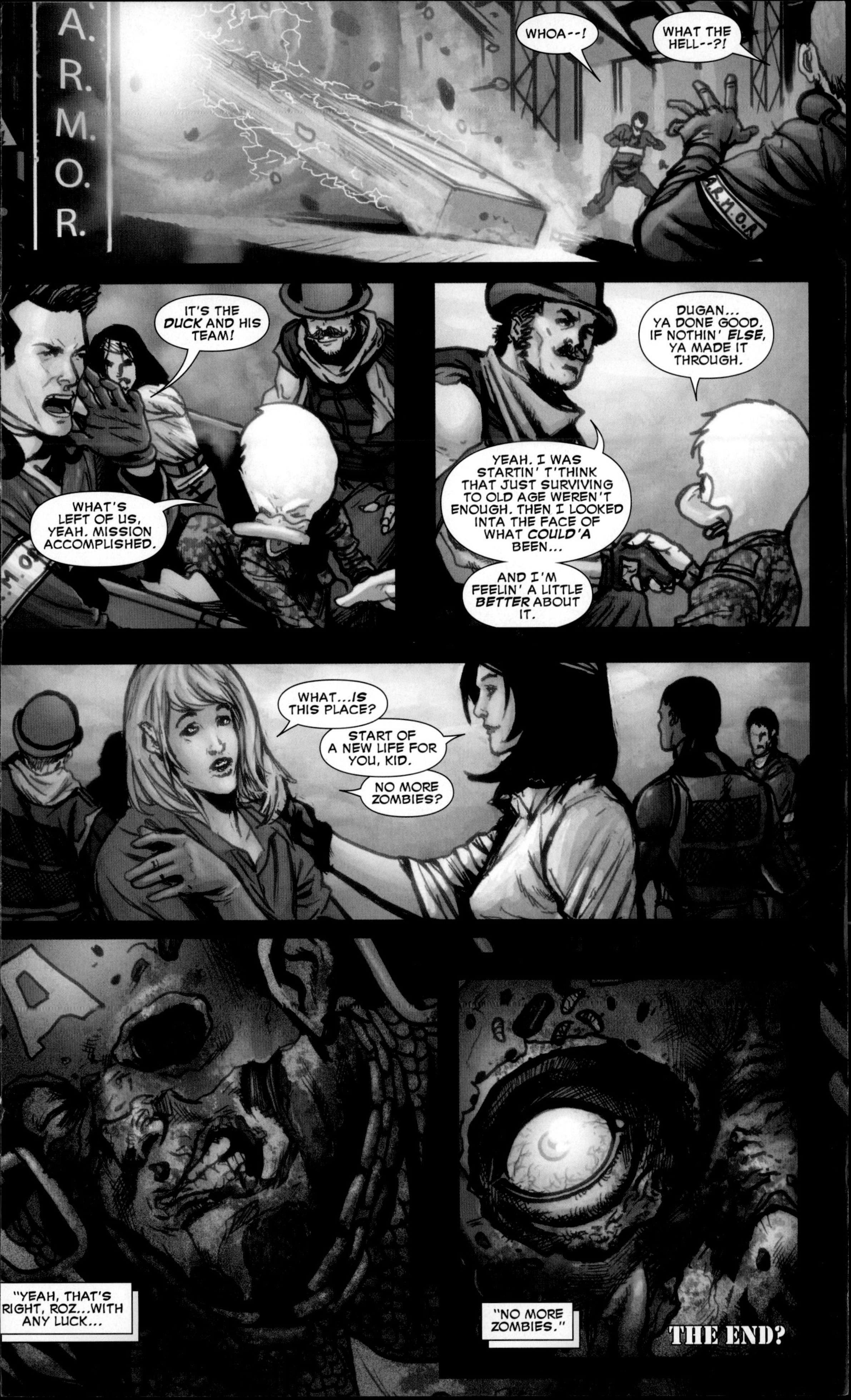
A.R.M.O.R.
WHOA--!
WHAT THE HELL--?!
IT'S THE DUCK AND HIS TEAM!
WHAT'S LEFT OF US, YEAH. MISSION ACCOMPLISHED.
DUGAN... YA DONE GOOD. IF NOTHIN' ELSE, YA MADE IT THROUGH.
YEAH. I WAS STARTIN' T'THINK THAT JUST SURVIVING TO OLD AGE WEREN'T ENOUGH. THEN I LOOKED INTA THE FACE OF WHAT COULD'A BEEN...
AND I'M FEELIN' A LITTLE BETTER ABOUT IT.
WHAT...IS THIS PLACE?
START OF A NEW LIFE FOR YOU, KID.
NO MORE ZOMBIES?
"YEAH, THAT'S RIGHT, ROZ...WITH ANY LUCK...
"NO MORE ZOMBIES."
THE END?

An undead letter from the editor

And thus ends another thrilling installment of Marvel Zombies! As a huge horror nerd and zombie fan, it's been an absolute dream to have worked on this project, and I wanted to take a moment to thank our awesome zombies team – Frank Marraffino, Peter David, Mirco Pierfederici, Al Barrionuevo, Garry Henderson, Michael Del Mundo, Mark Paniccia, Clayton Cowles, Joe Sabino and Irene Y. Lee for weathering a crazy schedule, illness, pestilence and plagues to get this book out, and they made it all look BRILLIANT.

Sometimes, when an editor is as close to a project as I was on this, they can get a little overzealous. To that end I'd like to particularly thank Mike and Irene for putting up with my crazy doodles and turning them into absolutely stellar covers and recap pages. As a glimpse into what it takes to get this kind of madness made, here are some of the doodles I sent. I encourage you to go back and check out the awesome art these were turned into! I hope you readers had even half as much fun reading this comic as I had making it.

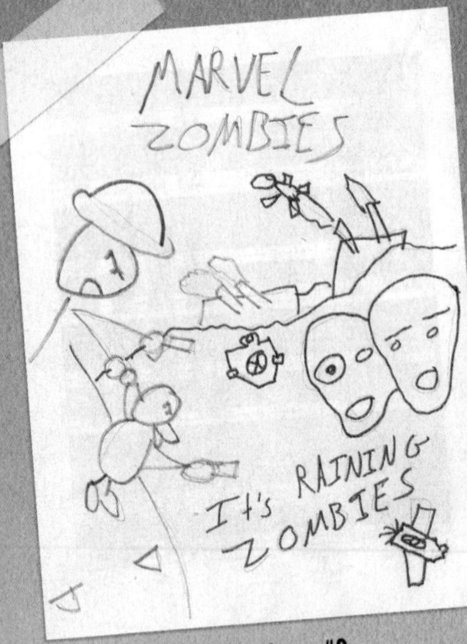

MARVEL ZOMBIES
It's RAINING ZOMBIES

Idea for Cover #2

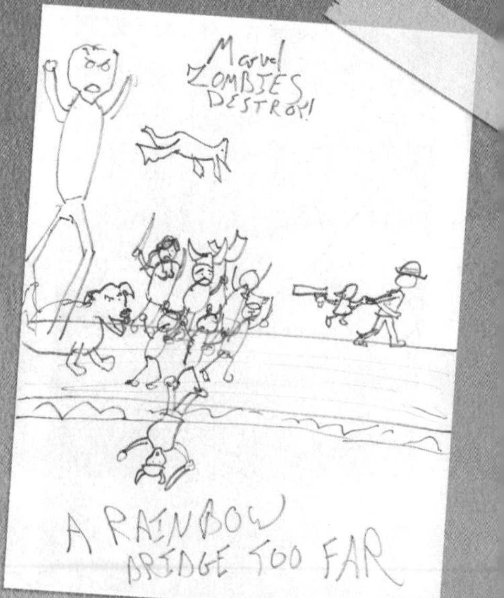

Marvel ZOMBIES DESTROY!
A RAINBOW BRIDGE TOO FAR

Idea for Cover #4

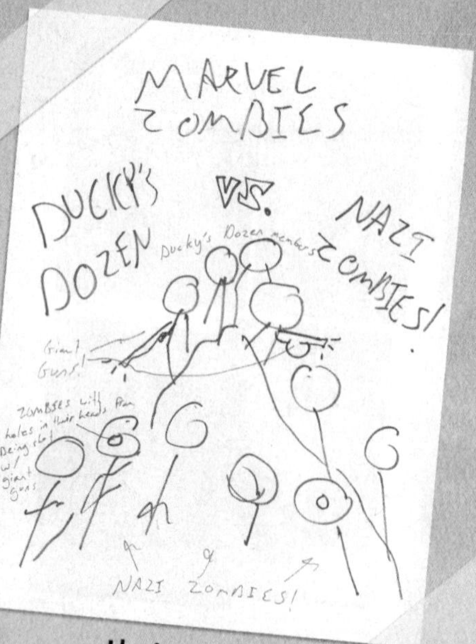

MARVEL ZOMBIES
DUCKY'S DOZEN VS. NAZI ZOMBIES!
Ducky's Dozen members
Giant Guns!
ZOMBIES with holes in their heads from being shot w/ giant guns
NAZI ZOMBIES!

Idea for Cover #1

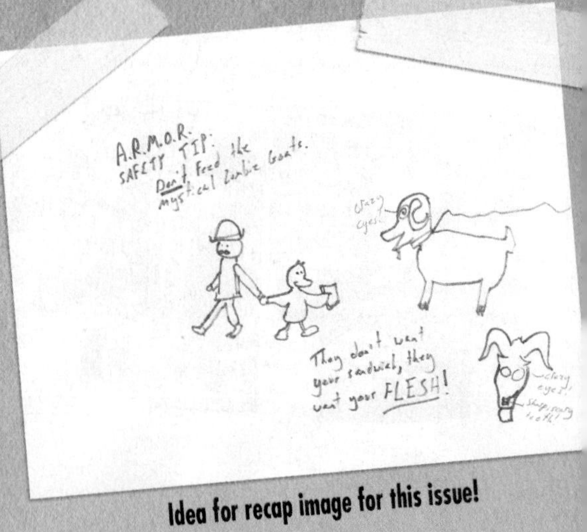

A.R.M.O.R. SAFETY TIP: Don't feed the mystical Zombie Goats.
Crazy eyes!
They don't want your sandwich, they want your FLESH!

Idea for recap image for this issue!

Stay Weird!

Jake T.

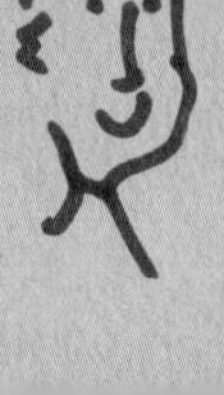

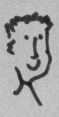

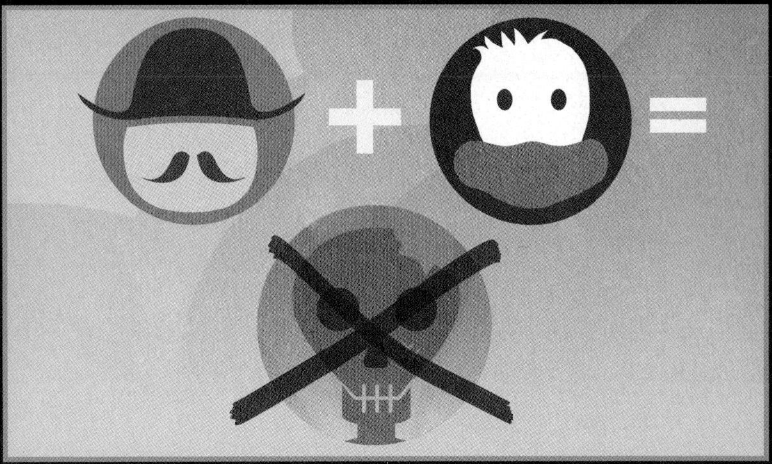

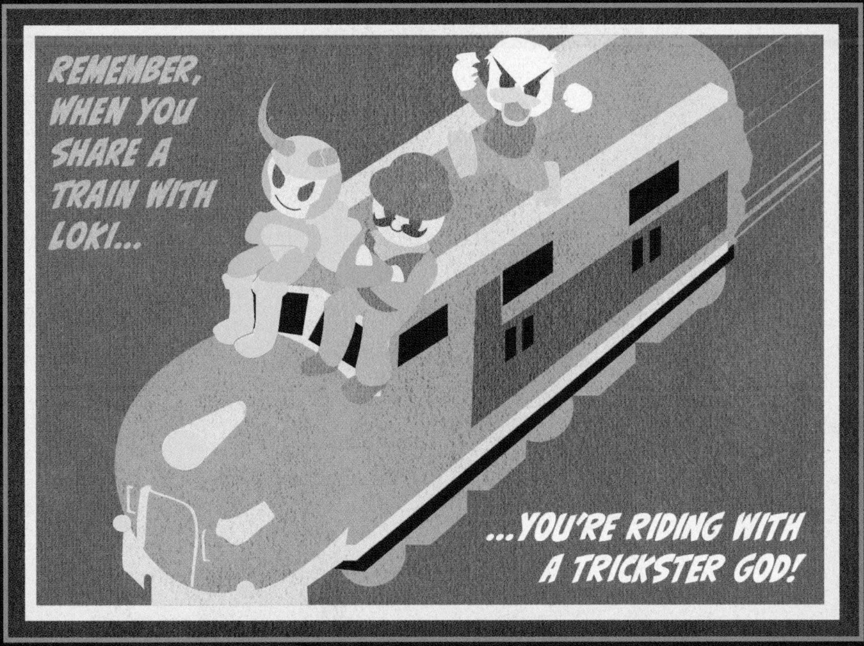
REMEMBER, WHEN YOU SHARE A TRAIN WITH LOKI...
...YOU'RE RIDING WITH A TRICKSTER GOD!

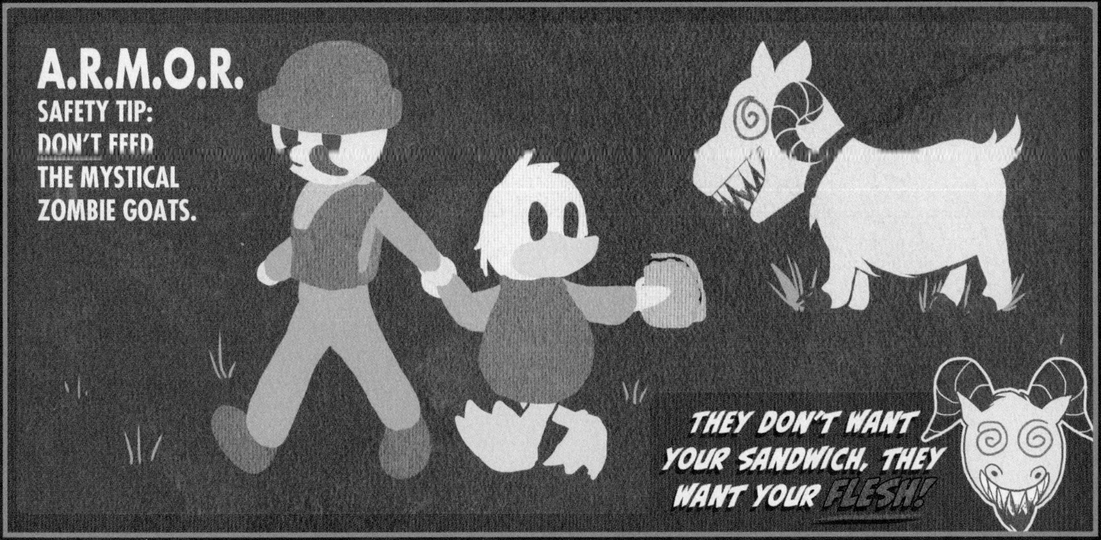
A.R.M.O.R.
SAFETY TIP: DON'T FEED THE MYSTICAL ZOMBIE GOATS.
THEY DON'T WANT YOUR SANDWICH, THEY WANT YOUR FLESH!

RECAP ART FROM ISSUES #2 & #4-5